BACK INTO THE STORM

BACK INTO THE STORM

A Design Engineer's Story
of Commodore Computers in the 1980s

by

Bil Herd

with

Margaret G. Morabito

Copyright © 2021 Bil Herd and Margaret Gorts Morabito
All Rights Reserved.

ISBN: 9798534584950

Cover: Photo editing and design assistance by Kristi Herd. Cover photos provided by Joel Herd (C116 top left and C128 center), Rob Clarke (C16 top right and C264 bottom left), Commodore-Info.com (C128D bottom right), and Raychel Sanner pexels.com (background).

Disclaimer: None of this is real. They are in fact the ravings of a madman and should not be taken seriously. The fact that somebody may sound like you, or share your name, depends on whether you like what it says. If you don't like it, it's not you. If it's not about you, but sounds disparaging or insulting about someone or something else, it must be more misperception concerning an imaginary person or product. Opinions expressed are made by a young man from 38 years ago who no longer exists and whose current day memory is fading.

The authors in no way represent any company, corporation, or brand mentioned herein. Some names and identifying features of characters in this book have been omitted to protect the identity of certain parties. In some cases, only first names were included. Full names of real characters have been included who gave their approval to include their name in this book, or who are highly praised in this book, or whose names and positions are in the public record and are included for historical purposes.

To my son, Joel. You inspire me.

Acknowledgment of Registered Trademarks, Tradenames, Service Marks

The companies listed below (in no particular order) are, or were, the owners of the registered trademarks, tradenames, and/or service marks of products/companies referenced in this text for informational and storyline purposes. Some might not still be in existence or have changed, but are listed for historical reference.

Apple Computer, Inc.: Apple II, Apple IIc; Arduino SA: Arduino; Atari Interactive, Inc.: Atari, joystick, 2600 games, Atari font; Bell Laboratories; THE OPEN GROUP LIMITED: UNIX; Butter Cup popcorn popper; Burger King Brands, Inc.: breakfast sandwich; KRAFT GENERAL FOODS, INC.: Cheez Whiz; Retrobrands USA LLC: Chiclets; Commodore International LLC: CBM 8032, C116, C264, Plus/4, C364, C16, C232, C64, C128, Amiga, 1541 disk drive, 1571 disk drive, 1660/Modem 300, 1670/Modem 1200, 1701 monitor, 1702 monitor, 1902 monitor, KIM-1, PET, SuperPET, VIC, VIC-20; Commodore Portable Typewriter; COMPUSERVE INCORPORATED: CompuServe; Consumer Electronics Association: Consumer Electronics Show (CES); NISSAN JIDOSHA KABUSHIKI KAISHA COMPANY: Datsun 260Z; Digital Equipment Corp.: DEC, VAX, VT100, Rainbow; INTERGALACTIC DIGITAL RESEARCH, INC. DOING BUSINESS AS DIGITAL RESEARCH CORPORATION: Digital Research, Inc., CP/M, CP/M-86, CP/M PLUS; EaglePicher Technologies, LLC; Electronic Arts Inc.; OHIO ART COMPANY: Etch a Sketch; Franklin Computer Corporation; FRITO-LAY NORTH AMERICA, INC.: Fritos; General Electric Company (GE); Hayes Microcomputer Products, Inc.: AT Hayes; Hewlett-Packard Development Company: RPN calculator; HERMAN MILLER, INC.: Herman Miller furniture; Harley Davidson: H-D Michigan, Inc.: Harley Davidson motorcycle; International Business Machines Corporation: IBM, IBM PCjr; Kaypro Corporation; Kimberly-Clark Corporation: Kleenex; TRANSFORM SR BRANDS LLC: KMart; K-Tron Technologies, Inc.; LEGO JURIS A/S CORPORATION: LEGO; Marriott International Inc.: Courtyard by Marriott; Microsoft Corporation; ANHEUSER-BUSCH, INCORPORATED: Michelob; MITSUMI ELECTRIC CO., LTD; Commodore Business Machines, Inc. of West Chester, PA: MOS; MGM Resorts International; NewTek, Inc.: Video Toaster; Osborne Computers: Osborne-1, Osborne-2; Pennsylvania Scale Company; PHILADELPHIA EAGLES FOOTBALL CLUB; PLR IP Holdings, LLC: Polaroid; Panasonic Corporation of North America: Quasar TV; TECHNOLOGY PROPERTIES, INC.: Radio Shack; RAND Corporation: random numbers; RCA Trademark Management: RCA; San Francisco 49ers; Scientific Calculations, Inc.: Scicards; RINGLING BROS. -BARNUM & BAILEY COMBINED SHOWS, INC.: Siegfried and Roy Show; SIGNETICS CORPORATION; TEXAS INSTRUMENTS INCORPORATED: Silent 700 modem; Tandy Corporation Ltd: Radio Shack; Tektronix, Inc.; Texas Instruments Incorporated: Speak & Spell, TI99; TIMEX COMPUTERS LTD, Sinclair Research LCD: Timex Sinclair, Spectrum, ZX80; General Mills IP Holdings II: Trix cereal; Washington Redskins (aka Football Team); WESTERN UNION TELEGRAPH COMPANY: telex; ZILOG, INC.: Z80, Z8000; 4th Generation; DOW CHEMICAL COMPANY: Styrofoam; DC COMICS Warner Communications Inc., DC Entertainment: *Mad Magazine*; DC COMICS E.C. Publications, Inc. and Warner Communications LLC: *Batman*; CW Communications/Peterborough, Inc.: *RUN Magazine*; Atari Interactive, Inc: *Asteroids*; Midway Amusement Games, LLC: *Wizard of Wor*; Commodore: *Magic Desk, Magic Voice, International Tennis, Mind Walker, Visible Solar System, International Soccer*; ADAMS, DOUGLAS INDIVIDUAL: *The Hitchhiker's Guide to the Galaxy*; MicroProse Software: *Kennedy Approach*; Epyx, Inc.: *Jumpman*; Electronic Arts: *Archon*; Atari Games Corporation: *Marble Madness*; ATARI, INC.: *Joust*; Universal Pictures, The Turman-Foster Company: *The Thing*; Access Software Inc.: *Mach 5*; The Malpaso Company: *Dirty Harry*; Koala Technologies Corporation, Audio Light Inc.: *KoalaPainter*; National Broadcasting Company, Inc.: *Late Night with David Letterman*; LUCASFILM LTD.: *Rescue on Fractalus*; HANNA-BARBERA PRODUCTIONS, INC.: *The Flintstones*; Columbia Pictures Industries, Inc.: *Ghostbusters*; *Solsbury Hill* (Peter Gabriel); *And We Danced* (The Hooters); Metro-Goldwyn-Mayer (MGM): *2001: A Space Odyssey, The Wizard of Oz*; Westinghouse Broadcasting Company, Mike Douglas Entertainment: *The Mike Douglas Show*; FarWorks, Inc.: *The Far Side* (Gary Larson); Harmony Gold USA, Inc.: *Macross, Robotech*; Manga Classics Inc.: *Manga*; VisiCorp CORPORATION; Wecora, LLC: *VisiCalc*; Wind Dancer Productions: *Home Improvement, Tim "The Tool-Man Taylor."*

Table of Contents

Authors' Preface ix

Acknowledgments xi

Introduction 1

1. Getting Started.. 5

    1.1 I Blew My Interview 5
    1.2 About CBM and Jack Tramiel 11
    1.3 CBM Family 16
    1.4 My First Day 17
    1.5 My First Week 20

2. Early TED.. 27

    2.1 Introducing the TED 27
    2.2 The C116 34
    2.3 TED Chip Problems 42
    2.4 The C264 and C364 46
    2.5 People, Places, Things 50
    2.6 West Chester 56

3. Middle TED... 63

    3.1 More Problems 63
    3.2 To Japan 65
    3.3 Fixing Things 72
    3.4 Fun in Japan 75
    3.5 Slight Detour 79
    3.6 Winter CES Las Vegas 1984 81
    3.7 TED Disk Drive 90

4. Late TED, LCD 97

    4.1 Back in West Chester 97
    4.2 TED Family Shrinks 104
    4.3 Games and Humor 108
    4.4 Summer CES Chicago 1984 115
    4.5 Moving on to the LCD 119
    4.6 LCD Components 121

5. Early C128 127

    5.1 Transitioning 127
    5.2 Beginning the New Nameless Machine 131
    5.3 Getting It Going 139
    5.4 Five Months and Counting 143
    5.5 Customized Chips 156
    5.6 80-Column Chip 8563 163
    5.7 Why the Z80 167

6. Middle C128 179

    6.1 Other Problems That Plagued the 8563 179
    6.2 Things Heating Up 186
    6.3 Comic Relief 198
    6.4 Lingering Problems 206
    6.5 Winter CES Las Vegas 1985 219

7. Late C128 235

    7.1 Finishing the C128 235
    7.2 The Weekend of Tears 243
    7.3 What Didn't Happen 254
    7.4 On a Lighter Note 258
    7.5 Nearing the End 263
    7.6 People with a Lasting Effect 266
    7.7 Back into the Storm 270

Glossary of Terms 273

Parting Shots 289

Authors' Preface

Back into the Storm: A Design Engineer's Story of Commodore Computers in the 1980s brings you on a journey recounting my and my team's experiences working at Commodore Business Machines from 1983 to 1986. These were years when the home computer wars were at their height, technology moved ahead at a fast pace, and Commodore was at its pinnacle.

This was a unique time in computer history, when a handful of (mostly) young individuals could craft a computer with the resources of one of the largest computer manufacturers at the time at our disposal, and yet there were no *design committees* nor *management oversight groups* to get in the way of true progress. As corny as it sounds (and it does sound corny), we designed from our hearts and for the five-month period that it took to get a computer from paper to CES, we lived, breathed, and ate everything dealing with how to get the computer done. We added features when we thought they were good ideas and did our best to dodge the bad ideas that were thrust in our direction. We had that cockiness that came from knowing that we would outlive these same bosses in the Commodore corporate culture, if we were successful, and providing we outlived the design cycle ourselves. We worked hard, we played hard.

My intention here is to put into writing, in one place, the story of a team as seen through the eyes of a kid. I was only in my early 20s when this all happened. This is a story of an exciting time, the story of a young man thrown into the deepest water doing what he loved.

I approached my co-author, Margaret Morabito, about working with me on this book in late 2019, the year that her book, the *Vintage Commodore 128 Personal Computer Handbook* came out. I was honored to write the Foreword for her book. This seemed like a good fit as Margaret was a technical editor and writer for *RUN Magazine*, coinciding with most of the years that I was at Commodore.

We hope you have fun on this journey. We did.

Bil Herd, Design Engineer   Margaret G. Morabito, Technical Editor

Acknowledgments

We would like to thank the Commodore community worldwide for their support and photo contributions to this book. When we needed a photo, we reached out to Commodore people--some who we knew and some who we didn't know--to ask if we could use photo(s) that we found on their web sites, and when needed, to get referrals to the original photographers. We even had people offer to retake photos that they felt could be improved upon, and we had two professional photographers who had taken photos back in the 1980s. We actually ended up with more photos than we could use.

In true Commodore spirit, everyone who we contacted gave permission for us to include their photos in this book, and we are truly thankful for their generosity. We would like to mention them here. In no particular order, they are Robert Bernardo (Fresno Commodore User Group, www.dickestel.com/fcug.htm), Thorsten Kuphaldt (cbmmuseum.kuto.de), Christian Simpson (www.perifractic.com), Chris Collins, Mark Corliss/MultiMedia Creations, Commodore-Info.com, Ian Matthews (commodore.ca), Deborah Porter-Hayes, and June Tate-Gans (https://nybblesandbytes.net/).

In particular, we would like to acknowledge and thank Rob Clarke, who took many photos of his TED computers and peripherals for us.

Special thanks to Terry Ryan and Dave Haynie, Bil's Commodore co-workers and lifelong friends, who provided photos of the CES shows and get-togethers back in the 1980s. Thanks also to Joel Herd, who took photos of Bil's equipment and did the C128 block diagram.

Thank you to Michael A. Morabito, Esq. for proofreading and editing assistance, and to Dr. Michael G. Morabito for handling final production of this book for publication.

Last but not least, thank you to the Commodore team itself, whose stories and memories are now etched in computer history throughout this book.

Introduction

It's sometime in the early 1980s and it is my second week working for Commodore Business Machines (CBM) in the heyday of home computers. Sitting across from me are several IC manufacturing engineers from MOS Technology, the Semiconductor Division, and my cranky RPN Hewlett Packard calculator has just quit on me. The fact that I am in the meeting at all apparently is punishment for being in the wrong place at the wrong time, something I would learn to better mitigate in the future by hiding faster … but more on how my boss delegated random little jobs later.

I glance up knowing that they can't tell that my calculator has just died and I take note of the way they are watching me. Since I am no longer focused on madly typing in timing parameters, I notice that they seem just a little too intent on what I am doing: there is something more than the timing specifications on the bad chips that is bothering them.

For the uninitiated, Commodore Business Machines, or CBM, was the absolute best and most prolific of makers of home computers ever, but then I am biased. Note that I said "home computers" and not "personal computers" as that vernacular didn't yet really exist.

I mutter something to the affirmative about what they think I am still working on. No reaction. I mutter something negative about the numbers. Again, no reaction. *They don't care about this number; it's a decoy* I realize. Looking them in the eyes, I nod in a way that probably means my agreement. I truthfully am not paying attention to the timing parameters either now; I am watching eyes and posture. They give another number and I pretend to type it in and make notes, the blank display of the calculator threatening to disclose that I really am a fraud and that I can't really do this.

Then there is something different about the next number, and I realize that this is what the meeting is all about. If they can get me to accept whatever problem there is with this batch of chips, over a quarter of a million dollars' worth I find out later, then the problem will be the Commodore Hardware Engineering Department's, not MOS Production Engineering's. The game played by MOS and CBM Engineering at this point in time is the "They bought it" game, but now I am on even footing without the pesky calculator to distract me.

What happened over the next 10 minutes was akin to playing chess where you put your finger on each piece and see if your opponent catches his breath. At the end of that time, they have led me straight to the problem and to the source of their fears. They now know I know. Their hopes that I would sign for something with a problem, because it remained hidden, are gone. The game changes. It is now, "What will you give me in return?"

One of the MOS engineers, Greg, whom I went on to become friends with, volunteered that they easily met another parameter. Now I have fallen into the lead role for this meeting through no fault of my own, and I start requesting that they type into their own calculators a string of numbers, working backwards from what they *can* give me in timing. I agree to sign for the one degraded spec, as long as they make up for it in another spec. They are so visibly relieved that I find myself glad that I don't work for MOS. It turns out that the MOS culture was one where it is hard to admit your mistakes for fear of retribution. These guys' careers were tied to the performance of these different batches of chips to some degree, and I just gave them a pass for the week.

I look them in the eyes and tell them, "Next time, *show* me the problem and I will work to find a way to make it work." We shook hands and we became friends over the next couple of years, and the relationship between chip makers and the guys using the chips changed a little that day.

I learned a couple of things that day: I knew that I needed to be able to say when I screwed up if I was not going to be paralyzed by fear of being wrong; and I learned that to survive at Commodore, it's not always about the technology and numbers.

Sometimes, it's about how well you can read the guy across the table. *Sometimes, it's about poker.*

Over the next year, I make sure that I proclaim my mistakes in public view: I hide little--most of the time. I create the expectation that I and my growing team are *supposed* to make a certain amount of mistakes or we aren't going fast enough. The culture changes a little bit: there are fewer witch hunts since it becomes known that I and my team are not hiding anything. People start to help us find errors; they start to help fix them. In that environment, it becomes possible to do things that defy the odds: things such as designing a new home computer from scratch and getting it to the much-vaunted Consumer Electronics Show (CES) in five months.

My team was a motley crew that in no way fit the standard definition of what engineers should look, or act, like for the day. Ultimately, Dave Haynie brought the phrase "the Animals" into the vernacular, which would later become "the C128 Animals," referring to the core group of us as a whole who worked on the Commodore C128. The name fit and it was sheer coincidence that I myself had had the handle of "Animal" while I was in the Army National Guard, most likely due to my somewhat shaggy appearance. (I wore a short-haired wig over long hair my last four years in the Guard). Before it was over, I would be called Animal in more than one language.

I have often equated the story of Commodore Business Machines to a Greek tragedy in three acts. Here for your entertainment is Act II, the transition from the C64/PET era to the Amiga era.

My name is Bil Herd, I worked at Commodore, and I was the lead hardware engineer on the Commodore Plus/4 and C128 hardware. And, I was with the best team I have ever worked with. We beat the odds; hell, we did the damn near impossible; and we paid out some skin along the way.

And there are more than a few stories to tell ...

Chapter 1

Getting Started

I might as well start at the very beginning. This is the story about how I got a job at Commodore and my earliest experiences working there, along with my tribute to CBM's founder, Jack Tramiel, who affected my professional life in a very profound way.

1.1 I Blew My Interview

It seemed improbable that I would land a design engineering job at Commodore, given that it was the top-selling computer company in the world and I had little to no experience with home computers at the time.

At Least Three Times

I blew my interview to work at Commodore Business Machines, not once, but at least three times that I counted. It was sheer luck that I even got the job, or even knew about the opening in the first place. A friend of mine, Hedley Davis, from where we both worked as design engineers, knew that I was having boss troubles, meaning that I was thinking of decking the boss and would get in trouble. Hedley was taking a smoke in the cafeteria at the Pennsylvania Scale Company in Lancaster County, Pennsylvania when he read an ad for a job opening from the newspaper to me. I made a phone call and was in the CBM headhunter's office that night.

My first interview was with Frank Hughes and I recall thinking that it didn't go well. I was very excited to talk about electronics, too excited really. I don't think we called it technology back then. Well maybe the Quasar "Works in a Drawer" TV set--that seemed like technology. I remember that I was telling Frank that I had read in one of the electronics magazines of the day about how magneto optical drives worked by heating up the medium with a laser to the Curie temperature while in a magnetic field, and it would record that magnetic moment. In hindsight, I may have been a little over excited and I felt that Frank was probably a "no." Only years later, 38 to be exact, did I find out that I was wrong on this point, but, at that moment of that day, I was convinced I had blown my first interview.

Frank also recently reminded me that I had car trouble getting there that night, and by "car" I mean my 1969 faded blue and primer gray Ford van that had to be seen to be believed and yet was pretty typical for the 1980s. I knew that night that, if I got the job, I would need a better vehicle to get me there every day.

My next interviewer was Bob Russell. I knew I was talking to someone brilliant, but I could also tell that he was working a long day as we were there at eight o'clock at night, and I was just another kid with a 10-minute shot. I remember exactly when I felt that my luck changed, when Bob decided to at least put me in the pile of maybe's. He had given an example of assembly code and said, "Load X immediate zero five, (LDX $#05)" and I muttered under my breath, "A2 05," the operation code or opcode language instruction used to tell a 6502 processor to load its X register with the value of five. He stopped and started again, this time looking right at me: "Store accumulator absolute," and I am muttering, "8D," followed by the address. His body language changed at that moment, and I felt a little bit hopeful. I always felt that that was the moment that got me in. I kinda liked that, because what they were really looking for was people who lived, ate, and breathed this stuff. Bob later denied that that's when they decided to bring me in. He just remembered that he wanted to, but I remember the moment he decided.

The exact phrase Bob used was, "Stop by the plant," so I thought, "Cool, I get to see where chips are made!" He was just so nonchalant about it that I thought I was taking a tour the next day, not going for a job interview. The next day, I drove the two lane roads that some person with a can of paint had turned into four lanes (drive around Norristown--we referred to it as King of Prussia--in Pennsylvania, and you will know what I mean) and pulled my '69 Ford van into the parking lot of MOS Technology, home of the best processor of the day, the 6502. Since I was taking a tour, or so I thought, I had worn jeans and a t-shirt to what turned out to be my next round of interviews.

I remember very clearly walking into the Research and Development (R&D) section, also referred to as Engineering, of Commodore/MOS. The hallways had a kind of engineer's pachinko parlor type quality with the blips and bloops of video games, and there were monitors displaying vibrant color everywhere. Then there was the smell. I was used to the smell of unwashed programmers, but there was something more. We were, after all, on the second floor of a chip foundry, a place that takes dirty sand (silicon) and metamorphoses it into sounds and colors and computations. There were actual chip wafers lying around on people's desks. Later, I would find out just how far a wafer can sail when thrown correctly, and how they shattered like glass when you tried to cleave them on the edge of your desk. But, at that moment, it was the equivalent to a tray of diamonds: 5" diameter flat diamonds.

Bob met me and took me to the second floor, the altar of silicon-ness. I had seen pictures of wafers in the magazines, but this is where *they were made*. We then walked into a room of workbenches and narrow isles, the hardware lab. The hardware lab was in fact two rooms joined, and they weren't much bigger than two living rooms and crammed full of stuff.

Bob turned me over to Benny Pruden who just happened to have gone to high school with Hughes in Louisiana and somehow ended up at the same place in Pennsylvania. Benny was a delight to meet and we are friends to this day. He liked to laugh and I liked to make people laugh, so we got along swimmingly. At one point, Bob returned to the entrance to the lab where the huge, loud photocopier was located. He was its heaviest user as he was always researching something, and these were the days before the Internet: to know something, you had to have had someone tell you or you would have had to read it in a book, magazine, or on a cereal box.

At some point, Pruden said something to Russell over the noise of the photocopier that Bob didn't hear, and he responded by replying gibberish, to which Benny replied back in gibberish. (This is actually a form of garbage-in-garbage-out.) I objected loudly that they had in fact made up a secret language and were now talking about me in it, in front of my face. For the next minute, only gibberish was spoken, and I knew I would enjoy working with these people.

Benny then showed me CBM's newest hit machine, the Commodore C64. He listed a small routine written in BASIC and then scrolled up the screen and changed a line. My jaw dropped. Any part of the screen could be considered to be part of a screen editor! I didn't know it then, but I was looking at the works of John Feagans. However, I did know that suddenly I wanted to actually work at Commodore. Up until now, I had been keeping that mental state of "eh" as the odds were that I wouldn't get a job here, not an unlearned, long-haired person such as myself who showed up for a job interview in a t-shirt and jeans. Now, I wanted to work here: this was exciting, but would most likely end in disappointment.

Next, they showed me the part of the lab where they were working on the Z8000 machine, a 16-bit business computer, based on the Zilog Z8000 processor and running UNIX. I remember, at one point, someone mentioned that no one knew the root password on one of the lab machines, and Frank told them to edit the password file to make the password field empty. I liked the trick and swore to remember it.

Finally, they brought me to Shiraz Shivji's office. All of Systems Development worked for him. Shiraz wasn't in, so I plopped down in a comfortable chair facing the desk and the window behind it. I remembered that that was the first time I noticed that, strangely enough, there was a golf course in the middle of an industrial park where they made chips. The next thing I remember is the voice of Shivji: "Excuse me, you are in my chair." Great. Turns out that he liked viewing the golf course, too, and I had been sitting in his chair, at his desk, staring out his windows. I was set on recovering stride and getting through the fact that I may have blown the interview again, when I proceeded to blow it really good.

"Where's your resume?" Shiraz asked the long-haired kid in a t-shirt and jeans who had been daydreaming while sitting in his office chair. I could only reply that I didn't bring one. I don't think I tried to tell him why. Army Basic Training had taught me to own my mistakes, and I knew I had just blown it completely. At this point, Frank stopped by and was leaning against the door frame, when he volunteered that he had a copy of my resume from last night. Suddenly, Frank, who I was convinced had been a "no" the night before, had come to my rescue.

Shiraz grilled me and we talked solid electronics. I was actually holding my own considering I had only taken Electronics 1 & 2 and a TV repair class in high school. We got on the subject of digital scales, as I was then working at Pennsylvania Scale Company, when Hughes mentioned the vibrating wire scale. This was a subject that I knew something about! The technology was owned by K-Tron and their advertising message was that their weighing technology worked equally well on the Moon as it did on Earth. I summed it up by stating that the weight of an object could be determined by the ratio of the frequencies of a vibrating wire attached between a test weight and the object to be weighed. Shiraz turned and looked at me through huge glasses that were popular in the 1980s and corrected me: "Close," he said, "but it's mass, not weight."

I looked at him and realized I had just been hired.

My Unconventional Background

Now, to understand the enormity of my hiring, let me tell you a little bit about my background at that time. You might already know some of this. My background illustrates what could be achieved back then, without higher education, but with some smarts and lots of determination. Simply put, I was passionate about all things electronic.

My career in electronics goes back to the fifth grade when my dad gave me four dollars for fixing a blown SCR (silicon controlled rectifier) in what we called a light organ: those things that pulse lights to the music. Later, I would become a TV repairman at the age of 18, as I had become licensed while in high school, though I didn't graduate (that's another story). I was also licensed to do CB repair and Master Antenna work which meant I climbed my share of antenna towers, sometimes during the very storm that took the antenna out. I trained other kids in my small hometown in Indiana to drag TV chassis that they might find thrown away in the alleys to my backyard. I would get the tubes and other components out of them, and then I'd go around fixing other TVs and stuff. So, it's fair to say, I was extremely interested in electronics in all its forms, from my middle teens on up. I was basically living, breathing, and eating electronics (something that would help me get the Commodore job years later).

Instead of finishing high school, I entered the Army National Guard where I served in an Armoured Cavalry unit and then later in a Medic unit. Later, I moved to Pennsylvania where I took a job as a technician at Pennsylvania Scale Company. Ultimately, I made a deal with the head of manufacturing that if I could do all of my job by lunch, I would be allowed to troubleshoot the top-of-the-line digital scales for the rest of the day, which I did. I stopped short of offering to pay for the privilege of troubleshooting high tech stuff, but it crossed my mind. When finally asked how I could troubleshoot so quickly, I showed them my simple trick: I spent five minutes inspecting each unit, especially the inevitable (for the day) cuts and jumpers. I fixed over 50% of the units just by looking at them! This was how I was taught to repair TVs by my teacher, Larry Davis, back at Marion High School in Indiana. Once you have to troubleshoot something for real and can't repair it just from using memory or looking at it, then the repairman loses money on the deal, as we got paid the same commission whether it took two minutes to fix or half the day. Mr. Davis had told me that it was okay to shut up and figure things out myself, which I have been doing ever since.

Come to think about it, being one of the people who understood what the engineers were trying to fix (I was a production technician, or tech for short) was how I got into the Engineering Department (aka R&D). I would occasionally reply to a change request with a write-up derived from databooks. In one case, I saw that they were using the wrong chip select to ensure that data didn't get corrupted when transitioning to battery power in the 1980s no less.

This led me to eventually becoming an Associate Engineer and finally a Design Engineer, having worked my way up from production. I was learning that I could do whatever I applied myself to. Hiring me into engineering had been a form of "put up or shut up," and it turned out I had a knack.

I was self-taught to the point where I was able to get into engineering, where the schooling started, as I was fortunate to work amongst some brilliant engineers. The culture in an R&D lab was that we shared our knowledge freely amongst ourselves. So, that's when my schooling really began. I tell people that I got my Bachelors at Pennsylvania Scale Company and my Masters at Commodore.

1.2 About CBM and Jack Tramiel

There is a long and well-documented story about Commodore, and most of you know the story, but in case you don't, here is a quick overview of CBM's highlights and its founder, Jack Tramiel.

About Commodore

Commodore Business Machines was one of the first companies to design, produce, and sell a self-contained home computer, known later as the personal computer.

Around 1958, the Commodore company was set up in Toronto, Canada, as a manufacturer of portable typewriters, then adding machines, and eventually electronic calculators. CBM later entered the U.S. market and by 1967, it had become established as an international business machines company, Commodore International, with subsidiaries in Japan, Germany, and Switzerland. In the early 1970s, CBM became a vertically integrated component manufacturer, making its own parts for the products it manufactured. Throughout the 70s, the company surged ahead in designing and producing computers, notably the KIM-1 and the PET.

It was in the 1980s that the computer market boomed and Commodore was most prolific. They came out with a line of 80-column display business computers, the CBM 8000 series, followed by the B128. But, the most famous computers that Commodore came out with in the '80s were the VIC-20 and the Commodore 64. Both were huge successes in the home computer market. The Plus/4 soon followed, and in 1985, the Commodore 128 made its appearance as one of the last 8-bit computers.

Commodore took another leap around then and bought the Amiga corporation, which was developing a computer, based on the Motorola 68000 microprocessor. This would be the first in CBM's line of 16/32-bit personal computers. There were other computers that CBM designed, yet were not produced. You'll read about some of these later in this book. Despite its lofty achievements, Commodore went out of business in 1994, about 10 years after its founder left.

About Jack Tramiel

The founder and driving force behind Commodore was Jack Tramiel, born in Poland in 1928. After the Germans invaded Poland in 1939, Mr. Tramiel's family was sent to the Auschwitz concentration camp. He ended up in a labor camp from which he was rescued by the U.S. Army in 1945. In 1947, he moved to the U.S. and joined the Army, where he learned how to repair office equipment and typewriters. In the early 1950s, Mr. Tramiel bought a shop in the Bronx, New York, for fixing office machinery. He called it Commodore Portable Typewriter, using the word "commodore" as a way of incorporating a military name into his company. He ended up in Toronto later, with the company evolving into Commodore Business Machines, and, as they say, "The rest is history."

My Tribute to Jack Tramiel

I worked at Commodore from 1983 to the beginning of 1986. I didn't even talk to Jack Tramiel until after he had left the company, but I was dedicated to him (see Fig. 1-1). In short, I was a company man. It wasn't until the 1985 Winter CES show that I talked to him in person for the first time, yet I felt that I was one of his guys. As a team member, you would do anything there to do his wishes. I was only three levels under Jack: a vice president (VP), a director, and then my boss, Shiraz Shivji. My boss, Shiraz, would talk directly to Jack Tramiel. We called it "going up the mountain," like Moses, where he would meet with Jack and get marching orders.

Fig. 1-1 Jack Tramiel and Bil Herd at the 25th Anniversary of the C64 in 2007.
Photo courtesy of Robert Bernardo (www.dickestel.com/fcug.htm).

On hearing that Jack had died in 2012 ...

I sat my son down and explained who Jack Tramiel was, what he had done for people with home computers, how he made himself, how he was a survivor, and how my identity as an engineer and entrepreneur was intertwined with the business that he built. The best way I could think to honor him was to make sure the next generation knew.

I have really never understood the negative connotations regarding Jack Tramiel, and part of it is that I tend to not listen to opinions of people who would have no way of knowing.

Here is what I believe about Jack Tramiel:

How you were treated by Jack, and your future in his employ, was pretty much up to you. If you said you would do something or had been told to do it, and by a certain time, then you had better have it done. Anything else was an excuse. Yes, sometimes, legitimate game-changing things arose that may impact your ability to deliver, but those were the stakes to play at that level. If anyone knows of the Animals' history, we were children of the no-excuse culture and still got it done when even the chips didn't work right. People got offended with the fact that we stepped on their backs and shoulders as they bent over looking for excuses. We can and have lived with that as a fair assessment.

To understand the stories about people being fired when they didn't agree with Jack Tramiel, I think it helps to understand how things work in the Army. It's the job, if so asked, of those in the chain of command to render the information and opinions so that the superior officer can make an informed decision, though the decision may not look to you like your input mattered (and it might not have).

Once the decision is made, it is up to you to carry it out with all of your resources and intent. Unlike in the Army, if you don't like it, you can quit your job. Applying this to the people who came to Tramiel and said that they couldn't "work that way," he did the equivalent of them quitting, which is they got fired--which was him living by the standards he set, in my opinion. Any stories of sudden firings sounded fair in this light.

If you made a mistake, you might get fired. Your best hope was to explain that you screwed up and that you learned from it. I think you had to legitimately feel this way as I believe Jack Tramiel was a shrewd judge of character and would know if you were just mouthing the words.

I believe that his sense of fairness was pervasive in his business dealings. We didn't charge as much as we could, or that the market would bear for something: we charged a fair price. He also expected the distributors of his products to do likewise, which I would imagine caused a lot of friction.

I believe that Jack Tramiel didn't believe that the company was there to serve us; we were there to serve the company. I believe he felt likewise, even though he was the founder. He paid for his own lunch in the cafeteria, and I believe that he didn't like that the chairman of the board used company assets like they were his personal property to use.

I believe that he could, and would, make decisions quickly and with finality. One could argue that with more review, sometimes a third and better option might have been available, but again I will go back to the Army. "You can go left, you can go right, but pick a direction and go," is a belief baked into the culture.

When I heard how Jack Tramiel decided to leave, it fit my understanding of him: he applied these values and he made a decision, and one day he walked out the door.

1.3 CBM Family

After I was hired, I soon found out that I would be working with some of the most talented people in the industry. It became obvious that this was a small group of experts. To be clear, there were some less enthused employees who just hung on the periphery and were there just to play video games at work, but the core group exuded a passion and excitement for what they did, all while making it look perfectly normal.

It was a decision-making environment. You didn't complain about a chip that didn't do what you wanted: you changed the chip, or you changed a design in a way that would affect millions of units.

Extended Family

As my time at Commodore grew, our team became more like an extended family. We went to each other's houses; we partied together; we got to know each other, too well sometimes, and sometimes not well enough. To this day, I would drop whatever I was doing if one of my Commodore family were to call and ask for my help.

The other day, I put on a t-shirt that had printed on it one of the computers I had worked on while at Commodore. I almost took it for granted, and then stopped and grinned at the sudden flash of all of the memories of my friends, who together, made it possible. At Commodore, I got to do what I loved and also worked with amazing people, and I'm pretty sure they loved what they did as well.

1.4 My First Day

I arrived for work in my *new* used Datsun 260ZX, a car that I bought just to get me to my job reliably. This would be my first "Z" of a series that would grace the parking lot, especially on long nights and weekends. I bought my car from a Vietnam vet who was suffering from the effects of Agent Orange. He had to wrap his hand with a rubber band to hold the pen while he signed the title, making the car mine. It became apparent that there was a problem with the engine, and this vet not only fixed my engine for free, but made sure I had it in time to start my new job.

On my first full day at Commodore, they didn't know what to do with me, literally, and so they put me temporarily in Benny Pruden's office since he was out for the week.

Benny and Fred's Office

The first thing I noticed upon entering Benny's office, which he shared with Fred Bowen, was the cascade of spider plants on the window. The second thing I noticed was the wall of disk drives belonging to Fred. Every model of Commodore disk drive was represented there, and Fred was known for being able to convert any format to any format. The third thing I noticed was the big stack of green and white paper that was being shoved in my direction, saying, "Learn this, as you're now a coder for Benny, doing 6502 assembly code for disk drives." This sounds like a bad thing for a hardware engineer, but for me, I was just happy to be there and was willing to do whatever it took to be a valued member of MOS and Commodore. People had hired me, in spite of me not having any formal education, and I was determined to prove myself.

Fred Bowen

The first thing I noticed about Fred was that he seemed to know something about everything involving the happenings at Commodore. I mentally dubbed him "one of the sages of Commodore," and I was not alone, as there was a constant stream of people coming in to show him different things or to get his opinion. Fred went on to become a good friend, the kind of friend that I could stop by his house at 1:00 in the morning if I saw the lights on and just sit and watch TV with him, not necessarily saying anything or talking: just sitting and watching bad TV.

There is a time and place for common sense, something I had not known, as I would just barrel through a problem without regard for what the easiest path might actually be. Thanks to Fred, I became a little less of a bull in a china shop.

At one point, somebody had stopped by to show him something. When it didn't work correctly, I remembered that someone had changed one of the jumpers on the cartridge in question, and I volunteered that fact. It turned out that was the problem, and when they removed the jumper off of the cartridge, it proceeded to work. Fred looked over his glasses at me, pointed his finger, and said, "Very good." I had just fixed my first crashed computer system, in my first week. Even if it was a small deal, it was a good way to start. I also learned the purpose of two jumpers on the Commodore cartridge, called /EXROM and /GAME, and that knowledge would surface later when I went to troubleshoot the *Magic Voice* cartridge for the Commodore 128 a couple of years later.

In short, my education had already started.

I would end up teamed with Fred on almost every project that I did for Commodore. We learned each other's capabilities and, more importantly, learned to trust each other. I knew that whenever the hardware would get to a critical step, Fred and Terry Ryan, his cohort, would be there with the appropriate code to make it work.

Terry Ryan

Speaking of Terry Ryan, I was immediately impressed by him as someone who seemed to already know the answers and was just waiting for the rest of us to catch up. I remember that he would have a small smile as he waited for us to work through what would have been obvious to him all along. One of my goals was to be able to turn that smile into a laugh, as his sense of humor was very dry and cynical. If I could make him laugh, I was on my game that day.

Terry and I also stayed lifelong friends and worked at several places together over the years. He claims these days not to remember having written BASIC versions 3.5 and 7 (used by millions of people), which would be a shame, if true, as we had a blast doing what we did back then. With that said, it means that I can attribute anything I want to Terry and he can't rightly deny it.

I worked with the most wonderful people. In this book, I hope that I can capture their personalities in a way that can make people smile.

1.5 My First Week

My first week working at Commodore was a mix of putting my nose to the grindstone and wandering like a kid lost at the county fair. I remember oscillating between focusing intently on what I was supposed to be doing and what I *wanted* to be doing, which was to poke my nose into every magical corner and crevice. These were the wizards of the day and the workplace was unlike anything I had ever conceived of. The sounds of 8-bit games burst from offices and no one was getting in trouble. Walking the halls, my head swiveled like the kid in the candy store, as I had gone from not ever even having seen a home computer to working in the R&D Department of the makers of the Commodore 64, the best home computer ever.

Chip Lab

One place I wandered into that first week was the chip lab, which was a rather small room, albeit directly above a chip fabrication facility! The room had a row or two of workbenches and there, on top of a brown Commodore brand file cabinet, was a small portable TV. Yes, a TV set designed in the 1970s, if you can picture that. On the set was an eternal game of race car that seemed to always have somebody slack-of-jaw and drooling while playing it. It turned out that this TV/Commodore 64 combination was a vital pressure-coping mechanism. I would spend several tens of hours navigating that 8-bit track, all the while not thinking about the problem of the moment, allowing things to unconsciously gestate and having the answer form in my mind. 8-bit racing was like getting an idea in the shower, but without getting wet.

The Physics of Light

One day that first week, I noticed that the designers of the TED chip (more on that later) were clustered around a microscope and murmuring to themselves. I listened intently without acting like I was listening at all, and at one point, I heard Bruce Ahearns, the lead designer, say, "Turn on the microscope light; now turn off the light. Are we in NTSC mode? Good."

The engineers were doing what's called "probing." They had an integrated circuit powered up underneath the microscope. In this particular instance, they used a couple of chips that had been specially made, and the protective layer called "passivation," an insulation layer to protect the chip from the air, had not been applied to the chip die. They would use these tiny wires, called whiskers, to gently tear down into the layers of the chip and try to make contact so that they could analyze a chip that did not work. This was the great challenge of the day: there was no onboard test circuitry and no "boundary scan" logic. The reality was that, when making chips in the 1980s, we did not have the tools that would tell us why a chip didn't work. Simply put, the tools didn't exist yet to verify that the way we made the chip was to the chip engineer's design or schematic, so we had to find that out for ourselves. I used to say that the chip started out as an approximation of a schematic and got better as it went along.

What had happened on this day was that one of the address lines, address line 9 (A9), had cut cleanly across the other address lines, A8 and A7. Had they only gotten too close, the design rule check software (DRC) would have said it's too close, but since the address line cut *cleanly* across A8 and A7, the DRC thought it was a very clean short (as opposed to a dirty one) and therefore an intentional short. What this meant was that the brand new chip could not be talked to: the registers could not be read from or written to, which was a problem.

I interrupted Bruce. "Wait. Did you just use the photons from the microscope light to flood the register, knocking it into NTSC mode?" Without even looking up from the scope, Bruce affirmed, "Yeah, um-huh." Let me state that again. They used the light from the microscope to influence what they were trying to measure. I realized in that moment that I was working in the best place in the world for doing what I wanted to do. I was home.

I still had a lot to learn, but I got very comfortable sauntering in to talk to the guys as they probed their chip day after day. One time, I walked in a little too relaxed and casually threw my hip against the table as a way of leaning. Three heads suddenly popped up like chickens watching a ping pong match. By jamming the table the way I had, I had ruined their morning's worth of probing, as the shock of my hip hitting the table was enough to dislodge the probe tip. I quickly left the room, doing my best sheepish, "I screwed up," conciliatory apology for having messed up so monumentally within a few seconds of entering the room.

Speaking of probing, occasionally a chip needed to be probed that had its passivation layer still intact. Bruce called this the "push and pillage" method of probing, where they would use the probe tip to *plow* through the passivation, usually making a microscopic mess in the process. I swear they would grin maniacally while doing this method.

Lab Technicians

I got to know the lab technicians around this time, too. These were the ones who did pretty much every part of the job, except for computer design. They built and re-worked prototypes and pre-release systems, troubleshot anything broken, set up the CES booth, and have been known to paint units for photography for the Marketing Department. They made sure we had the right test equipment and the stock of parts to pull off whatever small miracle needed to be done that day.

They were Gale Moyer, the head of the lab; his right hand man, Lucky Kolakowski; and the tech, Jeff, who let me know I was the fricking new guy (FNG) of the group and would have to earn my stripes; Claude Guay, our resident Canadian; and Curt, who sometimes went by the name of "Chip," but later would be referred to as "Curtis" and occasionally "Arlo." Later, Dan Faust and Kim Constein would join the group, all dedicated technicians and assemblers that rivaled small company production in some ways. To this day, I've never met a better group of R&D technicians than I met that first day at Commodore, or somebody with so many nicknames as Curt had.

On the run up to anything important, we always got what we needed from the lab. The guys were great: if I needed a tech, I had a tech--day or night. Likewise, if I needed a fresh tube of parts, it was mine as quick as I could ask for it. Gale and all of the R&D techs were as committed as any of us were to getting our projects done, and on time. Without their help, us lowly engineers would not have gotten anywhere.

Head of TED

One of the other labs that I walked into that first week was the hardware lab, where I met a young engineer who told me that he only had two weeks left at Commodore, and that he was working on the TED project, a series of computers that used the TED chip. He explained that TED meant TExt DIsplay and that naming chips was a normal thing in the biz. He also explained that even though he was the lead engineer on TED, he hadn't designed the TED. The engineer before him had done most of the prototype work.

I noticed that the prototype before me was built around the VIC-II chip, the core chip of the C64. To someone, that made sense since TED didn't yet exist, but I thought that was bonkers myself.

While talking to the engineer, I realized what they were doing: they were splitting the bus between the graphics processor and the microprocessor, the venerable and popular 6502. I described in excited tones how I was doing the *exact same thing* at home on a development board I had adapted. I had been learning a split bus structure for the 6845 video processor, where you basically sat and waited for the vertical retrace or horizontal retrace. I had taught the 6502 and the 6845 to share the same bus. Instead of only accessing video during the video retrace times (a small percentage of the time), I was splitting the bus on every cycle exactly like he was describing. I remember the engineer verifying that I wasn't just talking out my ass, and the more we talked the more I realized that I knew this design. I asked how he refreshed the DRAMs (dynamic random-access memory). I asked how they stole cycles when they needed them, and I asked how to manage the DMA (direct memory access) for the microprocessor. The answer to all of these was TED: the TExt Display chip that the entire computer was designed around.

This was Commodore's first *single-chip computer*, even though it had more than one chip in it. The entire computer was centered around one chip. Sure, there was a microprocessor in there, but now it was an add-on chip to the main brains of the outfit, TED.

Something must have clicked as, later that day, Shiraz came into my office (actually Benny's office) and told me that I was now the new head of the TED project. He called me into his office and opened his Commodore brand file cabinet and pulled out a Sinclair Spectrum. "This is what we're going after," he told me. Years later, I would find out that Jack Tramiel had considered the C64 the *Apple Killer* and that TED was supposed to be the *Sinclair Killer*. Jack really wanted to shut out Sinclair from the American market for inexpensive computers and also to open the market for small business computers, hence the text display. This was not your mother's gaming computer.

It must have been a good fit as I didn't even blink when I was told that I was now in charge of a project already. This is what I was made to do. This is what I had been doing before I joined Commodore, working as a project engineer responsible for designing digital equipment from the ground up, and at the ripe old age of 24.

I only found out later that I had originally been hired as a technician. I was then assigned as a programmer for some future Commodore disk drive and soon became the lead design engineer for the newest Commodore computer. I started in the middle of the C116's phase of development, the C116 being the first in a family of TED computers. There was a design, but no printed circuit boards (PCBs) and no chips, yet.

I waited until the current TED engineer officially left before I took over. In my first official act, I walked over to the prototype that was based on the VIC-II chip and dropped it in the trash can. I did this as a joke with Gale Moyer, the head of the lab, in attendance. He did retrieve it out of the trash can for safekeeping, but I never again had it on the desk.

I talked with Gale, the TED guys and others, and started a new prototype design for what the TED chip would be when it did work. I can only surmise that the attitude had been, "Well, since the TED chip won't be done for six more months, let's prototype with another chip that's completely different." To a young engineer, this was invaluable as it meant that older people didn't always do what made sense and maybe I actually could contribute. The weirdest thing for me was that I had all of this confidence. I knew how to design this computer, and I'd only worked here a week. I knew what was important and I knew that the current prototype was not. With all of that said, dropping it in the trash was simply a fun thing to do.

My Superpowers

When the engineer first showed me the prototype, he made a grunt of anguish. Someone had stolen the VIC-II chip and replaced it with an older chip that "sparkled." (We'll talk about sparkle later.)

I found out that this was common at the time, and this was the second time someone had liberated the VIC-II chip from this particular board. Since everyone that worked at CBM had a C64, courtesy of CBM, the number of people that could use the most modern, non-sparkling version of the chip was close to 100% of the staff.

One of the superpowers that I learned I had was the ability to "send downstairs" for parts. I did what was considered to be radical at the time and *sent downstairs* for a tube of VIC-II chips. I deliberately left them on the bench with a sign that said, "Need one, take one." Within a couple of days, the tube was empty, and I set out a second tube which only became halfway depleted and stayed there for anybody needing a VIC-II chip for their personal C64. I had saturated the market for good VIC-II chips and ensured the safety of the remaining units in the hardware lab.

This action would be repeated, sometimes at notable events, such as when I needed a 6529 to fix the joystick port--I *sent downstairs* and had parts within an hour. Later, when we moved to West Chester, I could still send for chips and have them arrive via our couriers that traveled between the two sites.

We also had other shortages, such as jumper leads. I ordered extra jumper leads and started hanging them where anybody could get one. I was told that my jumper leads would get stolen if I didn't keep them hidden, and my reply was, "Not if I saturate the market." Eventually, I did and the sight of jumper leads hanging on each of the magnifying lights in the hardware lab was a trademark of my attitude. Superpowers aside, now it was time for me to take the reins on this new project and develop my leadership skills.

Chapter 2

Early TED

This was a time when I was getting my feet wet at Commodore and quickly learned that the job entailed not just the ups and downs of designing computers from a technical aspect, but also included dealing with the unexpected animosity between departments and a major relocation. Throughout all of this, as a team, we kept and finely-tuned our sense of humor.

2.1 Introducing the TED

The TED chip was to be used in an entire family of new computers, and now I found myself in charge of this expansive project that ultimately spanned continents.

My Happy Time

The days and weeks that followed for the next several months were my happy time at Commodore. My life was not in a complete, tumultuous uproar, and the environment was calm enough that I could really pour myself into the making of the next computer.

I quickly developed a schedule of working until about 8:00 to 9:00 at night, taking a break in the afternoon and then one again in the evening. It was during one of these evening breaks that I would run into Dave DiOrio, one of the chip designers of TED and who would go on to become one of my best friends ever. Apparently, Dave had the same work ethic as I did, and this became one of the first things we realized we had in common. Dave started to teach me about chip design, a process that went on for my entire time at Commodore, and I started to teach him about the outside world banging on the door of the chip. I talked about real-life influences such as noises, dropouts, and how the capacitive load of the bus or an impedance mismatch can change timings, etc. In short, I started to make Dave a systems designer.

Above all else, I learned not to take for granted the way the chip worked. I could look past the pin of the chip to the circuitry on the inside. Maybe not all of it, but, in my mind, I could certainly see the circuitry that I interfaced with. The computer became an extension of the chip, and the chip an extension of the computer.

I found out that even though CBM had designed the most popular home computer, the Commodore 64, those engineers were now gone. We were like the owners of a work of art and yet had lost the recipe ourselves to some degree. I was surprised when I picked up the schematic of TED and immediately started making changes to the component values for better producibility, as I had come from production. I'd been a production technician before becoming an associate engineer before becoming a computer design engineer: I usually knew what worked and what didn't.

The TED Family

The word TED describes both the chip itself--TExt Display--and the family of computers that used this chip (see Fig. 2-1).

The MOS 7360 TED chip itself, made by MOS Technology, was multi-function and served as the basis for the entire family of computers. It was a video chip, but it also contained sound generation and other features that I'll explain soon.

The TED family started out as three models: the C116, the C264, and the C364. The entry model, C116, had chiclet keys, 16 kB of RAM, and was meant to take on the Timex Sinclair ZX Spectrum head on. The C264 was a full-blown business computer for the day with 64 kB of RAM, including a family of accessories to include printers, joysticks, cassette recorders, and monitors. The C364 was a C264 with 64 kB and an even bigger keyboard, as it had a numeric keypad. It also talked, with built-in speech processing. The computer was to ship with talking *Magic Desk* software, and it was to be our high-end entry, doing something new that computers of the day couldn't do--talk. It was called by various names: C364, CV364, V364, or C364V. The V stood for "Voice."

We felt that the driving force behind the TED family was Jack Tramiel, and we had the full support of Commodore Tokyo and Commodore Texas in producing this computer. Once Jack Tramiel left, the TED series started to be reimagined by different parties, not all of them qualified to parallel park a car, let alone to reimagine a computer. Marketing wanted to charge close to $400 for the same computer and needed an excuse, so they built in some average software and the C264 was now called the Plus/4, in reference to the software that had been added.

Commodore TED Family

PRODUCED & SOLD

- **C116** — 16 kB Memory, Europe
- **C16** — 16 kB Memory, North America, Argentina, Europe
- **Plus/4** — 64 kB Memory, North America, Europe

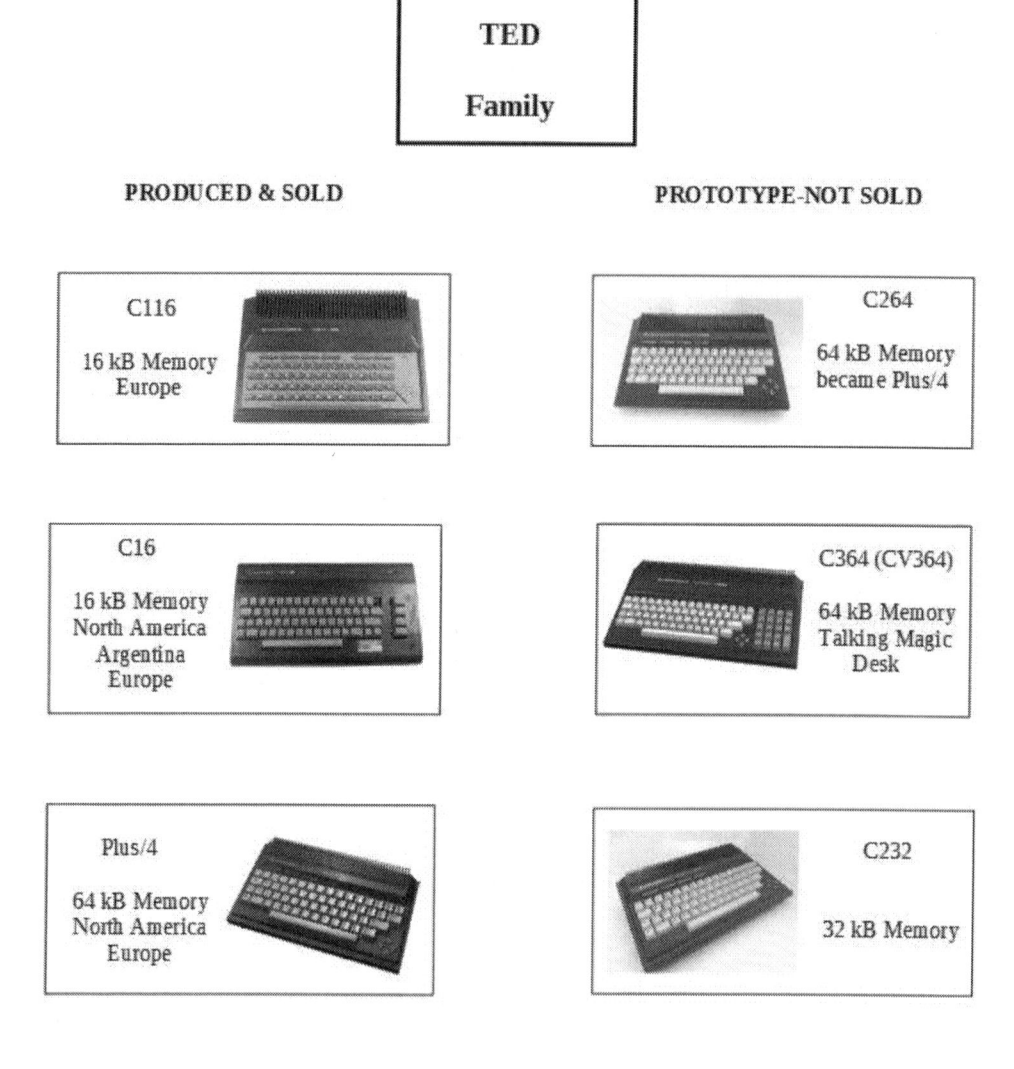

PROTOTYPE-NOT SOLD

- **C264** — 64 kB Memory, became Plus/4
- **C364 (CV364)** — 64 kB Memory, Talking Magic Desk
- **C232** — 32 kB Memory

Fig. 2-1 TED Family.
Photos courtesy of Bil Herd (c128.com) C116, Rob Clarke C264, Bil Herd C16, Thorsten Kuphaldt (cbmmuseum.kuto.de) C364 and Plus/4, Rob Clarke C232.

Other Versions

Meanwhile, Commodore Japan tried various other versions to reduce cost, and while they worked with us during these other models, they took the lead. One such computer was the Commodore C232 (see Fig. 2-2). It was a C264, but with only 32 kB of RAM. This doesn't sound like a big deal, but what it meant was that there were only four RAM chips instead of eight.

Fig. 2-2 C232 prototype.
Photo courtesy of Rob Clarke.

Looks like a Plus/4. You'll notice from the photos in this chapter that most of these TED family members looked quite similar. The one that stood out the most as looking different from the others was the C16, which was to be the most inexpensive computer Commodore would make. I'll talk about the C16 a bit later.

I'd been kept in the loop, though off the radar, throughout the production of these off models, thanks to my relationship with the Commodore Japan office. Once the designs showed up in West Chester, they came under my purview, and ultimately, I ended up signing off on all of these variations to the TED--all interesting, none of them hitting the mark like the original design did.

What Made TED Different

The TED computer was supposed to be as close to a single-chip computer as we could get in the 1980s. It was actually one of the first of this kind of computer, and certainly a first for Commodore, laying the groundwork for future single-chip systems--thanks to the versatile TED chip.

The TED chip provided the entire graphics display, including both NTSC and PAL modes, which were different television standards throughout the world. In the past before TED, we had to produce a chip for one mode and another chip for another mode. This would be our first chip that could be switched between the two modes, which was not easy, trust me. To make the math work, the chip had to wake up in PAL mode, the broadcast standard prevalent in Europe. If it woke up in NTSC mode (the American standard) and it was really a PAL computer, it would crash. But it could wake up in PAL mode in an NTSC computer and be okay. So we woke them up in PAL mode. This was the mode I witnessed in the microscope that one day (remember that story?) when the chip woke up in PAL mode and they needed a way to test the NTSC timings in spite of the fact they couldn't write to the chip.

In addition to the different video processor, the TED chip also produced sound, but was nothing like the SID (Sound Interface Device) chip of the Commodore 64. It did, however, produce enough sound effects for *business applications* on a small home computer, which was its purpose. TED also was the source of all the I/O (Input/Output) lines and scanned the keyboard itself. Unfortunately, the designers of TED thought they could use the data lines connected to the keyboard, which is not really recommended.

TED also directly controlled the DRAMs, a technique learned on the C64 and improved upon in TED. The chip designers for TED nailed the DRAM timings. I don't believe that I had to do any fixing of DRAM-related issues along the way.

Squawking Noises and Blame Game

This was not to say that everything was rosy however. When I got there, finger-pointing was in full bloom. The chip designers were blaming the hardware engineers; the programmers were blaming the chip designers. This resulted in Terry Ryan, who was writing BASIC for the TED, writing a memo in what he described as the "raucous, squawking noises" of the TED sound system.

The major complaint about sound was that the white noise was not white. It sounded like a bumblebee buzz or a rumbling freight train late at night. White noise is supposed to be composed of all frequencies at random values and amplitudes. It is not colored by prominent frequencies; it is, in effect, "white noise." If it is not random, the human ear will discern a pattern and that's what we had. This was a repeating pattern that was not random, so it had kind of a rock 'n roll beat to it, something we call "pink noise" on a good day and other names on days that weren't going so well.

This was truly a learning experience, as the designer, Dave DiOrio, had a 256 bit shift register and thought it would initialize randomly. I would have thought that, too. In real life, variances in fabrication and layout caused a bias to the white noise and it became the rumbling, rackety sounds that we ended up with. Dave and I had a conversation about randomization and random numbers in general. This is an ongoing topic in computer design and there was no great answer. At the end of the day, I believe Dave looked up some random numbers (the RAND Corporation sold a book of random number tables back then), and then he hard-coded them so that the same pseudorandom number would come up for every TED chip.

I had been a little surprised at the animosity between the various groups, and this was the first time real-life bickering had entered my perfect world where I found myself working at Commodore. I made a note to myself that, if I was ever in a position to prevent this kind of animosity again, I would do something about it.

2.2 The C116

So, the first member of the TED family was the C116, and while this was to be a big competitor in the low-cost computer market, history shows that it became the nearly unheard-of computer.

What It Was Supposed To Be

The main thing about the C116 was that it was meant to be a low-cost *business computer*, to sell for only $49, and not to compete with the Commodore 64. It was the last computer that I know of, in my belief, that Jack Tramiel basically had ordained or said, "This is what we're going to do at Commodore."

Now, look at the photo of the C116 (see Fig. 2-3). It's got a chiclet keyboard, but other than that, it's a full-blown system with 128 colors. Well, actually 121 colors, as eight shades of black is still black, so it really only has 121 colors. It does have sound, but, if you want music with the filters and everything, go buy a C64. TED didn't have sprites. Again, if you want to play games, buy a C64.

Fig. 2-3 C116 donated by Rob Clarke to Bil Herd.
Photo courtesy of Joel Herd.

The TED series was a niche-focused computer, and it wasn't meant to compete with the Commodore 64 nor to be a Commodore 64 in any light. Marketing apparently didn't get the message, and here Commodore lost its way after Jack Tramiel left. The people in marketing and whatnot couldn't tell the difference between the success of the Commodore C64 and this new machine called the TED, so they tried to turn it into a Commodore C64.

Now guess what? You can buy an Arduino board (single-board microcontroller for building digital devices) these days for the equivalent of $49, but usually with no keyboard, no sound, no case, no power supply. You can't buy any other computer with a keyboard, with sound, and power supply, or any of those things for that amount. So, in this, the C116 was ahead of its time.

The C116 was much smaller than the C64 and PET series of computers. Every single thing was in its place; every available space was used and nothing wasted. The number and sizes of the connectors, along with the keyboard, set the minimum size for the C116. The very first thing the C116 got a bad wrap about was the joystick port. The joystick ports weren't the standard Commodore joystick ports. I hadn't even seen a DIN connector this small until I saw the one in the C116, and it fit perfectly in the port size available. The big Atari joystick connector simply didn't fit, and again, if you wanted to play games, go buy a C64.

Ira Velensky Design

The TED series turned out to be a work of art, thanks to Ira Velensky who worked out of the Commodore Japan office. The classic computer design, the design of the computer case itself, was exemplified in both the C116 and C264 housings. These were pure Ira Velensky, and I learned to identify Ira's work, just as I would a fellow engineer's hardware design. I could look at a piece of plastic and tell whether Ira had designed it. I loved his work.

Ira Velensky had also designed other business systems and designed the case for the Digital Equipment Corporation (DEC) Rainbow. We found this out when he was in my office one time, and someone (Joe Myshko, who helped run the DEC VAXs) had brought in a foam packing piece for a keyboard to fit into a box. Ira looked at it and said, "This is from a DEC Rainbow," and he had the start of a smile that I would come to recognize when he was proud of something and could tell it was his baby just by looking at the packaging material.

Ira was a consummate designer and took pride in the title of designer. One time in the Tokyo office, he suddenly became obsessed with the appearance of his phone. For 10 minutes he could not be bothered with anything else while he found a simple but elegant way to dress up his phone with the addition of color--just a touch of it to the center of the dial of his Japanese phone. It was the '80s when phones tended to be dial phones. I learned the Japanese word for cellophane tape as he finished the modification with a flourish and pronounced his phone "designed." I had to admit that it looked better when done.

DRAM

What made the C116 possible in the first place was that the memory known as DRAM, for dynamic random-access memory, had come out in a new size, the 16 kB x 4 bit size, which meant that 16 kB x 8 could be done with just two memory chips. The local memory distributor was beside himself with joy when he learned that we would be buying millions of the 16 kB x 4 memory. Then I remember hearing his jaw drop over the phone when he realized that the C116 would be built in Japan with parts being sourced overseas, resulting in the fact that the parts would be bought from outside his territory. Feeling his pain, I wrote a letter to his company specifying that his support was instrumental in CBM adopting the 16 kB x 4 architecture.

Adding a Reset Circuit

The heart of the C116's design is the custom TED chip and the custom version of the 6502, known first as the 7501 in its HMOS version and 8501 in the HMOS II families, which basically were ways to make the chips go faster and use less power.

The philosophy of the TED computer family is that it was based on the minimum number of chips possible. When I got there, that was nine chips for the C116. Real quick, I realized that the reset circuit was a non-starter and would be problematic, as I noticed that the circuit itself was practically non-existent. It was overly simplified in a way that I was sure would not work right. It was a simple RC into a hex inverter and that doesn't work; it just doesn't work.

At my previous job at Pennsylvania Scale Company, I had made an art out of screwing up digital weighing instrumentations' reset circuits, using a Variable AC Transformer on the AC line. One of my special projects had been to make the reset circuit and voltage protection circuit for the battery backup RAM. Perfect. I knew more ways to break a reset circuit than anybody at Commodore at the time, and I immediately broke the one in the C116 design.

I went to Shiraz, my boss, and said we needed a foolproof reset circuit, that I was sure of this, and how the addition of one more chip--the venerable 555--would make a very serviceable reset circuit. I made a case that, if they wanted to go to mass production with this, they needed to increase the minimum number of chips.

I was told that Jack Tramiel himself had said there will be only nine chips in this computer. The technicians in the labs and a couple of engineers laughed and shook my hand, saying it was good working with me while I had been there, but that I was about to become an ex-Commodore engineer. This was apparently because I was going to violate Tramiel's mandate about nine chips, when we needed 10, and that I would consequently be fired for breaking the rule.

A funny thing happened. Much to everyone's surprise, I didn't get fired that week or the week after. In hindsight, Jack probably had not said nine chips total: he probably said that the system had to have a minimal number of chips. I added a 555 reset circuit, our problems went away, and I never had to revisit the reset circuit again on TED.

I still have my old TED schematic. Below, you can see my handwritten addition of the 555, showing where I taped it onto the schematic (see Fig. 2-4).

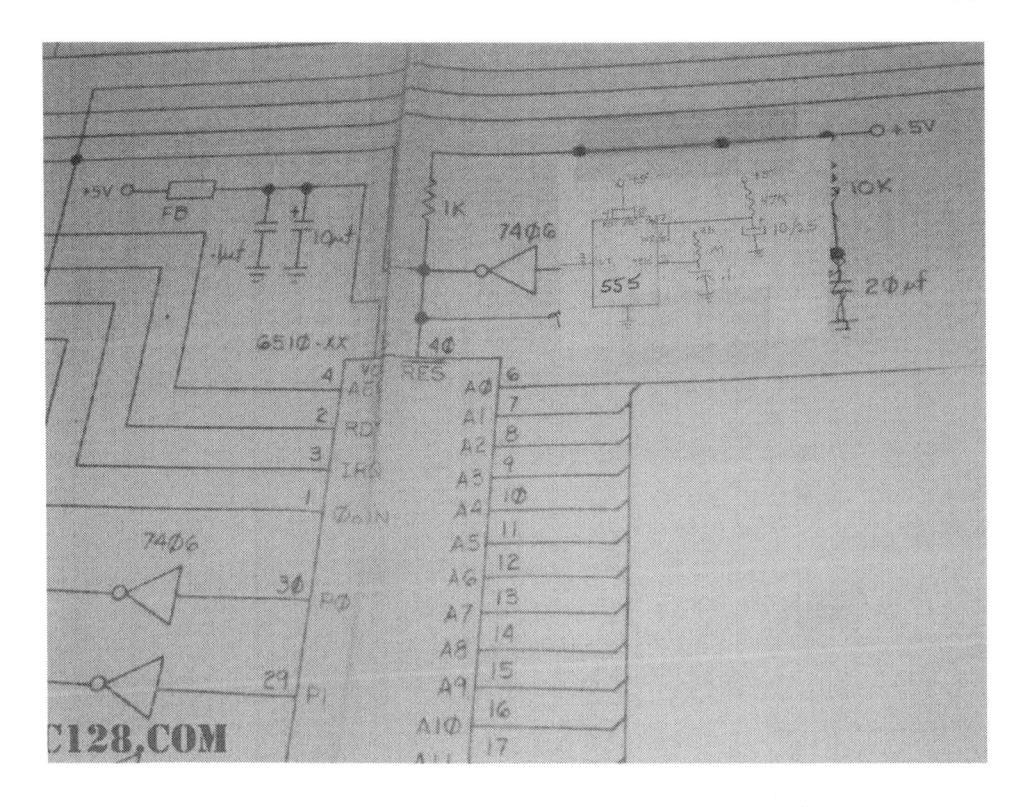

Fig. 2-4 Adding the 555 reset circuit to the TED schematic. Photo courtesy of Bil Herd (c128.com).

I think that if I had to pick a time when my boss started to believe that I really knew what I was doing, it might have been around now.

Taking Ownership and the TED Team

I had started to adopt the TED design as my own, though I still made a couple of mistakes, one being of not taking full ownership early enough, but more on that later. I had been carrying around the schematics of the TED under my arm for a couple of months now, but I still didn't feel like the owner of the design. I felt like the design came from the chip, and I was merely helping the chip to work.

The TED chip itself had been designed by Bruce Ahearns, Dave DiOrio, Eric Yang, and Bob Raible. It took a team to make the TED family. The people who worked on the TED computers were Fred Bowen, Terry Ryan, John Cooper, Dave Haynie, Hedley Davis, and myself.

ROM Monitor

One of the things that Fred and Terry built in right off the bat was a ROM monitor. This gave us the ability to disassemble our own work while working, to display and modify memory, and in short, to have a real time view into what was going on inside the computer. It was excellent. We actually got a telex from one of the heads of Commodore UK that said, "You've now created the perfect machine for piracy." And I sent back a telex that said, "Thank you." (It actually said, "thx" which was telex-speak for "thank you," since telex charged per character.)

Understand, I was a long-haired kid with no formal learning who had to be told not to eat with his feet.

Atari ROMs

Speaking of ROMs, it was during this time that I found out that MOS made all of the ROMs for the Atari 2600 games, or at least most of the ROMs. I asked if we had the code--what we called the font back then--that went in these ROMs, and proceeded to receive a tape with every single Atari game on it that MOS made. I would sit and stare at this tape and ponder the day when I would make a special ROM cartridge for my Atari 2600 at home, where I could reload any game I wanted. Alas, working at Commodore did not leave enough time to go home and work on computers in your spare time. If you had an ounce or a second, it needed to go to Commodore.

I Finally Got My Own C116

For 30 years, I didn't even own a C116 until Rob Clarke sent me one in 2015. The one that I have is a PAL version. I noticed that it's got some kind of European symbol on it. After all those years, I was feeling kind of sad when I mentioned it to my son because I wanted to show him what the TED PCB looked like (see Fig. 2-5).

I thought that it was a work of art.

Fig. 2-5 C116 PCB, donated to Bil by Rob Clarke.
Photo courtesy of Bil Herd.

2.3 TED Chip Problems

Back to the inner workings of the TED and how we overcame obstacles ...

Emulation

We needed a new TED chip and were waiting for that. The fact that the TED chip needed a revision was actually good from a system designer's point of view since we really didn't have anything to plug the chip into!

The wirewrap prototype that I had nixed, when I first took over, was based on the VIC-II chip, and while schematics existed for the newest TED machine, the C116, there wasn't a PCB to go along with it (see Fig. 2-6).

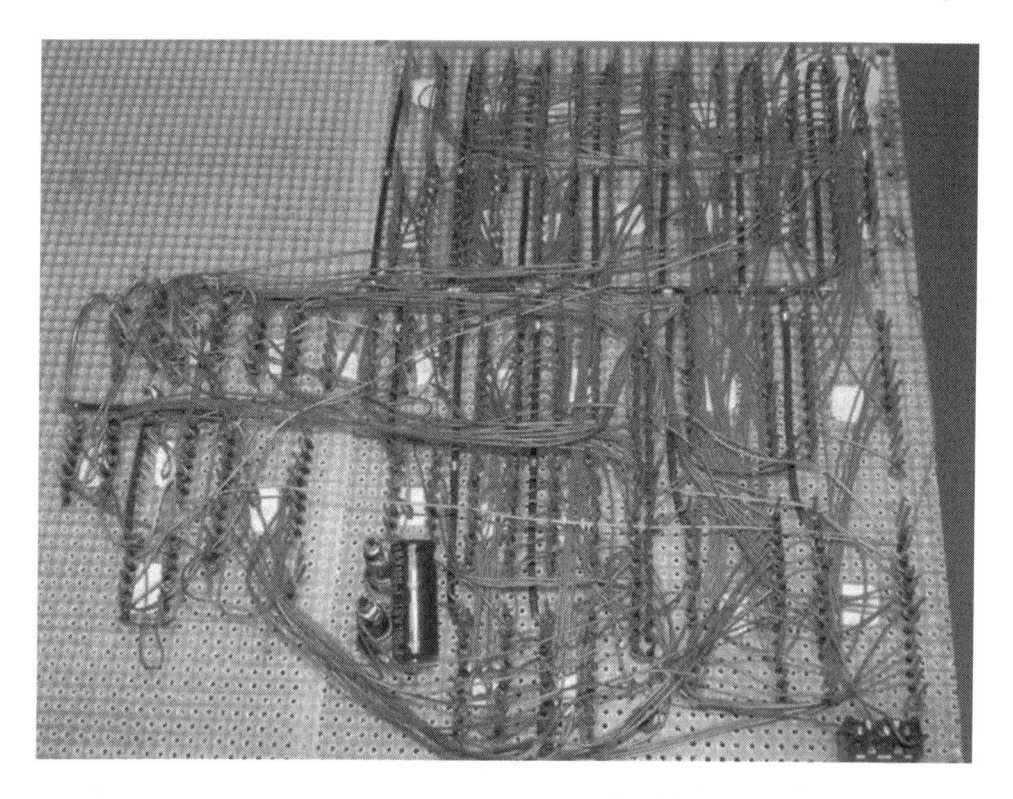

Fig. 2-6 Example of wirewrap construction.
Photo courtesy of Bil Herd.

We scrambled to create a PCB in the ensuing weeks and got the first PCBs in before we got the next revision of the TED chip. This left only one major stumbling block: we also needed a working version of the new microprocessor, which would become known as the 7501/8501.

Since the new TED chip was ready before the new processor chip, I had to build something to simulate the processor. I did this so that we could test the TED chip sooner than later, as we were always pushing forward and couldn't just wait while other chips, like the processor, were being revised. This would become a recurring theme through my tenure at CBM, and I realized early on that having access to custom chips, like only Commodore could do, meant that we often would need a way to simulate the completed chip prior to it being ready.

In preparation for the arrival of the (hopefully working) next revision of the TED chip, I designed a small hand built circuit we called a "tower" that we could plug into the microprocessor socket on the brand new PCB. With the tower and a few other chips, we made a standard 6510 (the microprocessor found in the C64) act enough like a 7501 (soon-to-be 8501) to test the TED system design.

We didn't know it then, but this technique of making "chip emulators," or small circuits to pretend to be the final version of custom silicon, would come to define how we kept to aggressive schedules.

Nothing Happened

When we plugged the new TED chip into our contraption, nothing happened. Nothing. This is the worst-case scenario in bringing up a microprocessor as everything has to work at least a little before anything works at all, and *nothing* was working. I sat there and stared at it, and what I was doing was loading the entire design into my head: the processor, the TED, and what I knew about it. I got quiet. Shiraz called a halt for the day. Terry Ryan reminded me that that night was his Bad Beer-and-Bad Movies party. I nodded to him and let him know I'd be there, but I was still real quiet, uncharacteristically quiet. I was doing something I had learned to do, which was to solve a problem subconsciously.

Bad Beer-and-Bad Movies Party

So engrossed in the problem was I, as I drove to the party that night, that I almost hit another car. I had to steer my Datsun 260Z between a telephone pole and the guy wire perfectly, without scratching my Z, as I avoided the car that I swerved to miss. I don't believe I stopped thinking about the problem, even as I backed my car out from between the pole and the wire, as I was that engrossed.

I got to the party, started drinking heavily, and, what's worse, is that I started taking it out on some innocent programmers. This would become a running joke from then on--to try not to kill more programmers than one can eat (a Terry Ryan-ism). At one point, I grabbed a young programmer, who I was still pissed at for rifling through my stuff one time, and told him to "drink with me." At one point, he had been drinking more than he could handle and went running out the back screen door. Unfortunately, he did not open the screen door before running through it and went out and puked in the middle of the backyard. I had my first kill for the night and went looking for my second.

Around 9:00 that night, I figured out what was wrong with the circuit. The flip flop was hooked up wrong on the little tower that we had made for the 7501. I was sure of it. I started drinking in earnest and killed two more programmers. The next morning, which was a Saturday, I walked into work, moved a single wire and the TED booted up. I'd been right the night before as to what the problem was. This would become my MO for solving really complex problems--to solve them holistically--to load the entire design, or as much as I could fit into my head, and think of the whole problem at once. Years later, I'm lucky to trim my fingernails evenly, let alone decipher minor discrepancies in macro timing diagrams in my head.

Black Dots--Add Two Diodes

Once we got the original TED chip to work, I noticed something right off. When I brought the computer close to the display monitor, little black dots would appear on the monitor. I threw an oscilloscope (scope) probe on the main signals and saw that they were stopping and restarting. Having learned from my friend Dave DiOrio about how MOS tested the chips as part of the production process, I knew that the test engineer needed a known starting place in order to test that the chip outputs were correct. They had probably built in a function to aid with this. Sure enough, I went back to Dave and I said, "Did you try and reuse this one pin as a test pin?" and the response was "Yes, how did you know?"

I brought the chip guys into the lab and showed them that the extreme sensitivity of the input pin made stray voltage sources, like your finger, trip the reset function. This effect also included the electric field from the monitor itself. When I touched it with my finger, the computer would literally freeze up. I ended up adding two germanium diodes to each TED chip. The diodes fixed the problem at the design level for a future revision by keeping the pins from ever getting more than .3 volts above 5 volts.

2.4 The C264 and C364

The two big brothers to the C116 were the C264 and the C364, both quite similar but with major differences and unexpected futures.

C264

The C264 was supposed to be the mainstay of the TED family (see Fig. 2-7). It had a full keyboard and 64 kB of RAM.

Fig. 2-7 C264 prototype.
Photo courtesy of Rob Clarke.

As I recall, it was supposed to sell for only $79, but I think that marketing ended up charging $349 and renamed it the Plus/4 after putting the Plus/4 software in it. The Plus/4 software was a way for the people in marketing to increase the sale price of the TED. I have never actually used the software, but I just didn't think that any software was worth the difference between $79 and $349.

Another feature of the 264 and other TED computers was the separate arrow-shaped cursor keys in a grouping at the bottom right of the keyboard. This new look and placement of cursor keys differed greatly from prior Commodore hits, like the VIC-20 and the C64 (see Fig. 2-8). While some people criticized them for being too difficult to manipulate when typing, on a positive note, they did provide an attractive layout to the keyboard (thanks to Ira) and were in an easy-to-find location relative to the main typing area.

Fig. 2-8 Plus/4 keyboard and cursor keys.
Photo courtesy of Christian Simpson (www.perifractic.com)

Ultimately, the C264 and the Plus/4 were identical in look, aside from the identity logo.

My First Japanese Word

During this time, I learned my first Japanese word. The keyboard for the C264 had arrived and Yash Terakura picked it up. When he flipped it over, there was a Japanese symbol written on it. "Ohmoi," he read out loud and then laughed. "Ohmoi" was Japanese for "heavy" among its multiple meanings.

Yash had been part of the original C64 team and he became my mentor for many things, including Japanese and different Japanese accents. At one time, I could tell an Osakan accent from Tokyo standard, thanks to Yash.

C364 Talking Desktop

The C364 had additional keys and it *spoke*. The idea was that you could have an entire desktop arrangement--we called it *Magic Desk*--to do business from this small computer. Yes, *before* the Macintosh, Commodore was already doing the *desktop environment*!

We added speech to it, so that you could say things like "Delete file." To do speech, we went to the top of the mountain, as it were in the '80s, and hired the team from Texas Instruments (TI) *Speak & Spell* to work at Commodore's Texas office. It was during this time that I met Tom Brightman and Dr. Richard Wiggins of the TI *Speak & Spell* crew. Tom and I became friends, and while everybody was uptight around Dr. Wiggins, I was known for leaning into his car trying to convince him to come to the bar with the rest of us and called him Richie in the process. I did get him to smile and laugh, even though he never did join us at the bar.

I had the pleasure of walking through the CES show with Dr. Wiggins. He would stop at every booth that was doing any kind of text-to-speech and would chat with the lead programmers or program managers. I learned ways to test text-to-speech, for example, with the word "hobo." I must have been a sight, a long-haired kid in his element, walking the CES show in the company of one of the scientists behind one of the main products of the day, my head on a swivel as I drank in the technology of the 1980s in all its glory. To this day, I've only grown older, but I have not grown up.

You know, it was a real honor to meet and work with those kinds of people, and it was an interesting thing to do. I don't know if the C364 had a target market audience, but in typical (post-Jack Tramiel) Commodore fashion, we put tremendous effort into making a talking version of this and then didn't sell it.

More TED Chip Revs

It had been a couple of months since I joined Commodore and the TED chip still wasn't working properly. The chip guys continued to work on TED in the background. About every three to four weeks, a new revision (rev) of the chip would show up. Inevitably, many things would be fixed, but a few things might break that had worked previously.

EPROM Emulator

One of the programmers had made his own EPROM emulator. This allowed him to make rapid changes to code and try it on the real computer. Ultimately, we copied his design and had two or three of them for the programmers to use. The only problem with the EPROM emulator was that sometimes it wouldn't start up right, and the only way to make it start then was to turn it off and turn it on. I started to look at the design, and the programmer gave me such a disgusted look that I stopped, as he was proud that he could do hardware also.

Finally, after a couple weeks of this problem, somebody noticed that it worked differently if it was frozen with cold spray. I did look at his design and realized that the programmer had thought that the 74LS157 was the same as the 74LS257, which it is not. Late one night after he had left, I snuck into his office and replaced the 157s with the 257s, and the problem went away. I may have done this without telling anyone, as I did not want to suffer another disgusting look.

2.5 People, Places, Things

You'll discover some diversions here and there throughout this book, such as this section. What made work life appealing was that our team members grew to be friends, in and out of work, and we could clown around without too much notice or interference from above.

Last Names

Thanks to my time in the Army, I had a tendency to call everybody by their last names. That was a common thing since we all had our last names plastered right on our uniforms. So, even though we were best of friends, you could hear me shouting down the hallway, hailing people by their last names in what we called The Commodore Paging System. I was Herd, Dave Haynie was Haynie, Greg Berlin was Berlin, and Terry Ryan was Ryan. You could hear me holler down the row of offices, "Yo, Bowen!" when I wanted Freddy's attention. The running joke was to tell our co-workers that it was tee-off time or that they had a call by the pool.

We walked around on a last-name basis with our friends, unless the name was confusing. For example, for some people like Hedley Davis, we used his first name, given that his name was so unique. But, for others, who we might not have liked that much, we called them by their first name. There were many managers who thought we were being very polite when in reality we might have been being a little sarcastic.

Bill Who?

One day, I walked into Bob Russell's office and somebody was on the phone, rather excitedly, with Microsoft. My memory is that the person kept saying, "No, Bill, listen," and finally asked to talk to Paul. This is at a time when Microsoft only had eight people working there and we were one of their customers. I have no idea if this memory is correct or just the imagination of a warped mind.

My MOS Office

My office at MOS ultimately was an 8-by-6 room with three people in it: three desks, three file cabinets, and a door. I never once felt cramped or out of place there, and I was just so excited to be working at Commodore/MOS. My office mates were John Ramage and Kong Su, who mostly worked in the business end of things, but we would spend at least an hour a day exchanging our technical knowledge with each other about whatever we were working on. We also knew who had to be quiet in such cramped surroundings, so that each other could work.

Greg Berlin

Greg Berlin joined MOS Technology at around the same time I did. I think maybe even the same week. As I had just fallen into being in charge of the TED hardware, Greg was next in the queue and got put in charge of the TED disk drive hardware. This meant that Greg and I were on the same schedules, vying for the same resources and planning for the same shows. It also meant that both of our products had to work before either product was considered to be workable, and so we were vested in each other's success even more than normal R&D camaraderie.

Greg would do the disk drives for every computer that I would work on during my time at Commodore. We formed a unique bond since we were under the exact same pressure, on the exact same schedules, and each in charge of our own computer. Disk drives were actually computers that just happened to support the reading of 1's and 0's stored on floppy media: in short, the drives were just as complex as the computer itself.

The first thing one noticed about Greg was his six-foot-eight height. He broke the mold of what people thought an engineer should look like, in much the same way I did with my long hair and tendency to not wear shoes.

Greg also lived a lot closer to Commodore than I did, and there would be many a night when I crashed on his couch or even his floor--and once in his yard when he wasn't home. (If you're going to sleep in someone's yard, make sure it's someone you know.) This wasn't as brutal as it sounds; the Army had taught me to lay down and sleep wherever and whenever I needed sleep.

Bunnies

Early on when we were still at the MOS building, Terry Ryan hung a picture of a rabbit (a sketch really) that he had photocopied, outside his room. To know Terry was to know this picture, as he was being cynical about the way we were crammed into our warrens like bunnies. At least, I assume so, although he may have been more cutting with his humor and I missed the point.

But I do know that bunnies multiply, and so one night I took down his photocopy, and I made a hundred more photocopies of it. I then proceeded to carefully hide each and every photocopy in a unique place. I would put one or two bunnies several kleenexes down in his Kleenex box. I went through his filing system, carefully filing pictures of bunnies. I basically abused his entire work area with pictures of bunnies. Part of our humor was then not fessing up to it, so poor Ryan walked around the halls wondering why there were bunnies jumping out at him from everywhere. I remember, two years later, Terry opening something only to find a bunny. I was rewarded with a quick giggle and "Ah, a bunny!"

My New Boss

One day, I got a new boss. I could hear him coming down the hall, stopping at each office to discuss each person's project with him, so that when he got to my office I was all prepared. I had timing diagrams, schedules, bills of materials--all the things he had been discussing with the people before me. I hate to say it, but I learned this trick in the Army while standing in line to talk to the drill sergeant. He made a point to tell us that we should be listening to the discussions of the people before us, so that we knew how to respond correctly. My boss and I got along from that day on, as we clearly had the same goals of getting the product out the door.

(Laughing) I remember one old-timer not doing so well and accusing our new boss (I had several over time) of not being his real father, or real manager, or similar. Needless to say, this joke didn't go over well. What had been the status quo with the prior boss was now different. From my viewpoint, I liked this new one (though we didn't always agree) in that he allowed me to own the design and did not micromanage me as long as I provided the information requested of me, which was part of the job description after all.

Jack's Brilliant Idea

Jack Tramiel had the brilliant idea of offering $100 off on a Commodore 64, if the home user sent us another brand of computer. This was brilliant in that it got all of those computers off the streets in addition to the sale of another Commodore 64. We had skids of third-party computers downstairs. Yash sent for a skid and had it brought up to the hall. We all took turns picking through this pile, and one of my claims that day was a Timex Sinclair ZX80. There were hundreds of them--brand new--as they were available for $50.

Sinclair Doorstops

So people were buying Sinclairs for $50 and sending them to Commodore for $100 off a new C64. We didn't care. As I had already stolen a door and modified my office to now have a door, I needed a doorstop, and the Timex Sinclair ZX80 was perfect. A couple of weeks later, somebody from marketing stopped by my office and saw my doorstop. Within a couple of days, every marketing door had a Timex Sinclair holding it open.

In addition, we probably got some Spectrums and tons of TI99s. We really took a swipe at all competitors. I also got a KIM-1 from the pile. I didn't see any Apples now that I think about it; they were way too expensive for this deal.

Pistol-Packing

A couple of other things that I grabbed out of the pile were plastic pistols that were meant for arcade shooter games where you pointed them at the TV screen. These pistols were life-like enough that I would carry them with me into corporate meetings, if I had a major bone to pick. I would come in, sit down, and put my guns on the table--literally. What no one really noticed was that I tended to leave the guns pointed at the person I was having a problem with, kind of as a pointer to who I was going to go after first.

My First Hire--Dave Haynie

It was about this time that I did my first hire of my career, who was a young man named David Haynie.

Twelve-hour days were a common work day for the core engineering and admin staff. So, it was not unusual to work eight hours at the office only to then caravan to the "headhunters'" offices which ultimately were spread up and down the Route 202 corridor outside of Philly. We were on a mission to fatten up our staff any way that we could. We were literally casting nets for the best and the brightest in the Philly area who might be open to a new job.

On one of those nights, we visited Al Etskovitz (aka Al White), one of our favorite headhunters. The headhunters became such an integral part of our environment that we used to consider them as good friends and invited them to our keg parties. It could be thought that the headhunters of the Philadelphia region were part of the team that made what we did in the 1980s possible.

One evening, I traveled to the headhunter's office with my boss. The headhunter left me in the lobby while he set us up with an interviewing room, and in bopped the first applicant, Dave. He more like *diddlebopped* (Yes, this is a word.) into the lobby, full of energy and aspiration. He plopped down in the chair next to me full of nervous energy, and I gave him a minute or two before I engaged him in conversation. Basically, I interviewed Dave without him knowing that he was being interviewed by one of the people from Commodore, right there in the lobby. I found out what he was doing and why he wanted a new job, and honestly, had he said some of the things he said to me in the lobby during the *real* interview, I might have questioned them. The line that sticks out in my mind is that Dave was writing high-level code basically for missiles for GE, and as he said that night sitting in the lobby, "I don't want to kill anybody." I totally believed him, and what he didn't know at that moment was that he had just been hired, even before he got to the interview room.

The running joke is that I even had a magazine upside down while I was talking to him, and Dave didn't notice, but the reality is I wouldn't have noticed if the magazine was upside down either at that point.

So, Dave joined us at the MOS building which was still in King of Prussia. We would become part of an elite group of engineers that had worked in the MOS building.

2.6 West Chester

Like all good things, living life crammed and being overstuffed into small offices had come to an end and Commodore purchased the QVC building in West Chester, Pennsylvania--a huge, beautiful building with lots of windows and woods surrounding it.

Moving Along

So, right in the middle of producing the TED computer systems, we up and moved the entire division: the hardware lab, programmers' offices, chip labs--all moved during the course of a week. I remember helping the guys in the lab carry the lab workbenches down a circular stair flight in the center of MOS singing at the top of my lungs 'cuz I knew it annoyed them. I was still being treated as the FNG and so I was going to have as much fun with it as I could. I think when they realized that I didn't *have* to be there carrying these awesomely heavy tables down the stairs that they started to cut me some slack.

No one actually complained about moving offices in the middle of a CES cycle, as we were that hurting for office space. And no one was actually in charge of the move in our area, so someone had taped a drawing of the office layout to the wall. Some industrious engineer pencilled in his name on the office he wanted. At that point, it became a free-for-all and the mad rush was on as we all started selecting the offices we wanted, oftentimes erasing someone else's name in the process. It became a game of musical chairs to be the last one with their name on a window office. Suddenly it was time to move.

All of us from the original MOS building ended up with window offices. That's a sign of seniority. For me, it was a sign of sanity as I would often stare out the window and wonder about things, such as whether 8 was the right number of bits to have for a computer.

Games Group

Moving the offices to West Chester had the effect of bringing the Commodore Games Group together in the same building as we were. The group was headed by Andy Finkel at the time, who I knew as one of the wise sages of Commodore; he knew the stories going back to the earlier times. The Games Group was cool, and I was friendly with every person there. Plus, they had their own arcade room. Yes, long before the Silicon Valley attitude of a ping-pong table, we had our own room full of video arcade games, some that were used by the people who ultimately would create computer games of the same (or similar) title. On a late night, I could grab a beer and go play an arcade game of *Wizard of Wor* or *Asteroids*.

Some of the members of the Games Group, in no particular order, were Carolyn Scheppner, Judy Braddick, Ric Cotton, Steve Finkel, Jeff Bruette, Steve Beats, and the head of the group, Andy Finkel (see Fig. 2-9 and Fig. 2-10).

Fig. 2-9 Bil Herd and Judy Braddick at Las Vegas Airport after CES 1985.
Photo courtesy of Terry Ryan.

I got so that I knew the different programmers by the software titles they had worked on. I remember Judy, who developed *International Tennis*, talking about the physics of the ball in tennis and that Jeff, who programmed *Wizard of Wor*, had a little 3D module of a spacecraft on his cabinet that he used as a visual aide to create the spacecraft as viewed from all angles. A tidbit that I found out later was that Ric (aka Eric) had set the clock on the Amiga desktop to the time when the Challenger shuttle exploded.

Fig. 2-10 Games Group Manager Andy Finkel (right in jeans) and Carolyn Scheppner (center). Hedley Davis (left). Summer 1985. Photo courtesy of Dave Haynie.

Ditching the PET

During this time, I finally had it with trying to do all my work on a PET 8032. One day, they caught me screaming while holding the PET over my head in the hallway--something about losing an entire night's work--and I was going to throw the PET if nobody took it from me. Thankfully, an engineer named Ric stepped up to save the day, calmly removing the computer from over my head and taking it for himself as he had not warranted having one yet, in the minds of management. I figured that there was a limit to what I could get away with, and at that time, throwing a PET in the hall (complete with CRT tube) would have most likely exceeded the limit. I probably could have gotten away with it a year later though.

I went to the chip guys and asked if I could be on their computer system. They all had ASCII terminals connected into several VAXs that acted as our core network. This was much more similar to what I was used to where

I came from in the small digital scale company. The answer I received was that there *was* an open terminal but no one to run the wires for it, so therefore, the answer was "no." I laughed. "I'm a hardware engineer," I explained. I went to the terminal and ran my own wire, becoming the only member of hardware engineering to be on their VAX. Haynie and I found a way to share this line, and ultimately, I got him his own terminal connection since we actually used the computer. The word "spreadsheet" didn't yet exist for the day, so we used the VAX version of *VisiCalc* that allowed us to change the numbers in cells and have the recalculation occur in real time. Trust me, I had done timing diagrams manually more times than I can count, and suddenly we didn't have to worry about stupid little mistakes interfering with our engineering.

Lake Herd

My West Chester office looked out over part of the roof above Production where a huge lake would form on top of the flat roof when it rained. One whole side of my office was window and it looked out over this body of water which I promptly named Lake Herd. I went so far as to draw a beach and palm trees on the window using dry erase markers. Unfortunately, we found out that, when you write on reflective foil with a dry erase marker and then bake it for several months, it cannot be erased. Lake Herd, complete with palm trees and seagulls, became a permanent fixture.

Like in the old location, the chip lab was attached to the hardware lab, but there was a problem. Being on the second floor of a large building, the vibrations of the building--especially when the air conditioner was running--made chip probing problematic, if not impossible. The chip guys had to abandon their chip lab and find a whole new lab downstairs, on the concrete slab as we said, leaving us with twice the R&D lab space that we had started with. We were in heaven.

What's more, we now had two entrances to the hardware lab. We ended up with a set of warning signals for when a particular manager might happen to wander in the front door, as oftentimes he would have some obscure assignment and he would give it to the first person he found. The techs would start making their signal sound and several of us would duck down and go scurrying out the back door of the hardware lab.

During this time, TED finally started to work fully. Users were able to plug a computer into a monitor and have it work straight up. Things seemed to be moving along.

Chapter 3

Middle TED

Despite this shred of light from the TED actually booting up and working (for the most part), I wasn't lulled into euphoria. I figured that there would be other technical hurdles to overcome--and there were. And, to add onto those, I had an unexpected trip coming up, as well as the next CES show to deal with.

3.1 More Problems

The one aspect of the design that I wished I had taken ownership of earlier, which I did eventually get to, was the design of the keyboard-joystick interface. There was a problem in the very way the keyboard interface was conceived and it turned into a show stopping issue within minutes of its discovery.

Keyboard-Joystick Problem

Unfortunately, the artifact that showed up was that, once we plugged a joystick into the TED, the black dots came back, but for a different reason. These were interference on the data bus. I could tell by looking at them. I looked up my ever-present schematic that I walked around with, sometimes subconsciously, and suddenly realized something I had not really thought of before: the chip guys had thought that the data bus could run out to the keyboard, as a way to read the keyboard directly with the TED chip. This is a bad idea. The data bus is much too dynamic and much too noisy to be exposed to the real world, either to radiate or to absorb noise.

I laughed out loud when I realized that the data bus ran to the keyboard. My boss had shown up around this time, just as I took a joystick and held it up to the monitor and the entire computer crashed. I laughed out loud again.

Fix It, Or You're Fired

Meanwhile my new boss was not amused. "Fix it," he said, "or you're fired." I laughed yet again. He was still not amused.

Within a couple of hours, I had found a fix, and it was a pure Commodore type fix. I needed something to insulate the data bus from the keyboard and yet still had to put up with multiple keys being pressed, which would short the driver outputs together.

Looking at the *MOS Data Book*, I found a single port I/O chip which has soft outputs that Commodore themselves made. I loved this, as I hated being dependent on other companies' parts, especially for timely delivery. If I used an MOS part to fix this, then we would be in charge of our own production schedule. Enter the MOS 6529, a single port I/O chip that I never even heard of until that day, and I used it to fix the data-to-the-keyboard problem.

My boss walked back into the lab later that day, and I was standing there playing a video game, the *Wizard of Wor*, on the TED. He got mad and told me that he thought he had told me to fix the problem. I smiled and pointed at the monitor. He got more aggravated. I smiled again and pointed at the monitor and the joystick cable, but he still missed what I was showing him. Finally, I showed him that I had put a 10-foot joystick cable on the joystick, I had removed the housing off of the computer monitor, and I had wrapped the joystick cable around the high-voltage section. This was proof positive that no interference could now crash the computer. He grumbled something and walked away. I continued to play the *Wizard of Wor*, smiling.

My boss threatened to fire me twice during my tenure at Commodore. This was the first time and I had survived.

3.2 To Japan

Just as I was settling into the routine--I probably hadn't really settled in, but in hindsight it feels like I had--I found out my presence was needed in Japan, or they wanted to get me out of West Chester, one of the two ... maybe both.

Traveling to Japan was not a common thing back then. In fact, we had very little exposure to Japanese culture other than some cartoons that were the forerunners of today's *Manga* (*Star Blazers*, aka *Space Ship Yamato*).

The Trip

On Thursday, I was told to get my passport photo in downtown Philadelphia, which I did, and then Friday was spent in New York City getting my visa to Japan straightened away. This was the most travel I had done shy of joining the Army, but I got it all done in time. By the time I got to the front of the line in the Japanese Consulate, I had learned the answers to their questions by heart in Japanese by listening to the people in front of me.

It seems I had been born with a visual memory and if I could visualize something, even a foreign word, then I could remember that visualization easily. I found that the quickest way for me to learn Japanese was to write down whatever word I was learning, at least once. Since I learned most of my Japanese while sitting in bars, most of the Japanese words I had written down were on bar napkins.

I spent that weekend on a flight to Japan. If that sounds like a long time, it was. This being my first flight to Japan, I didn't know that I was supposed to ask for a "polar route" which goes north from New York and is the shortest flight to Japan. I, instead, found myself on a 23-hour flight that went straight west across the United States, landed in California to refuel, and then flew to Japan from there. This was also the first time I learned about something called "business class." I learned that business class had free drinks on it. I learned to drink myself into and out of a stupor three times on these long flights as a way to break up the monotony.

I landed in Japan, beat, worn out, and excited. Nobody had told me anything to do once I got there. To a young engineer from Commodore, this was just more excitement and finding my way in a foreign country was par for the course. It was at this time I learned that my luggage had failed to make the exciting trip across the Pacific and would not be joining me until the day it was time for me to leave Japan. I chalked it up to part of the adventure and moved on. As I was getting near the front of the airport, I noticed a young man holding a crudely drawn Commodore logo on a piece of paper. I walked up and started to talk to him before I realized he did not speak English. We figured out that I was indeed the person he was waiting for and he escorted me to the train that went from Narita Airport to Tokyo itself.

Now, I was born and lived in the country, had only been to New York City once or twice in my life, and only to Philadelphia for my passport and to attend the odd rock concert or two. Now, I found myself wandering the streets of a strange city, Tokyo. Yes. Not only were the people driving on the wrong side of the roads, the roads were only a couple of feet across. All of the sizes were miniaturized compared to American standards, including the cars and trucks that fit down those tiny little alleyways.

Team Japan

Here I met what was essentially the C64 design team, and this was a true team in Japanese fashion where no one person was given credit beyond that of a team member. It wasn't until decades later--like 2020--that I actually asked Yash Terakura for the names of the individuals on the C64 design team. You see, it's kind of a cultural thing not to ask someone how famous someone is, if one doesn't already know. The reply was typically Japanese: "C64 team: Tokai, Okubo, Yash, and gangs."

The engineers were run by a man named Okubo-san who became my friend and something of a mentor, whether he knew it or not. I would learn

Japanese style production engineering from him over the course of the next year.

I also met Ira Velensky, the case designer of the TED series and also of the B machines, as some of the business computers were called. Essentially, in the early '80s, any of Commodore's designs that didn't look like square sheet metal were done by Ira.

In true Japanese fashion, they gathered all the members of the Japan Tokyo office to meet me, where I stood in front of everybody and joked about having lost my luggage. I figured out quickly that not many people actually spoke a lot of English, but they laughed politely anyway.

I also met Sam Tramiel, son of founder Jack Tramiel. Sam's office was at the end of the big room that served as the office for everybody else and had a bit of a *Wizard of Oz* feel to it. Sam kept a humidifier running right by the door to his office, and so the effect was a never-ending blanket of steam that flowed out of his office as if the wizard was at work. I talked with Sam only that one day, and even though he was in his office every single day that I was in the Japan office, our paths did not cross again; just the steam emanating from his office attested to his presence.

Samurai Desu

Unexpectedly, it was time for a team meeting, and I found myself in the conference room of Commodore Tokyo. Most everyone had filed in when one of the big Tokyo bosses entered the room, and I saw everyone's postures change. All of a sudden, the managers acted like their boss had just walked in. I was a little dismayed at this. These were strong managers who suddenly kowtowed to the big boss, who then walked over to one of the chairs and slapped the back of it. A manager immediately took his place in the seat and leaned on his hand, covering his mouth, in what I came to understand was a way of showing subservience.

I did what any headstrong, long-haired guy "gaijin" (foreigner) would do: I stared straight into the boss's eyes and put my feet up on the table in a direct challenge. The boss looked directly at me, and I quietly declared, so that he could hear me--in Japanese--"Samurai desu," meaning, "I am Samurai, (also)." He grunted and then took his seat; and after a minute or two, I took my feet off the table so that the meeting could commence. It's important to understand that there wasn't an ounce of subservience in the young Bil Herd: the only way I got anything done at Commodore was to run rampant over the obstacles, as if they didn't exist. Oh, and I was mad that my friend had had to show subservience, even if it was typical of the culture.

My Shrinking Desk

I was given a desk as part of an island of desks in the Japanese office motif. They prized communication in team spirit above all other attributes and didn't seem to have the Yankee need for privacy. They initially cleaned off my desk for me, but I soon learned that it was my responsibility to keep all the encroachment of other people's belongings off of my desk. In other words, my desk got smaller every day. I do remember that I mortified everybody when I went to the bathroom to get a roll of toilet paper and set it on my desk to use to blow my nose and to do general cleanup, in a typical gaijin fashion. One young lady, Rimi-chan, who quickly became my friend, ran out at lunch and bought me a box of Kleenexes and sternly took away my roll of toilet paper. "Please, B-san, no," she told me in a voice I have used with my own puppy.

After a day or two of sharing a common desk area, I was losing the battle to keep my desk from being encroached upon by the overflow from other people's desks. I did what I always do in these situations: I found a corner, back in the hardware lab and made "Fort Herd," using test equipment and shelves to build my own little workspace. I also learned that safety protocols, which we have in the States, didn't apply. For example, doors often opened inward, and I would walk straight into them. In the States, all doors open outward in case of a fire.

Another thing that I will never take for granted any more is the National Electrical Code. In Tokyo, everything from the fan to the oscilloscopes had voltage selection on it, and even had a frequency adjustment, as sometimes the main AC frequency was 60 hertz like in the States, but on the other side of the mountain, it was 50 hertz. Where I screwed up rather badly was when I plugged an oscilloscope set for 110 volts into a regular-looking outlet that was 220. Too late I noticed the little label that someone had put on the outlet saying 220, something that would not happen at home--ever! I remember the oscilloscope clicking and thought I smelled something, which brought my attention to the fact that I may have just ruined a Tektronix oscilloscope. It smelled expensive.

Japanese Food

That first night, I had my first sushi ever, and I am now spoiled because I had my first sushi in Tokyo, Japan. I also got hooked on things like octopus salad and various forms of seaweed: simply put, tastes that I had never experienced before in my life. We went out every night after work. It was part of the Japanese culture, especially with a visitor, though the reality is that people would only stay out for a couple of hours, whereas I tended to drink all night long.

One night, everybody took me out to a special dinner in my honor, and this would happen on every trip I made there. On one such event, I was served raw horse meat. On another, they cut up a live fish (ikizukuri) just as I was served it, which I would not touch. I told them this was cruel. They understood, but they also giggled each time the fish flopped on my plate.

I did draw the line though when I was served a special dish of very thin slices of whale meat. I was aghast. This was the only dish I was served where the cultural differences were never more apparent, and in my newfound Japanese baby talk, I told them that eating whale was "cold to heart." In English, I told the story about how whales used to be able to talk to each other over hundreds of miles, but that once humans started making noise in the ocean, whales could no longer talk to each other, except up close. And, I also expressed the fact that I liked whales more than I liked most middle managers.

Out of deference to me, the plate of whale meat sat there untouched. I'm sure that was hundreds of dollars' worth of food, and the reality is that it was now wasted food, but I couldn't eat it. I'm gaijin, I don't believe in killing whales, and I don't believe in eating them.

It was during one of these dinners that I related that one of my nicknames was "Animal," which translated to "Doobutsu" in Japanese, a nickname I still go by in both languages to this day. I also explained that my last name, "Herd," meant "many animals" in English, which made a lot of sense to the people I was telling this to, and they nodded appreciatively. I also knew the Japanese words for "dog" and a few other mammals, so when someone tried to modify my name (I heard someone call me a "big dog" at one point, probably due to the amount of hair that I had), I was able to respond immediately in Japanese that I was Animal, not a dog.

On subsequent trips to Japan, I noticed that they would play the game of "see what the gajin will eat" as they would serve dishes that they themselves weren't eating. When I commented on this fact, they replied rather slyly that they were for "guests." One of the dishes I took a pass on was smoked sparrow embryos or a dish we called "crunchy sparrow." Bob Russell did try the dish and was rewarded with not being able to go to the bathroom for over a week.

Long Flights to Japan

During my time at Commodore, I made several trips to Japan. By the time I got to my second or third trip to Japan, I had learned to deal with some of the discomforts of flying such a long trip, taking between 14 to 23 hours to arrive in Tokyo, depending on the route taken. One time, I was in business class, which I always tried to fly as I could get all the free drinks I wanted and free headsets. This was back when headsets in airplanes were these awful, uncomfortable acoustic pipe-driven things, but you had to pay for them if you were in economy class.

On this one flight, the economy class was basically empty. There were entire rows where one could lie down to sleep, whereas in business class, there were no open rows left. So, I loaded up with free drinks and a pile of free headsets, and I wandered back to economy class.

I often joke that I had to kick a chicken or two out of the way and bed down in some straw, but it wasn't quite that bad. I gave the Bloody Marys to the people around me in economy and handed out the headsets, in exchange for their help. While I was sleeping, if the flight attendant asked, they told her that I was not from business class, but was from economy. In other words, I bought their protection with vodka, tomato juice, and headsets.

Upstairs Lounge

My favorite place on my flights to Japan in the 747s of the day was in the Upstairs Lounge of the airplane. There was a row behind all of the other rows on the floor that was open and empty. On one flight, I got back behind the last row in the upstairs of the plane and slept on the floor for a good eight hours. You could see my feet sticking out into the aisle, but since it was the last row, there were no complaints issued, and you could see my feet turning over from time to time as I tossed in my sleep. I awoke with just a couple hours to go before arriving in Tokyo, and this, by far, was my best flight.

I had heard about how good the movie *War Games* was, but I had no time to go to the movies myself. Then, on one flight where I was miserable and bored, as the flight had just started, I had over 12 hours to kill. *War Games* came on, killing two hours, and I was the happiest engineer on the flight.

3.3 Fixing Things

In Japan, I had my first glimpse of the C116, as it was to be, as well as learned an interesting fix for the C64.

Power Resistor

The C116 was beautiful, a work of art. It had the smallest possible case you could design and contain a computer of the day. Something stood out to me though. I had learned that there was a heat problem, which we would have to address later when we needed to put together some prototype units. I could solve that by putting in a large heat sink in the prototype units, which had a larger housing. However, there was no room for a standard heat sink, and little room for even a custom one, in the smaller C116 housing that would be used in the production version. But something caught my eye. I noticed a 10-watt resistor near the power supply. I looked at this for a total of about six seconds before I started laughing. I knew what they had done: they had cheated in a most Commodorian fashion. They had routed most of the heat to this resistor by making the assumption that the computer would always draw a certain amount of current. They took this minimal amount of current and "threw it away in the power resistor." Even this kludge was beautiful; I got it, and that changed my life as an engineer. I was becoming a Commodore high-quantity, production-based design engineer, who spoke a smattering of Japanese.

The power resistor, while it solved the problem, felt like a little bit of a dirty trick, and I reveled in this dirtiness of doing whatever it took to get high quantity production out the door. This meant you couldn't overlook a single rule of physics! If someone missed anything at all, the mass quantities that we ran would be sure to roll up your problem and drop it at your feet times thousands. So, while the power resistor was a dirty little trick, it did indeed work, and it would have been worse to have no resistor at all.

C64 Noise aka Sparkle

Understanding the mentality of what I saw in the C116 allowed me to start "reading" the C64 schematic, as it was obvious that the C64 design was one where several major problems had needed to be fixed. They did get fixed and they got fixed in ways you would not ever design a computer from scratch to do, but they worked.

A major concern of the Commodore 64 was "electrical noise" that could be seen on the monitor, and this was something that nobody had known about until the computer was designed and done. There were two types of noise basically: the static unmoving noise and the dynamic moving noise. The dynamic moving noise was much more annoying to the human eye as there were flickers and herringbones racing across the screen, so much so that Commodore formed the "tiger team" to fix the Commodore 64.

Now, while this was before my time, one notable area was that on the home screen of light blue and dark blue, there were light blue flashes throughout the screen. This occurred when the foreground color would accidentally be mapped on top of the background color. Benny Pruden told me that one of the fixes that the team had come up with was to set any unused characters to be dark blue on a dark blue screen instead of light blue on dark blue. So, while it was still flashing foreground to background, they were both the same color and it *appeared* to be quieter. What I learned from this was that hardware could be fixed in software sometimes, or worse case, could be made to look to be fixed when nothing had really changed.

TED Easter Egg

Speaking of unseen things, in the '70s and '80s, it became popular for programmers to embed their names, and sometimes a message, into the operating system of the computer. It was known as the Easter egg, since it also became popular to search for these hidden prizes. Here is the Easter egg hidden in the Plus/4, which can be seen by entering SYS 52650 at the BASIC command prompt (see Fig. 3-1).

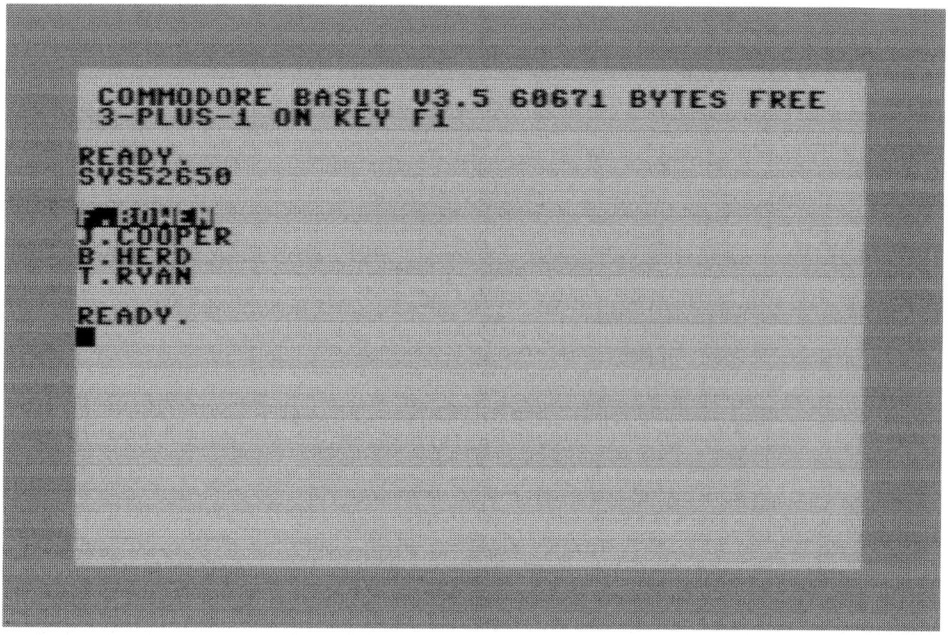

Fig. 3-1 Plus/4 Easter egg.
Photo courtesy of Rob Clarke.

3.4 Fun in Japan

One of the early things I learned from traveling to Japan was what jet lag really meant and how it affected me. And, as was my normal inclination back home, while in Japan, I naturally gravitated toward fun, both inside and outside of work.

Jet Lag and Macross

I couldn't sleep at night, I couldn't sleep in the morning. So I would spend my off time watching Japanese TV. I put on a show that had giant robots and a space carrier called Macross, and I was hooked. I couldn't understand a word that was being said, but that didn't matter. The sci-fi action and subject matter was so dear to my heart that I became a *Macross/Robotech* fan for life. This show, I later found out, was a predecessor to what later was known as *Anime*.

On future trips, I would collect the toys of the Macross collection. I almost missed a train one time as I was lying on my stomach pulling out old, dusty toys from the bottom shelf of a small toy store with the help of the owner, who was enthralled that a guy knew what Macross was and was eliminating some of his old, dusty inventory. Ray Hughes and Ira Velensky wanted to see one of my models while we were in a taxi, and so I opened the box of the Valkyrie fighter jet model. Just then, the cab driver announced the arrival at our destination. Everybody started to get out of the cab, and my Macross parts fell into the street of a busy downtown Tokyo intersection. We scrambled to get my parts off the road and had a good laugh, but I never again opened the box while we were in a cab.

Speaking of cabs, back then the cabs' doors would open for you as you approached the cab. There was a little lever mechanism inside each cab door, and boy did they get pissed when you slammed the door, like we do in the States, rather than wait for the driver to close it manually. More than once, I had to endure the stare of an irate cab driver after I forgot and slammed the cab door myself.

Yikes! Was I in the Women's Room?

While in Japan, I learned to not ask the instructions to the men's room in Japanese unless I was prepared to hear--and understand--the answer in Japanese. I learned that it was often best to just ask in English.

One time while in the men's room, I distinctly heard the sound of a woman sigh. At this point, I assumed that I'd walked into the wrong bathroom, having misread the sign. I was mortified. So I sat there quietly in the stall, waiting for the woman to leave. As it turns out, she was a cleaning woman, and I was in the men's room after all. I still waited for her to leave though.

Hard Rock Cafe

I bought a shirt from the Hard Rock Cafe back when there were only three of these cafes in the world, one being in Tokyo. The Hard Rock Cafe was in the section of Tokyo known as Roppongi, and it was known for where the gaijins hung out. I hung out there, too, though I would also trip over to the nearby pinball machine places. Nowadays, you can have a shirt made that says anything you want, but back then a Hard Rock Cafe shirt from Tokyo was really something. I bought two more on a return trip, but accidentally left them sitting in a restaurant.

Subway Maps

This reminds me. On one of my trips to Japan, I pulled out a map of Tokyo to try and figure out which subway I would need to take. A woman saw me and couldn't believe that I had a map of some place in Japan with me, let alone that I was using it. Pretty soon, the entire shuttle bus was asking me about my adventures and what a computer was. This happened to me a lot. If I so much as wore a Commodore t-shirt, I could bet on standing and talking with lots of wonderful people before the end of the night.

Time To Go Home

After seven days in Japan and learning firsthand what jet lag really means, something happened. I had been learning Japanese at a rapid rate, but suddenly my brain had filled up. I could learn no new words. In fact, I couldn't speak the ones I had already known. I started to stutter. It was time to go home.

As I prepared to leave to go back to the States, I found out about an old tradition at Commodore, called "muling," which is where you load up the person traveling with absolutely as much as they can carry, as if one were a mule. In my case, I had to carry various parts of mechanical assemblies, etc., anything needed by the R&D lab when we couldn't wait a month for it to travel by boat.

Customs' Mess

When I got to Customs in New York, they tore open my boxes, leaving me no way to reseal them and a big mess on my hands. In the future, when I would close each box, I would leave a roll of tape and a razor blade in each box to help reseal it. On my last time traveling to Japan, the only box I did not do this to was a box of keycaps, 10,000 of them. The Customs' agent said he'd never seen 10,000 of anything before and wanted to see what they looked like. He tore open the box: keycaps went everywhere. I laughed, told him he now owned a bunch of keycaps, and started to make my way towards the door. He objected. I said that I had no objection to leaving my materials with him in his safekeeping, and I left. When I found a pay phone (remember pay phones?), I called the Customs' broker for Commodore and told him that he may want to head down to Customs to claim some unclaimed material. The scene is still stuck in my memory of looking over my shoulder and seeing hundreds of keycaps strewn across a marble floor.

During my time in Japan, I had seen the entire TED family, including accessories: the printers, the monitors, everything new for this new family of computers. We agreed that we would continue to travel back and forth in efforts to make the two engineering departments closer. The fact that I was learning Japanese and was totally enamored with the Japanese lifestyle helped also.

Bad Habits

Actually, after I came home, I discovered that I had picked up the bad habit of turning off my headlights when stopping at intersections at night, as was the habit in Japan, which made wonderful sense when trying to figure out which vehicles were in motion or not. I had to stop doing this eventually, or I would have been pulled over for acting erratically in the States.

I often returned home with bad habits that would take me a week or two to overcome, like shouting "Hai!" to almost any question, meaning "Yes." Terry Ryan used to ask me questions that needed a "Yes" answer just to mess with me during this time.

3.5 Slight Detour

Sometime after I got back from Japan, I found out that we needed to take a detour. No problem.

TED Alpha Units

We needed to produce some proof-of-concept Alpha units so that third-party software programmers could start developing for our new computer series, in advance of the actual computer becoming available. The real computer would not be available until the day it was available, which certainly would be the day *after* CES. It was decided that we would release 30 Alpha units for early software development.

Basically, we took a C116 and slapped it into a Commodore 64 housing, using the venerable Commodore 64 power supply. We used one-off PC boards: these would be the last printed circuit boards where we went outside of Commodore for PCB layout, and they would not be re-used after this one time. We went to 4th Generation in Bristol, Pennsylvania, to have them laid out in good old-fashioned "hand tape" on mylar. There were 30 of these, and with the exception of a couple that got *liberated* from the hardware lab, we shipped these units to our best third-party developers. I am still irritated to this day about this event, since they had stolen something that we didn't have any to spare whatsoever--our time. Forget the $5,000 cost of each unit; it was the *time* we invested in them that cost us.

So, I was spending several hours on the road each day driving to Bristol and back, in addition to my regular duties. I had assigned Haynie to take care of everything else needed to get the Alpha units completed. While these units placed a huge drain on vital resources in the middle of a project, they were needed and showed Commodore's commitment to software support prior to the release of a computer. This was back when we were still planning, or at least pretending, to market our computers.

I consequently forgot about the Alpha units until some 20 years later when I saw a picture of one of the units, and I recognized the handwriting on the EPROM. Full recognition slowly dawned on me as I saw the handwriting of a 24-year old me all over the board, and I realized that this was one of the Alpha units that had been found in a basement somewhere in Europe. I can only hope that it achieved its mission that set it on such a long trip.

3.6 Winter CES Las Vegas 1984

Around this time, the pace started picking up. Tensions got a little higher, and people became a little more short-tempered. CES was in the air! The hardware lab became a staging area for what would be Commodore's booth at CES.

PERT

It was during this time that I started to teach myself a way to track all of these variables (i.e. scheduling). I had never been taught formally how to do this, and so I was trying to invent my own way to track things that affected so many other things. I started to write them down, circle them on a big piece of paper, and then show their influence on other circles on the paper. I didn't know it, but I had reinvented the PERT (Program Evaluation Review Technique) chart. Since I knew MOS's scheduling fairly well, I was able to put together some pretty accurate schedules. The effort making the PERT was always worthwhile when I realized that a chip wouldn't be done in time unless I reorganized when I asked for the chips. Simply put, I wasn't willing to substitute the answer that MOS couldn't deliver on time, a common excuse at the time, rather than succeed. Instead, I gamed the system and got every available slot I ever asked for, because I was asking for the right slot at the right time.

Gurple

The C364s were in and they talked! They really did. You typed what you wanted to say, and they would say any one of 256 words, clearly. They were using a single byte value to represent which word to say, otherwise known as a token. One oddity we found was that when saying the word "purple," the C364 would actually say the word "gurple." We left about 12 of them turned on one night, all saying the word "gurple" in loops written in BASIC, a present for the head of the lab the next morning. Back then, recording a reasonable quality dictionary actually required renting a sound studio; then a mask ROM of the phonemes and other sound pieces would be cut; and then finally it could talk. We figured that there wouldn't be an update just for the word "gurple," and there wasn't. So, if you can find one of these rare C364s, you will hear that it still says "gurple."

Then one day I received the bad news: I would need a sports jacket if I were to go to the CES show. Basically, they were telling me that my ever-present jeans and t-shirt were not appropriate attire to represent Commodore at the biggest show of the year. My response was that they hadn't yet seen me in a jacket--they might want to rethink that. Regardless, I went and got myself a corduroy jacket, not realizing that a silver jacket and brown slacks didn't really match, but I wore them anyway.

Late Night Flight to CES

Suddenly, it was time to go to the show. A mad flurry of activity culminated with me finding myself sitting in the Philadelphia airport late one night sometime around midnight with a box of TED power supplies that I was muling to the show. There were two women in the waiting area, both carrying boxes of their own. We started talking and found that we were all headed to the same CES booth at the same show. These women were from our International Marketing Department. The friendship I made that night in the airport would be helpful over and over in the years to come, as now I literally knew people in headquarters, and a marketing department at that.

The flight into Vegas was very rough that night. I remember the beer foaming out of my complimentary beer can due to the turbulence. What an adventure to be on, traveling to CES to show what I'd worked on for the last year of my life, and what everybody had worked on. We were coming together as a team and would only get better.

I also made another friend, the airline attendant, who asked me if I could hold her steady while she tried to pour drinks for other passengers. Such was the turbulence on our flight. I helped by reaching out and holding her by her hips as she served everybody in our area. Later, she came and sat down next to me, and we talked for a big portion of the trip into Vegas. I was starting to understand that I had an infectious personality and that my excitement and jubilance was predominant and genuine.

The Dump Hotel

I got in sometime in the early hours and checked in at our hotel, which was a mess. After we set up our booth that day (the day before the show started), we headed out into Vegas. I'm sure I didn't get in till 4:00 or 5:00 in the morning. Meanwhile, of our four or five rooms, only about two had a working lock; the others looked like they had been kicked in too many times to fix properly. So, to provide some semblance of security, we took the mattresses out of four different rooms and we all holed up in one hotel room, often with an engineer (preferably a hardware engineer) standing watch while the others slept.

I remember, as we stood around the next morning waiting to leave for the show, hearing a lion's roar in the parking lot. Something very primal about that sound caused the hair on the back of my neck to stand up: this was an old predator. We later figured out that it must have been a lion from the Siegfried & Roy Show nearby, or some similar act.

Commodore's CES Booth

The CES booth had a kind of three-ring circus feel to it. Out front, we had a magician who was doing tricks that combined a C64 with audience interaction, doing what looked like card tricks, for example. Then there was a mime whose job it was to rope in passersby. He used to throw an imaginary rope to people as they walked by, and then lead them over to one of the Commodore activity areas. His name was Egg, and we went on to become friends. One time, we bumped into each other at a show in Boston. He broke character and we talked at length. People noticed and asked, "How did you get him to talk to you? He doesn't talk!"

There was also a section of the booth where Jim Butterfield, a well-known Commodore personality, was doing his particular kind of audience interaction. There were other areas where people could play C64 games and otherwise explore Commodore's product offerings. This was a very consumer-oriented booth, and it had been put together by David Rogers, who previously was a producer on the Mike Douglas TV show out of Philadelphia. I didn't know this until we were sitting in a bar and David happened to drop that fact to a couple of women in the bar. I thought to myself, "That's the best pick-up line I've ever heard," and told him so.

Monitor Fuse Problem--Heat Variable Resistor

We were putting together the display stations, to be comprised of a TED, a TED monitor, and a printer, when we found our first issue. Truthfully, the issue was going to come up at some point or other; we just happened to find it at CES. If you rapidly turned off and on one of the monitors, it would blow its fuse. Basically, they hadn't gotten the "slow turn on" portion of firing up a monitor correct, something that was important for preventing inrush currents that were too large. A common trick was to use a heat variable resistor, and that was an issue. The problem was that when I turned the monitor off and on rapidly, the already hot variable resistor would allow a huge inrush of current, which would blow the monitor's fuse.

Unfortunately, the fuse was very deep in a block of epoxy. One of the engineers from Japan ran out to the local Radio Shack and bought some jumper leads, unfortunately getting into a mild fender bender in the process. He and I drove Phillips screwdrivers into this block of epoxy, using a hammer and a screwdriver, until each screwdriver shorted to each end of the fuse. We then clamped the alligator leads to the two screwdrivers, and, lo and behold, the monitors came back on. This was a real cheesy expedient! To that end, we only showed a handful of monitors working. I think we even removed the on-off knobs on a couple of monitors so that people wouldn't turn them on and off themselves while viewing them.

At the end of the day, we gathered in that happy, tired kind of way after a long day; I heard Okubo-san mutter the words "shinu mousugu" and asked him what he meant. "Soon die" was his response and I laughed. My response was that I was near death as well, but in a good way. But hey, we just made the CES show and pulled off everything that we had set out to do … what a way to go.

C364 Talking Magic Desk and Kmart Demo

The next day, I had one task and that was to go to the International Marketing suite with a couple of C364 Talking TEDs (see Fig. 3-2) where I would meet John Feagans, who would put in his EPROM for *Magic Desk*, creating a *Talking Magic Desk*. As I mentioned before, for those who don't know about *Magic Desk*, it was the desktop motif that Apple said--*much later*--that they *invented*. Yes, Commodore had already developed a desktop--complete with trash cans, file cabinets, pencils and paper--*years before* Apple.

Fig. 3-2 Commodore TED C364 (aka V364) prototype.
Photo courtesy of Thorsten Kuphaldt (cbmmuseum.kuto.de)

When I got to the International Marketing suite, I was greeted by the two women, now my friends, whom I had met on the flight from Philly out to Vegas. I learned that we were setting up to present the C364 Talking TED to be sold through Kmart (a sales channel that we nicknamed "Bubble Wrap," meaning it was made for the masses, not for the classes). I also met all the bigwigs and then I got to work setting up a TED for the demo.

John Feagans, who had written the Kernal so well-known for the Commodore 64, met me with some EPROMs in hand for *Talking Magic Desk*. We inserted the EPROM into the empty socket on the mainboard. This could have been reserved just for this particular EPROM, as it turns out. We turned on the computer, expecting something, but got nothing but raucous, squawking noises as the processor crashed from garbage data streaming to the sound chip. We turned it off and turned it back on with the same results. John and the entire room watched as I looked at the machine to try to figure out what was wrong. I remembered that I told the PC board layout guy that he could swap the gates on the 74LS175. It dawned on me that maybe he didn't realize that I had used both Q and /Q outputs, where the /Q output is actually the reversed polarity of the Q output; and perhaps when he had swapped them, he got the wrong pins in the process. This was a long shot, but easy to test as I knew the schematic of the TED *by heart* and the 74LS175. I opened the computer, traced the trace, and yes, it was in the wrong place.

The only problem at this point was that the only tool I had was a soldering iron, and I don't even know why I had that. I certainly had no solder or pliers or wire cutters or any of the tools I would normally use to fix a computer, but then this computer wasn't supposed to be broken--not with Kmart showing up in 15 minutes!

I had only two machines. John and I took apart both systems, using the brick hearth of the fireplace (it was a nice suite) as a work surface. Using the soldering iron, I built up solder on the tip from the sacrificial board, and further sacrificed the one C364 we had, by removing the jumper wires so that I could modify "chip selects," the Q outputs (see Fig. 3-3). That was scary, but there was no alternative.

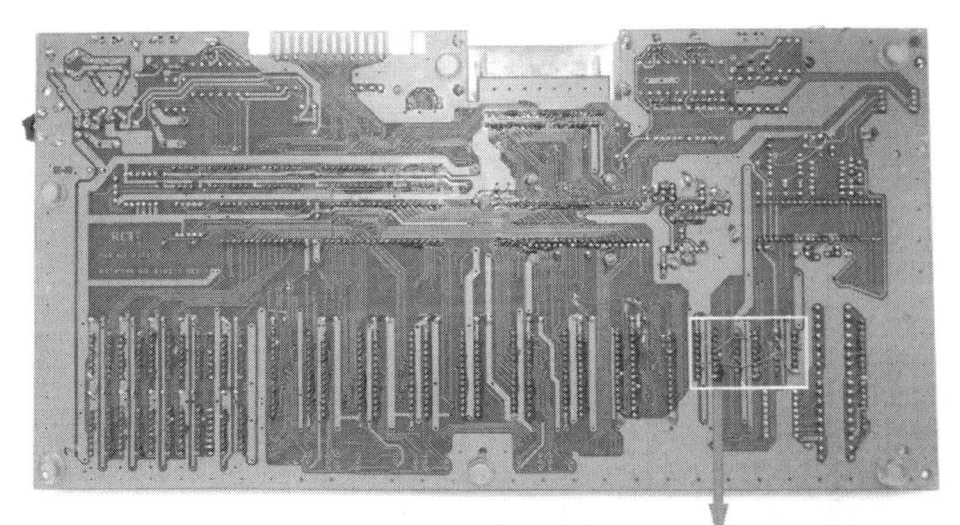

Zoom-in of Bil Herd's V364 soldering of wires for the Kmart demo.

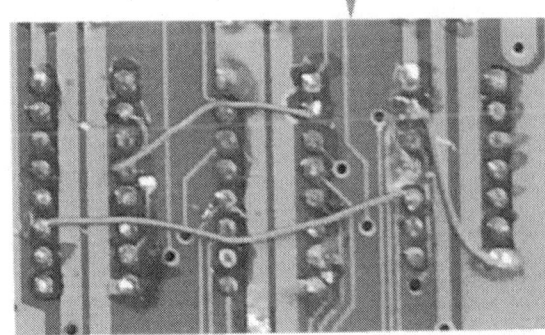

Fig. 3-3 V364 PCB bottom showing Bil's soldering fix for the Kmart demo.
PCB photo courtesy of Rob Clarke.

I didn't have needle-nosed pliers, so I burnt my fingers only a little bit more than normal as I removed a couple of wires from the donor machine to use on the broken machine. I used the tip of the soldering iron to tear up the offending trace--*from memory*--using wire with only the solder that was already on the PC board's jumper in the LS175, hoping that was the problem.

At the end of the day, we had no idea whether we were breaking the system further or fixing it.

Screaming Marketing Guy

Meanwhile, the head of marketing lost his eyeglasses and assumed that the only strangers in the room, me or John, had done something with them. He was now screaming at the top of his lungs at the two of us to stop doing what we were doing and help him find his glasses. A couple of times, he presented himself right in my field of vision while screaming, and I had thoughts of my Basic Training in the Army where the drill sergeant would get right in your face and scream at you, and you were expected to remain focused and unperturbed. I remained focused and unperturbed as I attempted to get Commodore's newest computer working, in spite of this slight distraction.

Finally, I had moved two wires, burnt my fingers, and ruined the donor machine. There was nothing more left to try except to turn it on. John and I turned on the computer, and it *spoke* in a wonderful, melodic voice, "Welcome to the Magic Desk." I almost didn't believe it was working and was wondering why the computer was now trying to fool me into thinking that it was pretending to work, but a glance at John's face told me that it indeed was doing what it was supposed to do.

With less than five minutes to spare before the Kmart demo, we were greatly relieved, quickly packed up the soldering iron, and started to head for the door. John and I went our separate ways and never really spoke again. I hope John remembers those precious minutes we spent in the trench together, and that we succeeded.

Just about that time, the head of marketing found his glasses. They had been in his upper left breast pocket! Kudos to my friend from International Marketing for asking him to look there.

On my way walking down the hall, I passed three guys in dark blue suits. I got about four paces past them and my legs wobbled, exactly once, as it was obvious that this was Kmart now showing up for their demo. I allowed my thoughts that I had just had my personal trial by fire at Commodore. I used my unique abilities and memory to fix a problem while under pressure, being screamed at no less, and with the reputation of the entire company boiled down to fixing a problem in 10 minutes' time. I hadn't wavered nor suffered from breaking my confidence. I knew at some level all along that I would fix the problem, but now I knew for sure that I could fix anything. This was my Commodore moment and I never again doubted my abilities to do the job that I needed to do for Commodore. In short, I had arrived.

Unhappy Software Developer

I didn't spend much time in the booth for the rest of the CES show. We tended to group up as engineers and do activities that we liked as a group, everything from doing the show to doing dinner. On one walk through the show, I was with Terry Ryan. We happened to mention to a software company that made its living writing software for Commodore that we were the engineers on the newest Commodore computer. There was a woman from the company who was fairly upset. "Come here. Let me show you something," she said. "This took me most of the year to write." She pointed to a piece of educational software. I remember this software to this day. It was composed of little, happy two-legged creatures that would crawl through a tunnel to answer a math problem and then do a little, happy dance once the problem was correctly solved. She looked right at me and then pointed at the screen. "This won't run on your newest computer." Now, I was mortified. I didn't know what to think, but this woman was distraught because clearly her livelihood depended on Commodore acting in predictable ways.

3.7 TED Disk Drive

Here are some more stories about Greg Berlin and the TED disk drive that he designed. Greg was a consummate designer and, as it turns out, a natural airplane pilot. I later found out that both design and airplanes were in his blood, when I spotted a picture that he had hanging up in his office showing his grandfather, Donovan Berlin, sitting in a P-40 Warhawk, the World War II plane made famous by the Flying Tigers. Turns out that Berlin's grandfather designed the P-40 while working at Curtiss and had learned how to fly with help from famous people like Jimmy Doolittle of *Thirty Seconds Over Tokyo* fame.

As I mentioned earlier, the first thing people notice about Greg Berlin when they first meet him is the fact that he's 6 feet 8 inches tall (see Fig. 3-4).

Fig. 3-4 Greg Berlin and normal-sized people at CES 1985.
Photo courtesy of Terry Ryan.

At the Bar

The stories I could tell of what it's like going to the bars with him. People would often line up to try to see if--or act like--they could take him on, as he often got the attention of being the tallest person in the place. It became so annoying when we were in a hurry to go off for some beer and get back to work, that I instituted a rule that said anybody who wanted to fight Greg needed to fight me first. This pretty much put a damper on the people wanting a fight as I was an unknown. They may get injured, and by an unknown and normal-sized guy at that. I also had a secret plan that if I did have to fight one of these yahoos, I was going to injure him enough that Greg could finish him off for me.

We were well-known at the local bars. One night, I was wrestling with Greg in the parking lot. I had years of Judo training, so I felt confident that I could handle the tall stature of my friend. On this night, I made a move where I grabbed his shirt lapels and kicked with my left foot, stopping his right foot and swinging to the side so that my weight would make him fall to kiss the ground. Greg was also familiar with this move, I'm thinking, because he reached out with his long arms and pulled me under him. Using me as an airbag, we both hit the parking lot hard, so hard in fact that I separated my shoulder. The displaced bone can be seen to this day when I take off my shirt. As our friend Curt said, being witness to the fall, "Yeah. Bil looked like a milk carton being smashed in the school cafeteria."

Another time, Greg and I ended up in a bar in Las Vegas at a CES show, watching the Washington Redskins take on the San Francisco 49ers. We were the only two people in the bar cheering for Washington, as they had defeated the Philadelphia Eagles that year to take the playoffs. Washington must have been doing okay, as I remember people getting seriously mad at the two of us. At one point, I emptied my mug and didn't refill it as its heft made it a versatile tool in this type of situation. We ultimately unassed the bar, as we used to say in the service, and went looking for more trouble, Vegas style.

1541 Disk Drive Urban Legend

Greg teamed up with Dave Siracusa for the 1551 disk drive for the TED system. We all knew, without being told, that speed would be a primary attribute, given the slow speed of our serial disk drives.

For some context, here are some details about the C64 disk drive, the 1541. There's a lot of urban legend associated with the serial bus of the 1541 disk drive, but I will say that even with all of its problems, the 1541 is probably the most sold home computer floppy drive ever made, given the number of Commodore 64s that were made.

The connection to the 1541 is via a cable of just a few wires, and the information is sent sequentially, earning it the name of "serial bus" for the serialized nature of the data. Originally, the data was going to be sent and received using a serial shift register built into the MOS 6526 I/O chip. Turns out that there was a "bug" in the chip. This is not uncommon for a company that makes their own chips, though it's frowned upon to actually sell chips with known bugs. The bug was this: when the shift register went from receiving data to "turning around" to transmit data, unfortunately, a charge would accumulate on a floating node while receiving, resulting in a glitch being transmitted when first turned to transmit. The glitch would freeze all of the other peripherals.

The urban legend part is that Jack Tramiel pointed to a spot on the desk and said, "Here's where the answer will be sitting Monday morning." Now, I don't know if this actually happened, but something like it probably did. There was a lot of urgency on fixing it. Bob Russell created a version of the serial bus in software. Unfortunately, at the speeds that computers ran back in the day, when the computer stopped to do just the disk drive, it took a long time. So, Bob had met the conditions that Jack Tramiel had demanded. It was done quickly, and it worked. It was just slow.

Bob went further and reconnected the two hardware shift register lines for the last rev of the VIC-20 PC board for production, which meant that we could do fast serial buses in the future. But, the engineers in Japan did not know that he was hedging his bets, and when they saw the extra lines, they thought they were an error. They painted it out on the film that would be used to create the PC boards, erasing Bob's fix. When I heard about this, I made a note that the problem had been poor communication between Norristown and Tokyo. The problem didn't have to happen, given that chip bugs do occur. It's how you fix them that matters, and wouldn't it be nice if we could actually talk these things through. I resolved to not fall victim to what had happened to the serial bus when my time at bat came.

1551 TED Drive

The new floppy disk drive for the TED, the black 1551, was parallel (see Fig. 3-5).

Fig. 3-5 Commodore 1551 TED disk drive.
Photo courtesy of Rob Clarke.

We figured it would run much faster, but we had no idea if that was true or not, as there are certain things that take a while, such as the spin of the disk. We didn't know how to take that into account just yet. When one engineer was asked how fast it would be, he replied, "I don't know ... an LDA, STA and a couple of NOP commands." That became our answer to anything we didn't know from then on: "a Load, a Store, and a couple of No

Ops." (That's LDA, STA, NOP, NOP for you 6502 fans.) I will say that the people who waited on our tables at the local bars were not much amused by this answer.

Ultimately, the new drive was a little less than five times as fast as the 1541, not as fast as we had wanted, but very serviceable by our standards.

Hot Dogs and Napping on a Disk Drive

A trick that I learned in the Army was that I could catch a nap at almost any time. Ten minutes here, five minutes there. After working so many 20-hour days, all of us were in nap-catching mode. One of the things Greg would do would be to put his ear to the new disk drive to listen to see if the stepper motors were still clicking. That would tell him that the software crashed, or that he was just waiting on a long load. As Greg said, "The floppy drive was warm, smooth, vibrating, and making a clicking noise." And, pretty soon he would fall asleep using the drive as a pillow.

One Saturday, I came in after stopping at the vending machine downstairs and loaded up on vending machine hot dogs. I came up to the R&D lab to find Greg asleep on one of his drives. I held the hot dog out away from his nose by about two inches. The smell woke him up, Greg snapping at the air much like you would imagine how a dog would wake up with a doggie treat. Greg had this huge impression of a disk drive on the side of his face, and we chilled out and ate vending machine hot dogs as if there was no tomorrow.

Japanese Subway Story

Greg and I were together on one of our Tokyo trips. Greg actually wasn't hitting his head as much as normal, as things were so low he could easily see them. I, on the other hand, was now whacking my head on something every other day. The worst one was when I was wearing a hat that blocked my vision of the doorways that were too low. When I went to hop off of the subway, I really whacked my head good to where I saw stars. I fell flat on my back and hit the back of my head on the concrete, resulting in more stars. I remember people continued to swarm around me on their way to work. You may have seen the pictures of busy subway stations on the news. Greg shuffled upstream to the flow of people until he stood looking down at me. "How's it feel?" he asked with a smirk. I may have replied, "Meep."

Universally Tall

I was paying the bill at a restaurant one evening in Tokyo and started talking to the gentleman in line next to me, in a mixture of Japanese and English. In English, I commented that he seemed to me to be very tall for Japanese. He thanked me in a sincere way, which made me think that commenting on his height was indeed a compliment. I continued, "In fact, you might be taller than me," to which he responded appreciatively. So now I did believe it was a compliment. (He was in fact an inch taller than me)

"But you are not taller than my friend," I said slyly. I turned and yelled for Berlin. We saw the shadow first. Greg was in a room off to the side, and the shadow that he cast into the hall spanned from floor to ceiling, as the creaks of his footsteps could be heard. Greg has a habit of slowing at doorways and bending down so that his head clears the rafters or door frames. So, a bent over Greg could be seen effectively squeezing through the door. Greg then stretched back up to full height dwarfing the door frame he had just come through. The effect on my new found friend was immediate, and he giggled nervously looking up at Greg. He may even have said, "Meep," which apparently is a universal term.

Friday Lunches

We tried a different place for our Friday lunches, which usually involved some prodigious drinking. One quick example is when we were at the seafood restaurant on the edge of town. The lab tech, nicknamed Arlo, hauled off and delivered a very solid 1" oyster cracker, doing a full baseball windup pitch, hitting Berlin square in the forehead from a distance of only four feet away, a truly brutal distance. The surprise blow snapped Greg's head back, but he came upright again--with this feral noise that is a real attention getter--and he started to go for Arlo.

Arlo got this look on his face, as he realized that his death may be met at the hands of the 6' 8" Berlin, who now had a big red impact dot in the center of his forehead. It turns out that throwing more oyster crackers was not a good defense, but he tried anyway. Before we left the restaurant, we were treated to the sight of Berlin holding Arlo from behind, by his belt and the scruff of the neck. Literally picking him up so his feet couldn't touch the floor, Greg was shoving him into the cushion in one of the booths, yelling, "Eat the cushion!"

Now, we had seen this before and figured the two were off to start the weekend partying early. The punch line of one such evening was that Arlo woke up the next morning on his couch with grass in his teeth and *Cheez Whiz* in his hair--neither Greg nor he could remember how it got there. His wife attested to his condition when she found him, and when he went to explain to her about the grass and *Cheez Whiz*, her answer was, "I don't want to know," with an early version of "the hand."

Onward

So, enough about Berlin and my antics. CES Vegas ended, and we headed home to face the next adventure.

Chapter 4

Late TED, LCD

I knew by now that there was no *normal* at Commodore, at least as most people would define that term. After we returned from CES, we immediately faced a new trauma, had to deal with a change in plans for the TED product family, and entered a totally new project--all within a matter of a few weeks. That was *our* normal, along with playing hard and breaking things on the way.

4.1 Back in West Chester

Once we got back to West Chester, we suffered the inevitable post-CES ho-hum drums. The CES cycle was nine months of mania, followed by three months of depression. The saying became, "Is there life after CES?" and the running joke was that the suicide rate would first climb and then plummet, as all those susceptible to suicide had already committed it. Well, hygiene went up as we slowly readjusted back to our normal schedules, which meant that it was still a busy and stressful time for us.

Without Our Leader

Oh yeah, and by the way, we found out that Jack Tramiel was no longer with the company.

We walked around discussing what this meant. Here I had this newfound confidence in my role at Commodore and now the big boss was missing. It really didn't matter at my level, at least not now, as I had clear marching orders. Little did I know that we were going to end up marching towards a cliff, if not off it, without Jack's leadership. And little did I know that this was the beginning of Commodore losing its way, but in hindsight, I should have.

We had just finished the show in early January, 1984; we had just found out about Jack's departure; and to compound things, we were opening a brand new present at our feet, called the Commodore LCD machine. However, even though we had one project closing and one project opening, we knew not to cut corners on the TED and so continued to work on it at least 2-6 hours a day, getting it ready for production.

Finishing TED

We had roughly a month to finish our Federal Communications Commission (FCC) submission if we hoped to be producing the TED in time for June, which is when we needed to produce it in time for Christmas. One of the tasks, in what we called the "endgame," was making sure that the FCC allowed us to sell our products without the luxury of being fined for every bad unit that we sold. One of our sayings was that to finish the last 5%, a whole new crew had to come in fresh, as the last 5% was often as hard as everything done to date!

We also needed to decide how to package the TED, what kind of box it would go in, the manuals, all the little stickers for it, even how many would be on a pallet. I had to take a completed unit over to Radiation Sciences in Pennsylvania and scan it very closely and carefully for any radio frequencies that might be leaking out. This is a process that took weeks, was nominally boring, and could make you feel helpless if you hadn't taken the time to make sure you passed FCC up front.

I loved FCC submission. It made other engineers nervous, so I dove into it with all the gusto of a high school dropout in a room full of degreed engineers. The TED flew through FCC pre-scanning. I had brought my notes from doing my own scans in the lab, and the engineer at the submission house was impressed at my accuracy, using just lab equipment in predicting how the final results would be. This would go on to become a very valuable relationship as I could get things through FCC quickly by telling them where to look, telling them where our worst problems were. And, if those passed, then we had it made.

I remember we got so bored with the non-critical scanning that we would go to the local bar for the afternoon. One day, a couple of us went to the bar, and I brought one of those little rubber band wind-up airplanes with me. Through much practice, I got it to take off from the bar, go flying through the adjoining room, only to come flying back in the other entry way, and land back on the bar. Yes, we were drunk and we were bored, but we worked for Commodore: it was a good day.

QA Manager's Drop Test

We started holding meetings on a weekly basis to summarize the status of TED as a computer system. At one point, the Quality Assurance (QA) manager mentioned in one of these meetings that the printers did not survive the "drop test." I knew that we had three units to test, so I was not worried: I figured they would fix the packaging and then have two more units for drop testing. The drop test simulates a six-foot drop off of a loading dock while something is still in its packaging, with the expectation of 100% survival.

The QA manager had bad news though. He had broken all three printers doing the drop test (see Fig. 4-1). I was flabbergasted to hear that they all broke through the packaging, and I asked him about this, incredulously. I remember the look on his face as he said, "Packaging?" I shut my mouth immediately and let the rest of the room pounce upon him. He clearly had destroyed $60,000 worth of Commodore property by not knowing how to do his job, and he endangered our submission to FCC and UL (Underwriter Laboratories). Just another day in Commodore Middle Managementville, I figured.

Fig. 4-1 TED printers. MPS 803 and DPS 1101.
Photos courtesy of Rob Clarke.

I would often conjure up in my mind the image of printer parts sliding out from under the door of the QA lab, as they threw their printers around the room, and I shared this imagery with my colleagues in Engineering. While these were just jokes, it showed our disdain for QA's lack of professionalism.

This QA manager would go on and try to get me fired on numerous occasions, but those are different stories.

Broken TED Joystick

In one such meeting, Ira Velensky joined us from Japan with all of the housings and everything that he had designed for the TED. It was a wonderful assortment of peripherals that showed a continuity across the family that I had not yet seen in the computer product line, especially a consumer product line. The high-visibility joystick stood out as being different. It had a different color, a different shape, a different design and used a different connector. What a great way to say this was a different computer.

One issue I had with the beautiful and elegant joystick though was that it looked too fragile: it had a real thin part, like a small thin neck, right where the handle met the body of the joystick (see Fig. 4-2). I was concerned that it would break and I told Ira this.

Fig. 4-2 TED Joystick.
Photo courtesy of Rob Clarke.

Ira assured me that it was fine as *designed* and would handle even the avid gamer. Normally this would have been good enough for me, but I knew that an anxious teenager could break almost anything in the throes of playing a video game. I knew this because I was little more than a teenager myself. He reassured me again. I remember that I was down near the end of the table closest to the window, and I made some noise, saying, "Okay, I agree to move on to another topic." And I let the rest of the meeting go on about some other detail.

When nobody was looking, I took the joystick and brought it below the table where it couldn't be seen; and I applied a fair amount of pressure to it, snapping off the top of it using just my bare hands. Yes, a loud, plastic, snapping noise proclaimed to the entire room that I had just broken a $20,000 soft-tooled joystick, something not meant to be played with, but to be *demonstrated* with. And that's what I had just done: I demonstrated that it could be broken.

To give Ira full credit, it took a lot more effort to break than I thought it would, but once I was committed to the act of vandalism, I went forward with gusto, simulating somebody who was very excited about playing a video game. I didn't want it to break and was hoping it wouldn't. But, alas, it did.

The entire room turned to look at me as I calmly pushed the joystick to the center of the table in two pieces, the fire button cable holding them together. While I acted as if it was an accident, we all knew full well that I had broken it on purpose to make a point. And I had made my point. If a rabid engineer could break a play joystick with a bit of effort, then certainly, very excited kids would wreak even more havoc.

Now, you have to understand that back then, to make plastic models like this, we had to have it "soft-tooled." It had to be carved in wood with plastic shot around it, a very time-intensive process. Yes, I broke a $20,000 joystick to save money later. I didn't say anything; the joystick said it all.

And, as a result of my input, it did get made thicker with some reinforcements before production. Now, Ira wasn't mad, but as payback, I had to be careful about what Japanese words he taught me, as a couple of them would get me into trouble later on.

Exchanging Ties for Shots

Commodore management decided to take both the American engineering team and the Japanese engineering team out to dinner to celebrate the success of the TED project, such as it was. We went to a fancy restaurant in Philadelphia. I remember I had to break out my CES jacket just for the occasion since it was the sort of place that normally would not allow somebody like me in.

I ended up making a deal with the bartender. I would bring him the ties of all the middle managers in the room and he would exchange them for tequila shots. This worked out for me, as every manager gave me his tie simply because I asked, not realizing that they would have to pay our bar tab to get their ties back.

4.2 TED Family Shrinks

After we found out that we had lost our founder, Jack Tramiel, we didn't imagine at the time that unfortunately this meant that the TED series of machines would basically die on the vine, to be replaced by a single computer called the Plus/4. The concept of a low-cost family of *business* machines apparently came from Jack and was now considered to be an outmoded way of thinking about the new line of computers. Commodore was used to selling the Commodore 64 and making a fair amount of money off of it. Commodore was also used to the Commodore 64 selling itself and didn't have a huge marketing engine behind it, as it didn't need one. There's a certain quality in being the highest-selling computer in the world: everybody's heard of you.

Plus/4

We started to hear *rumblings* about canceling all of the TED products, except for the C264. In fact, I was ordered to add more circuitry to the C264, a complete opposite direction from the original design specifications. I took the time to add a 6551 integrated circuit, making this the first consumer computer Commodore made with a real universal asynchronous receiver-transmitter (UART). Since the 6502 family of peripherals is driven by the phi clock, I had to generate a clock in programmable logic. I couldn't think of anybody better to do this. I was so well-checked out in the 6502 family of intricate timings; I lived and died by the nanosecond.

It was at this time that I became certain that the entire TED family had been reduced to the Plus/4 and eventually the C16. I knew this because I was in charge of FCC scanning of anything that was destined for production, and our family of TEDs was not being sent out for FCC approval. Our flock of computer models numbering around five or six had been reduced to only two. I'm not saying that was the wrong decision, but I am saying it was an incongruent decision, not taking into account why we had chosen this path to begin with, only to turn around and go for a cheap buck trying to resell into the Commodore 64 market.

Finally, the word came down from on high that the computer's name had been changed from the C264 to the Plus/4 by marketing and that it would now include what we called "function key software," which was software that can fit into an empty socket that we had designed in. That allowed add-on programs to be plugged in during production, or by an adventurous home user for that matter. From then on, this new computer was known as the Plus/4 after the name of its built-in productivity software: spreadsheet, word processor, database, and graphing. Instead of being sold as a business machine, it would now be a *productivity* machine.

The built-in productivity software was accessed through the function keys along the top of the Plus/4 (see Fig. 4-3). This was a unique feature at the time for Commodore computers, making for an easy way to boot up the various integrated application software.

Fig. 4-3 Plus/4 keyboard with function key-accessed software. Photo courtesy of Christian Simpson (www.perifractic.com)

As I mentioned before, unfortunately, the new computer would also sell for hundreds of dollars instead of the $79 that I designed it for. While this may have sounded like a winner to marketing, the Plus/4 sold poorly and was discontinued relatively soon after its release.

Recently, I heard somebody saying that the author of the Plus/4 software said that his software had gotten a bad rap, and that's a fair enough statement. I don't know anything about the guy or the software other than I knew it wasn't worth $200-plus in my opinion. It wasn't worth what it did to the computer. With that said, the only reason the expansion sockets were even in there for the software is that I had put them in the design after Jack had left, so my punishment for the innovative thinking was to be rewarded with the Plus/4 software being installed on an otherwise innocent C264.

C16

In an effort to use up some parts, for lack of a better way to describe it, we introduced several low-cost models, all based on the TED chip and the memory architecture. One of these became the well-known C16, nothing more than a TED chip stuck inside a C64 housing of which we had millions (see Fig. 4-4).

Originally, it was so cheap of a design that it was a single-sided PCB, a novel attempt at cheapness even in the 1980s. The original prototype used approximately 30 jumpers to complete the connectivity. We scrapped this as not being worth the cost of a single-sided versus double-sided PCB because single-sided boards were getting more expensive and harder to find. We went back to doing dual-layer PCBs and we never went back to a single-layer PCB again at Commodore.

Fig. 4-4 Bil's prototype C16 showing "soft-tooled" case.
Photo courtesy of Joel Herd.

The C16 became one of the more popular TED variants, although we at the engineering level didn't anticipate that. To this day, I get messages about the C16 and the impact it had on young people's lives. The odd thing about this is that we hadn't even planned for the C16 as part of the TED family when we began, but Commodore ended up selling over a million C16s. It's one of those unplanned occurrences that ended up being a hit.

4.3 Games and Humor

There were bright spots amid the darkness, and although life at Commodore was often nerve-wracking, we had fun along the way. The hardware lab had a great bunch of guys, and I would hang out there when I needed to laugh. We would practice laughing on bad days, so that on good days it would come naturally. And, the programmers I worked with were deadly. Terry Ryan would slice you with cynicism and then Fred Bowen would finish you off with common sense. Humor was a really important part of what we did. We worked way too many hours, under way too much stress, with way too many a**holes, to not have a relief valve.

Coffee Cup

One day, I noticed that my coffee cup was missing. I looked everywhere for it and finally, in the hardware lab, I started asking around. "Oh, that thing. It was disgusting," remarked Jeff, the technician. "So?" I replied. "So, I threw it away," he quipped back. Now, this coffee mug was a gift from my girlfriend and it was a really cute mug. I really liked it. "You what?" At that point, I got up, grabbed Jeff's coffee mug, and slammed it into the nearest trash can. From then on, every day, I would throw his coffee mug away. He would have to remember to get it out of the trash before the trash got emptied that day. Six months later, walking through the lab, I would slam dunk his cup.

Schematics at the Bar

We used to go to the local watering hole, Margaritas, during the afternoon. When nobody was in there, we'd push together several tables in the dining room and spread out schematics. Of course, we needed some way to keep the corners of the schematics from curling upward, so we would use beer mugs and sometimes a half-full pitcher of beer. If those schematics existed these days, one would be able to see the occasional wine glass ring, but mostly beer mug rings on the corners of the schematics.

Hitchhiker's Guide

One of the ways that we relieved the stress and the pressure of working 14-hour days was that we got into the series of books called *The Hitchhiker's Guide to the Galaxy*. These entertaining books sat near one of the workstations between the two labs, and often people from different projects would pull up a piece of floor and sit there to read part of one of the books. Sometimes, with multiple people, this would require somebody who was walking between the labs to have to step over the people reading the books. As it turned out, one of the first games for the TED series was *The Hitchhiker's Guide to the Galaxy*. This brought home to me a relationship between one of my favorite authors and the computer I was working on. I would never have thought to have had something in common in such an indirect way.

Unfortunately, I missed meeting Douglas Adams, author of *The Hitchhiker's Guide*, at a party one night. Let's just say I was at a different party. Andy Finkel, head of the Games Group, related to Douglas a bug in the software where he could move the cabinet to get the Babel fish. If you want to know more, you must read this unique series of books.

PC Board Hanging Mobile

One time, the R&D techs took it upon themselves to tease Greg Berlin by taking the various revisions of the PC boards for the floppy drive he was working on and making a hanging mobile out of them. As far as a multi-level, balanced mobile hanging in the corner of the R&D lab was concerned, it was actually quite well made. They had spent the time to balance each of the different PC boards on the different rods with strings that made it into a big sculpture. Greg wanted to be pissed, but he just grinned instead. Mind you, a 6'8" Berlin grinning can still be kind of scary to the uninitiated.

Playing Computer Games

On my first day at Commodore, I had noticed people playing computer games in their offices as I walked by, and no one was saying anything critical of this. I liked the thought that you would be judged on your work output and not on the appearance of doing work. But later on, I found out that a good number of the people I saw playing games didn't really do any useful other stuff … so much for the real version of Utopia. The "2nd shift" guys, who showed up only after management had left, basically gave up any pretense of working that we could discern. What we liked best about this arrangement was that it kept them out of our way for half the day, since as it turned out, our work day encompassed *both* shifts.

My favorite game was *Kennedy Approach*, an air traffic controller game. It was good enough that later, I would have dreams about the screams of people going down in the mountains outside of Denver due to my not being able to get them vectored for approach fast enough. I would walk out of the office shaking with clammy hands, eager to rejoin the mind-numbing stress of only working at CBM and not hearing the simulated voices of passengers as they went down with the plane.

I didn't play video games to relax as a rule; I played them so that life at Commodore seemed more normal by comparison.

Jumpman was probably the most popular game throughout Engineering and I assume some of the other departments. *Archon* was *great* on the C64; it lost something on the Amiga. I had been given *Archon* after crashing Electronic Arts' suite looking for a beer.

Flash forward: The last game I remember, other than *Marble Madness* (best use for an Amiga back then), was this weird Amiga game called *Mind Walker*, where you help return Sigmund Freud to sanity. It had this eerie music that just played continuously in the background, could be heard coming from several offices, and was probably still running on my Amiga the day I walked out of the office for the last time.

Packing Peanuts

As we were all working weekends on the run-up to the next CES show, I figured Dave DiOrio was at his office and I called him on Saturday, late in the morning. I'd already been there on this particular Saturday morning and I left him a gift. I called Dave and asked how his office looked and he said, "Fine." I asked him to lift his "flapper," the name we gave to the shelf on the Herman Miller furniture, which then released a mechanism that spilled packing peanuts all over his office--quite a lot in fact. I was very proud. "How about now?" I asked innocently. I was rewarded with Dave's chuckling, and I knew that I had helped to lift his spirits, if not my own.

Squirt Guns

My girlfriend and I started playing a game with squirt guns where we would hide them and then assassinate each other at unexpected times. One night, I heard her open the drawer next to her side of the bed, and I carefully slipped out of the covers only to have her shoot my now empty pillow with a water pistol. I was able to shoot her from the foot of the bed where I had crawled in the dark. I thought what a great game to take to work. So I purchased several water pistols all of the same type, and I took them to work, leaving them on various desks. Of course, mine held more water than anybody else's, but that was easy for them to figure out and correct, if they thought that I would give everybody an equal chance to get me wet. The squirt gun battles raged all day, waxing and waning up and down the hallways. If somebody was carrying something that absolutely couldn't get wet, they would declare so, knowing they would get soaked later that day as retribution.

Rubber Bands

On another day, I did pretty much the same thing, only using boxes of rubber bands. I remember that we had nine boxes of rubber bands in the shared supplies cabinet: not 10 boxes, but nine. Once again, I walked around leaving the boxes on various people's desks in order to instigate the Great Rubber Band Wars of '85. Since rubber bands could be reused and any number of people could join, the wars provided greater desolation. Eventually, rubber bands were everywhere throughout our section of the building. At one point, we tried to put a move on the mechanical designers and the chip guys by flanking to the left and going over the office walls. We got them in a basic military pincer movement only to see the engineer that had come to us from Franklin Computers go down with a rubber band in his eye. We rushed to his aid to find out if he had finished his design or not, and how this impacted us. Oh yeah, we also asked how his eye was.

On this particular day, we had a rare occurrence of a tornado warning. Being from the northeast section of Tornado Alley, having grown up in Marion, Indiana, I was all too familiar with the sudden change in air pressure. We lost power on one of these rare times. Commodore was completely dark in the engineering section. I had a window office and the hallway was lit by windows, but for some reason, most of us sought out the dark and ended up in the Calma Department (named after the brand of workstation that the chip layout folk used for doing the actual chip design and layout) in absolute darkness, sitting on the floor chuckling and laughing among friends.

At one point, the door burst open and the poorly lit hall backlit a manager. In fact, it was the manager of the Drafting Department who called into a dark room, "What is going on in here?" In the darkness, I heard the baritone voice of Terry Fisher (aka "Fish"), the PCB designer, as he exclaimed, "It's a dream come true," since we all still had our rubber bands and were proficient enough that we could fire them in the dark. It took the manager several seconds to realize that more than 20 people were firing rubber bands at him in the dark, and he quickly unassed the area.

The next day, Michael Angelina came to me and said he had a problem. Michael was the head of the Calma Group, the IC layout people, and a good friend, someone I respected, trusted, and went to lunch with. Michael led me to the Calma area, which was now littered with rubber bands. He showed me the $40,000 photo plotter which was now open, as somebody had had to clean a few rubber bands out of its insides. Michael was cool: he let me know this was now *my* problem, but if I solved it, there would be no problem. Clearly, I had to clean up the rubber bands, but if I was going to, I was going to do it my way and not just go crawling around on my hands and knees picking up rubber bands. So, I admitted that he was right; I had created this minor catastrophe pretty much on my own.

A few minutes later, I came back with a vacuum cleaner that we used to clean up small computers, strapped to my back. It had the long pickup nozzle that could reach all the way to the floor. To complete the effect, I had rubber gloves and goggles on so that I looked like I was pretty much sanitizing the place. I was able to walk around nonchalantly scooping up rubber bands off of the floor, while talking about everything but rubber bands. I was rewarded with a big smile later that day from the head of the Calma Department.

Brick at My Head

One day, I was carrying some papers just outside of Terry and Fred's office, when someone called my name. I walked into the office only to be met by five programmers, which was a little unusual, and someone (John) threw a brick at my head. "Catch," he said as he did it.

I had no doubt that there was now a brick speeding towards my head, and the papers in my right hand went flying as both hands automatically started to come up. Time slowed, the room got brighter, and I saw the brick hanging in mid-air as if it was suspended; I could see the ridges in the brick and there was mortar along the edges so this looked like a used brick that was about to clock me hard. By now, both hands had arrived at brick level, which was at shoulder height, as it made its way to my head. And, in one motion, I pumped the brick into a trash can just near my left foot.

I started to step forward towards John, who had thrown the brick, when my hands interrupted my thought process: "That didn't hurt," was the message that I got from my hands, "Huh." As I processed this new input, I realized that the impact of the brick didn't hurt my hands enough to be a real brick, as I had pumped the brick into the trashcan rather forcibly. I stopped myself before I shoved the offending programmer into the trash can along with the brick, but I remember the expression on all five people's faces as they looked at me. I was lucky that instead of this being a supremely embarrassing moment where I squealed like a little girl as a fake brick bounced off my noggin', I had impressed them with my reflexes and willingness to accept that violence was happening.

When I was younger, I had found that being willing to be violent suppressed people's desire to cast casual violence my way, and I think those hard edges showed through at times like this, even though I was in a civilized environment. My fight or flight mechanism was always just below the surface and still is to this day, to some extent. It's fair to say that my reflexes were fast enough in the old days, as my muscle memory would often kick in, and I became an observer myself as to what my body had thought was a good thing to do.

I also figured out at that moment that probably the reason there were five people in an office, that could barely hold that many, was that they had all been "bricked" and then took their turn watching other people undergo the process. Fair to say, I ruined the mood for such festivities and people wandered back to their respective jobs, as I gathered up the papers I had been carrying.

Fishing

While everything was going crazy around me, I went fishing. We had moved to a place closer to Commodore than my hour drive away, a drive I fell asleep during all too often and knocked the bumper off my car at one point. Now, I had a place close by, in Downingtown, that had a creek and a pond on the property. Just as we had done power designing, we did power recreation at my place. I would take various engineers up and down the creek or around the pond, either fishing or teaching them to fish.

We knew this was the calm before another storm: we worked at Commodore and there was always another storm on its way.

4.4 Summer CES Chicago 1984

Finally, we had the TED in the can, as they say, and it was time for the June CES show. This is when any last-minute sales of the year were to be solidified. I made the show with the vice president of R&D, Adam Chowaniec, and one of the managers of software development.

Manager Takes The Lead--Not

When we had landed at O'Hare Airport in Chicago, we went to look for transportation to the center where the CES show was being held. Our middle manager wanted to impress the VP by jumping in line at the bus shuttle terminal and immediately buying tickets for all three of us. Right after that, he realized that there was an hour-long wait for the bus, in spite of having tickets. So, then showing that same promise that had just failed, he immediately got into the end of the taxi cab line, which looked to be about 25 minutes long, and had about a hundred people in front of us.

This was not acceptable to the brash Bil Herd. I handed my briefcase to the manager and I said, "Wait here." I walked up the line of taxi cabs until I couldn't be seen by the cop directing traffic, leaned in on a cab, and said, "I got a cash tip for you if you'll take us, if you allow us to cut the line." He said, "Sure." I went and grabbed Adam and the manager, introducing the manager as the man who had the tip money for the cab driver. I told him to tip the cab driver at least $20. As we pulled away, the cop banged on the cab's hood, telling the driver that this was his one warning for the day for allowing us to cut the line. I didn't care; I had just gotten us a cab in less than five minutes.

At the Show

I didn't work the booth at this Chicago CES show, but I did attend for a short while (see Fig. 4-5). I had gotten out of that task, as I considered the Chicago show less important, though I would change my opinion later in life.

The reduced TED family was displayed at this CES. We still had some tweaking to be done here and there, but for the most part, things were working properly (see Fig. 4-6).

Dave Haynie made the show, too, arriving in style (see Fig. 4-7).

Fig. 4-5 Bil Herd and Adam Chowaniec (far left)
at the 1984 Chicago CES.
Photo courtesy of Dave Haynie.

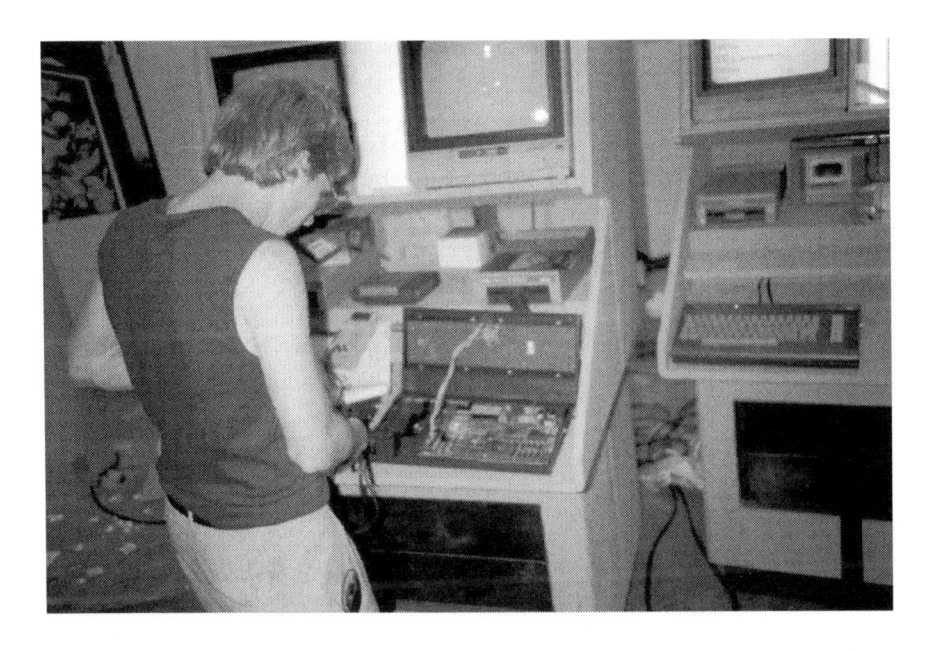

Fig. 4-6 Gale Moyer setting up TED computers at CES Chicago 1984.
Photo courtesy of Dave Haynie.

Fig. 4-7 Dave Haynie arriving at the Chicago CES 1984.
Photo courtesy of Dave Haynie.

Bumping into Irving Gould

It was at the Chicago CES show that I met Irving Gould, the chairman of the board at CBM. Being Bil Herd, I took this opportunity to express my opinion about the TED series of computers and the follow-through on them.

I told him about the woman who had complained about the lack of C64 compatibility, and I expressed my concern that the TED family of products was already ceasing to be a family. My point was that we could have a family compatible with itself, or compatible with our customer base; either would be okay, but a single computer incompatible with anything else was doomed to failure, regardless of how clever the hardware and operating system were.

I remember Irving just nodded sagely in tolerating this young engineer, who probably had beer on his breath, given that I was on a day off. He basically said nothing except to thank me for my input. Looking back, I'm probably lucky that I survived my brush with Irving Gould.

4.5 Moving on to the LCD

While we were wrapping up the TED during early 1984 and leading up to CES, we already had jumped into planning for what would be the next new computer, an actual evolutionary computer for Commodore: the Liquid Crystal Display (LCD) laptop. As it turns out, Commodore owned its own LCD manufacturing plant, EaglePicher, the only "glass plant" in America. At the time, all LCDs were made overseas, except for Commodore's. This put us in a great position to be the leader in computer manufacturers using this new technology.

CD-ROM

Someone from Commodore Texas had put together a design spec for this new computer, that could use a Write Once Read Many (WORM) laser drive--to try to break the memory barrier of 64 kB while providing non-volatile storage. The Compact Disc (CD) technology became available around this time, which opened the door in the mid-1980s to truly wonderful things. To us, this was right out of *The Hitchhiker's Guide to the Galaxy*. We saw the LCD machine, when coupled with something like an early CD-ROM, to be the ultimate reference device. As I used to say, you could look up everything from architecture to zoology. You should have seen our new portable computer.

The LCD Team

Now, everyone who had worked on TED was considered to be part of a seasoned design team. The way Commodore worked is that a lead person or two would take on a project and then politick for additional resources. Originally on the LCD, it was just me on the design team, but I quickly got Dave Haynie assigned to it to fly as my wing. We had also hired some of the fathers of the LCD industry, some who were at RCA in the early days when LCD first happened, to run our startup LCD enterprise. I remember one time I came flying around the corner and slammed into a guy named Dave, spilling his coffee all over him. He wasn't happy, I wasn't happy, and it was only later that I found out that I had just spilled coffee all over one of the fathers of the Liquid Crystal Display.

The Point

The idea behind the Commodore LCD machine was that it would be a transportable computer, maybe one that needed to be plugged in, but once you plugged it in, it would start up right away and you could continue typing in your document. To that end, we built in a variety of useful software, including BASIC 3.6, a word processor, file manager, spreadsheet, address book, scheduler, calculator, notepad, and a communications program for use with its built-in 300-baud modem.

4.6 LCD Components

My role in the LCD was on the initial design and architecture. I had specified how I was going to index the editor into the 25th line for the menu and how to index the editor right in memory, so you would not be rewriting to the video screen all the time.

LCD Editor

I laid down an architecture on the old 1/10 inch graph paper and was committed to having an editor that would "window" in memory. The computers of the day worked by transferring the text to a special buffer where the display could see it and scroll through it, refreshing every character, row by row. Unfortunately, the scrolling could take a very noticeable amount of time as it updated and moved every character location; while with a window, it just changed a pointer, and it all happened at 1 MHz. In other words, the LCD display was not a unique place in memory, but a window into the memory where a document was stored, an advanced concept for the day. This new concept required the use of a memory management unit (MMU), which became the core of the 6502-based LCD machine. We would also need LCD driver ICs. This task was assigned to one of the TED chip designers, Bob Raible.

Keyboard

Commodore worked with Mitsumi and produced this amazing keyboard that looks like a full-height keyboard, but had very clever beveled keys-- what we called "quarter stroke" keys. This meant that they didn't travel the full distance, even though they looked like full-size keys, yet felt as though they had (see Fig. 4-8).

Fig. 4-8 Bil's prototype LCD computer. Note the cool beveled keys. Photo courtesy of Bil Herd.

It was easy to type much faster and quicker than on our standard Commodore keyboards and would be the first thing a user would interact with on their new Commodore LCD. We were off to a good start.

Microprocessor

The Commodore LCD machine was an amazing machine. It relied on the relatively new 65C02 microprocessor, along with its counterpart, the 65C22 versatile interface adapter. We were using CMOS where we could, but back in the 1980s, we only had a certain amount of usable CMOS. We started out by using the CMOS that was available in the day and yet would still make a computer work, which meant I was going to start out by using some parts in NMOS (available in-house) and transfer to CMOS standard cell gate array or something similar as the project went on.

CMOS was like NMOS, only twice as complicated to make, as there were twice the number of steps to fabricate a CMOS device. It also required specialized equipment and environment; and fair to say, we had yet to produce usable CMOS internally. Consequently, we would design how we wanted the CMOS chips to work, but to meet our deadlines, we would have to buy them from people already producing CMOS. The good news was that a new technology known as standard cell gate array was becoming available, which allowed us to design exactly what we wanted, but have the parts made somewhere else.

Memory and Power

As far as memory went, we didn't have anything fancy to choose from. The only memory of the day that could be used for battery powered machines were 8 kB static RAMs. These were huge devices and relatively slow, and showed some of the obstacles back then. The current was also not so small. It was going to take regular old AA batteries to power this beast, and yet it represented a whole new evolution in computing.

Built-in Modem

Another feature of the new computer was a built-in modem. This had yet to really hit home computers, and all modems at this time were external devices. One of the items in the hardware lab was left over from the old Chuck Peddle (main designer of the MOS Technology 6502 microprocessor) days: a Silent 700 300-baud terminal where you physically put a phone into two rubber cups on the back of it, to make any phone into a modem. It was decided to design in a modem that could plug directly into the phone line without the need for the big silicone rubber cups that fit over the ubiquitous phone receiver. The thought of an RJ11 plug built directly into a computer was exciting, it was novel, and it was a really good way to get screwed by the FCC.

To accomplish this, we hired Jeff Porter, an engineer from AT&T and a fellow Hoosier out of Indiana, who was a modem expert (he was also a good engineer and a good project manager--two different things). Jeff had a lot of modem experience, including getting it to pass FCC Part 68 Subpart J, which pertained to the phone lines of the day. To legally let the computer touch a phone line, we needed our Subpart J certification. Jeff could actually whistle the tones that a modem used. He was an engineer's engineer, so we really did hire him for his brain and not his whistle.

What was cool about the LCD was that it exemplified how Commodore could start an idea in one location, start the engineering in another, and then transfer the bulk of it to our new headquarters in West Chester.

Ian's Poem

Ian Kirschemann was Jeff Porter's lieutenant and seemed to be a perfect match for what Jeff needed in a lieutenant (see Fig. 4-9). He and I would go on to have in common an EMS/trauma background.

On Ian's wall was a poem. I remembered it the first time I read it:

> who was this child,
> who screamed and ran wild,
> who spoke with his wings and the echo of gunfire

It seemed to capture my state of mind perfectly upon occasion.

Fig. 4-9 Ian Kirschemann (left) showing LCD at CES.
Photo courtesy of Terry Ryan.

My Dislocated Shoulder

Speaking of Ian ...

Ian had been a medic in Africa during some obscure action from back then. When we caught up for a reunion, we swapped medic stories. I remember one of his ended with "hand me that axe handle please."

Fred Bowen's wife tells the story about how, when she first met me at a party at their house, she went into a back room just in time to see me lunge my shoulder into a doorframe a couple of times, which was followed by a squishy pop noise. You see, I had dislocated my shoulder a while back, which used to pop out of place, due to an injury that I had gotten in Judo. I don't remember doing this on that particular night, as I had been drinking, and it wasn't all that uncommon back then that I had to do a little remedial repair. But, I know her story is true, as I hadn't told anybody about my shoulder prior to then. So, the fact that she knew that I had dislocated my shoulder (and could relocate it) rang true.

Years later, when I was an EMT on the streets of New Jersey, I would learn to identify the type of dislocation (anterior) at a single glance, though we left the relocation to the Emergency Room (so no axe handle for me).

LCD Schedule

Work progressed during the spring of '84 on the LCD computer. By now, the C364 and C116 had been cancelled and the C264 was on its strange trip to becoming the Plus/4. We could tell by the schedules and lack of urgency that the LCD laptop was most likely to be a two-year cycle, as opposed to a one-year cycle machine, meaning it might make the winter CES in January, 1985, but it wouldn't be available to the public in mass quantities for almost two years.

And, as quickly as all of this had happened, within just a matter of weeks as was our norm at Commodore, I was in for another abrupt change in plans ... and another beginning.

Chapter 5

Early C128

With the CES show behind us, we were finalizing the TED in its latest iterations and progressing on the new LCD. There didn't seem to be any rush on anything at this point. We had plenty of time to work on the existing projects that we had already begun. Of course, there would be something new coming up; we just didn't know quite what that would be, yet.

5.1 Transitioning

It was the summer of 1984, and I was in the hardware lab in West Chester. I was about three rows back on the right with my head bent over my bench, as I was working on something, either TED or LCD related. I kept hearing this muttering from behind me about something not being right. I focused on my task at hand and eventually finished what I was doing, but the muttering continued, so I finally turned around to see what was going on.

Genesis of the C128

Fred Bowen was sitting with the hardware engineer who had been assigned to the project that he was working on, basically working on one of the new business machines. After TED was officially finished on our part, we had split up as a group, each to find a different kind of home. This was actually fairly typical and didn't mean that we had worked together for the last time in a small place like Commodore.

I observed Fred observing *his* engineer who was exasperated at what the Tektronix 7D02 logic analyzer was doing in front of them. Now, this is an analyzer that I knew like the back of my hand. I'd spent many a night with it rather than partying with my friends in an effort to always stay on schedule. It's fair to say that I probably knew most every little nuance of it, so I offered a hand.

The problem that he was facing was simple. If you thought about it, the analyzer is just another piece of circuitry. It can be seductive to believe that the test equipment was omnipotent, but in this case, it was lying to the engineer operating it. It would show the clock cycles of the processor as it walked along doing its normal processor things only to finally trip up. It looked like three cycles had occurred in rapid succession in the time it took for just one cycle to occur. I had seen this before, and knew that if two outputs being measured got turned on at the same time, the contentious mess that occurred would confuse the analyzer. Simply, the ground would "lift" in the analyzer (meaning that ground stopped being ground--it wasn't even a reasonable opinion of what ground should be at this point), and the analyzer would think several processor clock cycles had gone by instead of just the one: in other words, exactly what the engineer was seeing.

I asked to see his terms for his PLA, his Programmable Logic Array, which was the cornerstone of almost all Commodore designs back then. It was a custom piece of integrated circuitry that Commodore had patterned after the Signetics 82S100 programmable logic array. Inside the chip R&D lab was a poster board full of Polaroid pictures taken through a microscope of the Signetics part. Someone had taken pictures of it and then laid out our chip to mimic their chip. I never heard of any bad ramifications from this, but I never felt good about it either.

My only consolation is that, by this time, the chip was our chip; it was no longer the Signetics chip. We turned it into a "non-field programmable," meaning the chip was programmed once by the engineer earlier in the design and then made cheaply and in millions. During development, however, we could use the tried-and-true 82S100 part, which could be programmed on the fly.

I looked at their PLA logic terms, basically a big chart of many columns and rows, and as I came down the column for each output, I noticed that the rightmost column had been cut off when it was photocopied. A whole column of terms was missing! One of these missing terms made it so that only one output at a time would turn on, but since it was missing, two outputs were turning on and the contention was shaking up the analyzer. I pointed out to the engineer that he had photocopied it wrong and needed to reprogram this part. Then, it would start working correctly and the analyzer wasn't really broken.

As I turned to go back to my work, I noticed Fred Bowen looking at me over the top of his glasses. I didn't think anything of it as I turned back to work, but then I turned back to look at him also and our eyes met. Then we both went back to work. Unfortunately, the seed had been planted when I absorbed the PLA's terms while looking at the bad photocopy. I understood in a single moment everything about the architecture of the computer since the PLA was at the center of it. I remember the day Fred looked over his glasses at me after I fixed their problem, and that moment was the true genesis of the C128. I remember this moment crystal clear up to this day.

LCD to the New Machine

Later that week, I stopped by Fred's office and asked him what he was working on. I remember it was a B128 or a D128, or some similar thing. (It turned out to be a D128.) It wasn't going to be compatible with anything, and it used a strange pair of processors. It was doomed to be yet another business machine that no one used. I didn't know much about our business machines, but I knew where we kept them. Just off the hallway, we had an alcove full of Ds and Bs, failed machines that looked really cool, but I never ever saw one in actual use.

I remember sitting in my boss's office at the end of the week, and I mentioned Fred's project. He replied, "Funny you should mention that. We've had a request for you." Bottom line was that we decided that Jeff Porter could take over the LCD machine, and I would become the co-manager of "the new machine," along with Fred Bowen, who would manage the software for that machine. This effectively made Fred the Father of the C128 in my mind, as he was on it first, which made me the Mother of the C128. This didn't bother me much as I had been called worse, though I did recommend that if someone wanted to liven up their day to step up close to me and call me a Mother. At least, I myself found what came next interesting.

As I mentioned earlier, we had hired Jeff Porter, who lived, breathed, and ate FCC Part 68 Subpart J, and the LCD was going to be very "modem-centric." He was the engineering equivalent of a rock star, so it made sense for him to take over the LCD as I switched to the C128. What I didn't know then was that the C128 would go on to interfere with the LCD machine and its competition for resources. Jeff and I had a good working relationship, and we tried to keep the demand for C128 time and materials out of the way of the LCD. I know I didn't always succeed, and it became harder to do as we got closer to the CES show.

5.2 Beginning the New Nameless Machine

And, so we begin ...

Okay, so what follows is a roller coaster ride. Fasten your seat belts as I try to portray for you the ups and downs and sideways of developing the C128. There are many parts to this story, as this thing went round and round during our mad dash to make the Winter '85 CES show. I'll try to go in order of things, but some things are best expressed when I jump ahead a bit and then back again. Some readers might recognize parts of this story from my 1993 posting on a CompuServe forum.

So, I was officially on this new machine, the new nameless machine.

While the C128 evolved organically in the beginning, I will say that the reason that there was a C128 was because no one stopped us. No one told us to do it, but no one stopped us either. This would be a computer conceived and implemented by a bunch of engineers, taking advantage of the void left by the departure of Jack Tramiel.

Early Concept

Now the very, very, very early concept of the C128 was based on the D128, a 6509-based creature. The engineers on that project had tacked a VIC-II chip onto the monochrome (6845-based) D128 in an effort to add some color to an otherwise drab machine. No one dreamed that C64 compatibility was possible, so no one ever thought along those lines. I was just coming off of finishing the Plus/4, and even though I had done exactly what I was told to do, I was not happy with the end result. I had decided to make the next machine compatible with *something* instead of making yet another incompatible CBM machine.

The C128 was to fill a gap of a year, maybe 18 months. In my mind, it was to get users and CBM used to the 80-column concept (monitors were scarce in the beginning). We made a decision to add C64 mode (we ourselves never said 100% compatible; the Marketing Department said that) and *not* to monkey with the definition of C64 by adding extra modes or features. (Not unlike inviting a guest into your house and they dig a big hole in the floor; not a polite way to treat the owners of the house.)

At this point, we had something like three weeks until the beginning of August, an ideal starting time if we agreed that what we were talking about was buildable.

I looked once at the existing schematics for the D128, and then started from scratch with a new design for the C128, based on C64-ness.

Those first three weeks were my favorite time of computer design. For me, this is where you use the right side of your brain, the artistic side, and design how you want something to look, feel, and operate. The running joke is that you then spend a year taking care of all the dirty, little details that you dreamed of the first month, but the time spent is still worth it.

The trick to design is balance. I tell people that it's like balancing a cookie sheet with some water on it. If it's not balanced, everything gets wet. The same in computer design: the processor can go really fast, but if the rest of the design doesn't go as fast, or there are any inefficiencies at speed, then the processor going fast doesn't help. In fact, sometimes it can hurt if it's going too much faster than the rest of the circuitry.

In order to design the C128 to have C64 compatibility, we needed to look closer at the problems that we knew existed with the C64. The C64 was all about two major components: the VIC-II chip and the DRAM.

C64 VIC-II

Through no fault of its own, the VIC-II did not have enough accurate clock edges to precisely create control signals for the DRAM. This meant that the designers tried to use a falling edge of a clock that wasn't accurately controlled like the rising edge, which meant that major control signals like Row Address Strobe - /RAS and Column Address Strobe - /CAS could move around a little too much, especially for mass production.

The Production Department was under pressure to ship product, and to accomplish this, they sometimes made modifications on their own. One of the tricks that the Production people would do was to solder capacitors on the /RAS and /CAS signals to try to delay the signals just a bit. What they actually did was to change the slew rate, which is different and actually made the signal sloppier rather than simply delaying it. Slew rate is the length of time it takes for a signal to go from one state to another. The best signals went quickly or had a high slew rate. Slow signals that took a long time transitioning from one valid state to another had slow slew rates and spent longer with the signal outside of the valid states. It was this length of time that it spent in an illegal state (not a digital zero and not a one) that was the root of several problems.

Now, if the /RAS and /CAS signals took too long just to rise or fall, they could create all new problems, in addition to the troublesome and annoying problems that we already dealt with. This failure is ultimately one of the reasons that the "sparkle problem" was so predominant on the C64. Nonetheless, Production had found that the units more often passed their QA test with the capacitors on those two signals. In other words, they had tried to fix a symptom rather than fixing a problem. Ultimately, I couldn't change their behavior when it came to the C64.

I resolved to make the C128 work correctly in the first place, as a way to assure that no one started tacking on parts *randomly* in production.

C64 DRAM

Again, dealing with the C64, we also had trouble getting DRAM memory that worked in the quantities we needed. We ended up suing one of the DRAM makers, who ended up suing us over the DRAMs, or so my memory goes. The question was whether the DRAM didn't work due to the DRAM chips themselves or due to the way the C64 tried to use the DRAMs. I had noted that the DRAMs did fail more often, but showed that it was in part due to the way we used it and in part the DRAM itself. In the end, CBM came to some kind of agreement, or at least I think they did, as we ended up buying the DRAM production design in an attempt to make them ourselves.

Hey, if something doesn't work, you might as well buy it up.

Also, when I saw this, I resolved that, if I ever designed a C64-compatible computer, I would create a better version of these control signals. Gee, it's not like I ever got a chance to put my money where my mouth was. Before it was over, I assigned Dave Haynie to bat cleanup on getting the DRAM timings in the C128 correct, and he ended up knocking it out of the park.

First Week

So, we had to figure out what we were going to build, the architecture of how to build it, and then, last but not least, all the little details that go with it.

I spent a lot of time with Terry and Fred as we talked about what it was that we could build. I asked them what they needed and what they expected. We blue-skyed in a way that only a few people could do. We were dreaming up the next computer, and we had a billion dollar company behind us, if we could pull it off. Not once did any of us ever say that this was too much pressure or we weren't suited to pick out how the next generation of computer would work. We were just doing our jobs. This is what we did, and Commodore was the place we did it.

While I was talking with Fred and Terry about what could be, I started the conversation with Dave DiOrio regarding what we could pull off in silicon (custom ICs), about how to do it. We would have to design the computer *twice*. We would need the final version that used custom integrated circuits in time for CES; but we would need something workable that emulated the custom chips much sooner, so that the programmers would have their own C128 systems to work on. It should be noted that nobody had even said the word "CES." At this time, we just knew. We needed a version that would work in as little as a month. It was wonderful being able to conjure up custom silicon for a new computer design. However, we paid for it by having a period of time where there was no custom chip, and we would have to emulate them using regular chips.

My design philosophy just happened to complement the time constraints that we were working under, and that dealt with speed. While some engineers would take weeks to do something and get it approved, I simply ran the calculation that I could get more done by being wrong a certain amount of time and fixing it, rather than taking more time, all of the time. Eventually, I got my black belt in "how to cut corners" without sacrificing *important* design principles.

Dave DiOrio was a lot like me in that he didn't always take a conventional approach for scheduling and specifying features, and this was the time for the programmers to get their favorite attribute built in. In talking with him, we started planning for a faster revision of the project, one that would be ugly, dirty, but would work early on in the process, using drop-in PC boards in place of special ICs. Again, the custom integrated circuits would not be done until near the end, but the programmers needed them almost right away, so the need for immediate emulation. Of the five chips needed, four would have to be emulated: the MMU, the CPU, the PLA, and the VIC-II chip. These were all emulated using wirewrap boards and handfuls of chips that otherwise wouldn't be needed later once the custom ICs were available (see Fig. 5-1).

Fig. 5-1 C128 prototype PCB bottom.
Photo courtesy of Bil Herd.

We talked about being compatible with the Commodore 64. We had one amazing legacy in the C64 and, until now, we had not used that legacy. I remembered the woman from the CES show in Vegas who told me how her new software wouldn't work on the TED. I felt like we had let her down (and other people whom I had not met). As they had supported us, we supported them. It was a symbiotic relationship: we needed them as much as they needed us.

Fred and I talked several times during this early design stage, and the idea of a Commodore C64-compatible machine at its core became more and more attractive. First off, no one anywhere else could do one of these, only Commodore. And even then, we were afraid that we might have already lost the recipe as nobody could tell us quite how all of the things were made to work in the C64. There were some amazing last-minute kludges made to get it into production and keep it there.

In addition to the processor, I had to take into account the bandwidth of the DRAMs and the behavior of the VIC-II chip. The result was a very busy main data/address bus. Quite simply, this is one of the reasons why there is visible noise on a C64: there is a *lot* going on.

What made the final decision in favor of C64 compatibility, for me, was the thought that this was a way to give back to the community that had supported us. I could give them a brand new machine, and yet, their old software would run on it. It would also give them a platform to write brand new software. I believe my feelings were shared by everybody. We loved the C64 ourselves. It's not like we had to be talked into it for the corporate line. Like many of those who bought the C64, when we had a moment and wanted to decompress, we would play a C64 game.

So, we decided that the new machine really could be C64-compatible, which would open the door to calling this the "C128."

Fred and I had hammered out not only C64 compatibility, but also an upgrade to 128 kB. And, I pushed for a continuance of the 80-column chip that was common in the business machines. We would have two outputs: the regular TV 40-column output and a simultaneous 80-column output for the terminals of the day. I had designed computers with the 6845 CRT controller, which was normally monochrome (one color, such as green on black or white on black). It was an old friend, and I was certain I could make it do color in 80-columns in a very controlled period of time.

By now, I was absorbing the design, as it were, and then reached for a brand new piece of 1/10 inch graph paper, my engineering pencil, and my ever-present collection of stencils.

Second Week

I disappeared into my office, which was slightly unusual for an outbound personality such as myself, but this was the best time--when you had a blank piece of paper and a head full of ideas. People knew when I was in design mode as I would wear sweatbands on my wrists, so that I could slide my wrists across the graph paper without smearing it.

In that second week, I laid down the architecture in a block diagram. I drew all of the signals and groups of signals, called buses--like data bus, address bus, etc.--for how I thought a computer could work that did all of the things we described in the previous week. I was adamant about this step. I never skip the architecture step or just dive right into "hooking parts together." To me, it is important to know everything about what the end result should look like before starting to draw the schematic. That's not to say the expectations won't change along the way. The point being: I always, always try to know where I'm going with my design.

Third Week

In the third week, it was time to actually draw the schematic. I took an ANSI B-sized tablet of the real light graph paper on 1/10 inch centers and my favorite stencils, loaded hard lead into my mechanical pencil, and put my sweatbands on my wrists. I laid down the design on paper; every data line, every address line, and every major piece of circuitry was represented that third week on that piece of paper. I started grinning maniacally, which can be scary to those around me, but ultimately, it meant that I saw a way that we could pull this off.

We Can Do It

It was the beginning of August. I knew it was doable now; I knew I could do it; I knew *we* could do it.

Too Many Middle Managers

Rather than asking the managers what they thought about the new machine, which would not have been particularly helpful, we went ahead and started calling it the C128. Every manager then who heard the name assumed that some other manager had picked the name and therefore couldn't change it.

It should be noted that middle management was starting to appear out of the woodwork around this time, without Jack Tramiel around to keep some sense of normalcy. With regard to the number of workers versus the amount of work done, our department exploded. The only thing was--it was still the same 8 to 10 of us doing all the work; the other people were filling in jobs that we had gotten away with not needing done up until now.

5.3 Getting It Going

Things just seemed to go so smoothly at the beginning. You could say that this was one of the best times of my life, these three weeks of doing sheer design. Now it was time to throw it into gear and start moving.

Proposing the C128

So, we went to the powers-that-be and we proposed the C128: Yes, the name that had grown up early on when we had the discussion about being C64-compatible. I had written the memo, "Yes, Virginia, there is compatibility," and it was time to put my money where my mouth was. I worked for the only company that could do a Commodore 64-compatible computer. I worked for the only company that could even do the chips that went in a Commodore 64-compatible computer, let alone know what that even means.

Surprisingly, upper management jumped right on the idea. For one thing, it was easy to say "Yes" to a Commodore 64-compatible machine. Secondly, there was nothing else in this slot. We were literally vying for an empty slot in our capability, and we knew it. We also knew that we needed something to present at the CES show, in addition to the LCD machine, something that seemed to us to have escaped management's notice.

Our boss didn't negatively comment on the name, and so C128 was now officially the new name of the project.

Putting the Band Back Together

I asked for people to help me pull off the impossible, as it was already a given that we had to make the next CES. The TED had turned out to be an ideal product, as it was a good exercise of all pieces and departments for what we needed to do on the C128. I have wondered to this day whether they would have trusted me or us to handle the C128--lock, stock, and barrel--if they hadn't seen us wrap up the TED series the way we did. Terry and Fred were already the choice by everyone for the software, having delivered on time and on spec for the C264 (Plus/4). I also got Dave Haynie assigned to the project for the same reasons. I talked with Bob Olah, the head of chip design, and got Dave DiOrio formally assigned to manage everything about the C128's IC needs, regardless of which designer might get tasked to do each specific project. This was good since Dave knew about what a chip was supposed to do, in a system, not just in a test jig. He was another from the Plus/4 band. We needed his guidance to steer all the chips, as we needed approximately four or five custom ICs to be done in five months, something that I hadn't seen done before, but DiOrio was the guy who could do it.

A Family of Two

Almost as soon as the C128 became official, we decided to do two versions of it: the first was known as the "flat" C128 with the keyboard built into the system, and the second was called the C128D, the "D" meaning that it had a built-in disk drive (see Fig. 5-2). This was an exciting version of the C128 and it became my favorite. While not really a portable computer, it had a handle and the external keyboard clipped up under it so you could carry your entire computer in one hand, except for the monitor.

Commodore C128 Family

C128

System, Internal Keyboard External Disk Drive. Flat.

North America 1985

C128D

System, External Keyboard Internal Disk Drive.

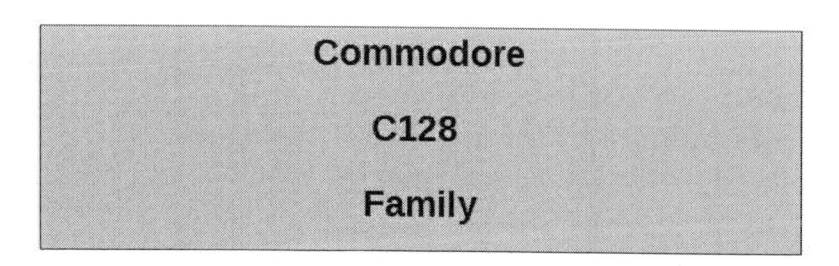

Europe 1986

Fig. 5-2 C128 and C128D were displayed at the 1985 Winter CES in Las Vegas.
Photos courtesy of Mark Corliss Photography/Multi-media Creations (www.markcorliss.com) C128 and Commodore-Info.com C128D.

We made sure that whatever we did for the C128 was 100% usable on the C128D, including the exact same PC boards in both (both the main PCB and the 1571 disk drive PCB). This would increase the number of things that we had to get right in the initial design, since we were essentially designing two computers at the same time. This was a big win in our book as the computer had already become a family of two. This also emphasized the fact that the development of the disk drive had to be in lockstep with the C128 itself.

Notable in the PCB design of the C128 to accommodate the C128D version are holes in the PC board for the support structure holding the internal disk drive. That severely limited our ability to get traces from one side of the board to the other. But we didn't once think about getting rid of the obstructions, as we were all committed to doing two versions at once.

Not by Committee

Our decision-making method consisted of short, quick little meetings, often in the halls, where we would decide things and move on. We made a lot of decisions in the hallway and at the photocopier. We were the antithesis of holding big committee meetings to decide small details, as we made small decisions all the time and would float the bigger ones to each other. It was in one of these impromptu meetings that I remembered the finger-pointing of the TED days.

I turned to the programmers and said that now was the time to ask for anything they might need in the chips, and that Dave DiOrio would get them (most) everything they asked for in the beginning. The price they would have to pay is that they would be required to fix any last-minute bugs, whether from hardware or a chip or software. I made it clear that there *would be* bugs in the hardware and chips. Of course there would be bugs--this was big, this was hard, and we were going to be ready for the CES show only five months away.

5.4 Five Months and Counting

So, it was the beginning of August, we had five months until CES, and we had just been given the green light. We were already behind schedule the moment we got the project started, but I was good with that. We would work enough to get a day ahead on the schedule and stay there throughout the design phase, meaning that we finished literally the day before CES. Yes, that happened. We got done with about four hours to spare. I remember specifically those four hours, because I sat down, drank a beer, and took a nap.

End of the 8-Bit Era

As the project progressed, we realized that this most likely was going to be the final 8-bit system to come out of Commodore. We began shoving in as many features as could fit in a five-month time frame. Before we were done, the C128 would have dual processors, three operating systems, dual monitors (40 and 80 column simultaneously), and would be one of the first, if not *the* first home computer to break the 64 kB barrier. I started referring to it as nine pounds of poop in a five-pound bag; we couldn't quite get 10 pounds to fit. If you had stopped us in the hall and told us that no one would really use a feature or two or three, our response would have been "maybe not," but our job was to offer as much of a machine as possible, in the time we had, and let the users figure out what worked for them. We joked about turning out the lights on our way out the door, as we knew that the 8-bit era was coming to a close and this would be a last hurrah.

Architecture

The architecture of the new C128 was still centered around the VIC-II chip, which necessitated that the new machine would be locked into an 8-bit architecture with VIC-II as the bus master (see Fig. 5-3). We had five months to modify five custom ICs. There would be no changing to a magical 16-bit machine or anything like that; we would be lucky to make this 8-bit machine work when we were done.

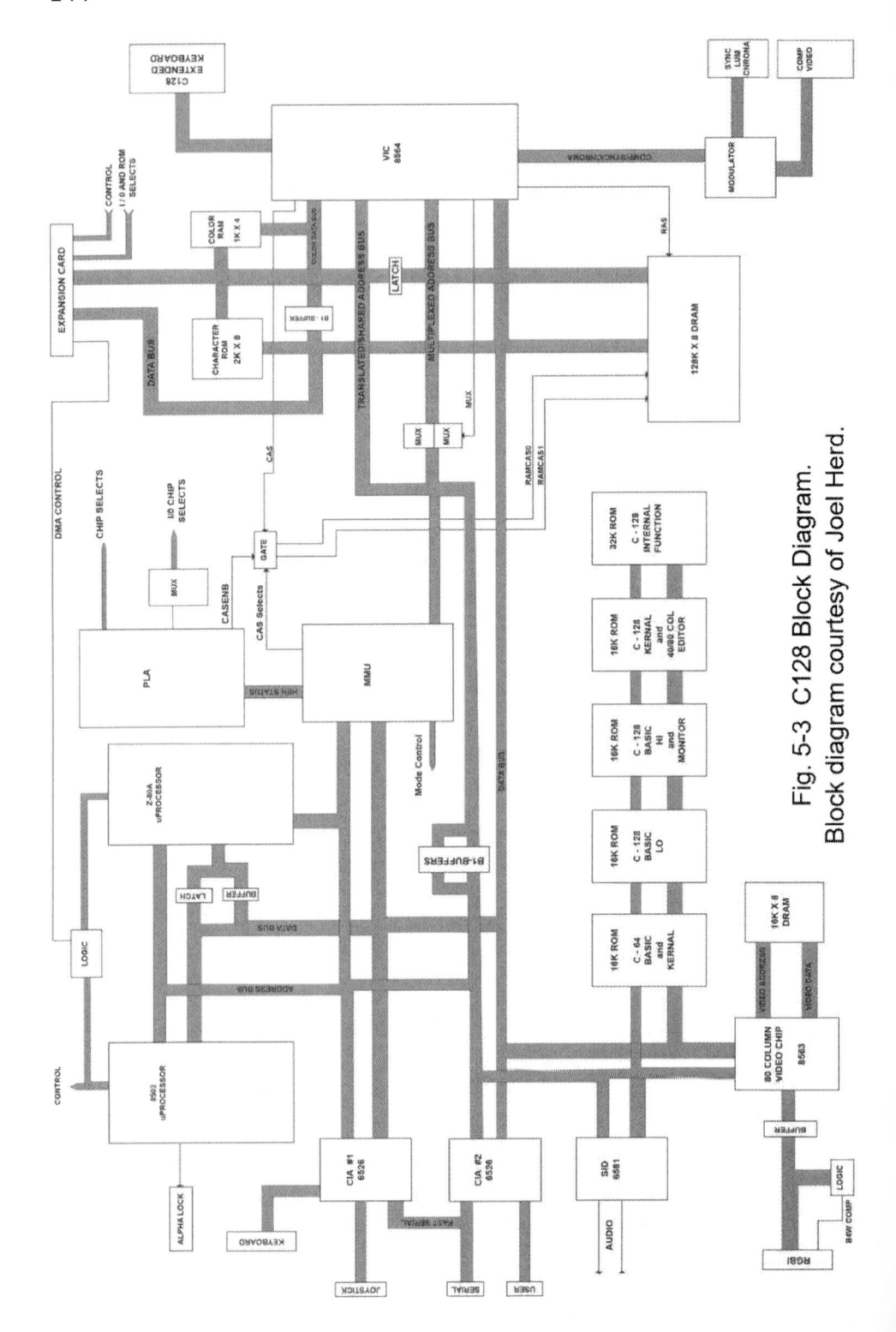

Fig. 5-3 C128 Block Diagram. Block diagram courtesy of Joel Herd.

The C128 would require four brand new 48-pin custom chips: a Memory Management Unit (MMU); a Programmable Logic Array (PLA); 8563 Video Display Controller (VDC); and a variation of the venerable, but scary, VIC-II video core chip--and before it was over, a new font ROM.

Did I mention that I loved working at Commodore?

Chip Emulators

Dave Haynie started on the emulation of the PLA chip, meaning that we made a wirewrap circuit that did everything, or mostly everything, that the final chip was supposed to do. In short, we emulated its behavior. I started on the emulation of the MMU chip. In addition to all of our other duties, we were now officially working two shifts, as we were working on the real machine and on what we called the software developers' machines. This was also a time to get all our ducks in a row, as the longer we waited to fix something, the harder it would be.

Very early, around September (pretty much as soon as the chip emulators were working), I showed the C128 playing *Joust* on a board that was half wirewrap and half PCB (it made me think of the movie, *The Thing*, where the dog was half dog and half squishy monster). This was a strong demo, as the colors and sounds were very exciting, and it was easy to be confused by the polish of the game alongside the rudimentary collection of wires and boards that it took to make the game run in all its sound and video glory.

Our boss took this time to present the C128 to the rest of the company, and so there was a stream of people that he led in to show them *Joust* running on it. He also took this time to present me as "the genius behind it" (his words), but again the sounds and colors were part of an internal sales pitch and easily obscured whether it was plain ole engineering or something more. At this point, zero of the custom chips were available, and I would guess that only about 60% of the games worked. The real genius of what we had done, so far, was that we had emulated hardware for 3-4 custom ICs in only 4-5 weeks (see Fig. 5-4).

Looking back, my long hair and wanton style added to the mystique of saying we could get a working unit showable at CES with only four months remaining. With that said, we were already a team and the simple *Joust* demonstration would not have been possible without the hundreds of hours of time put in by the programmers and the lab techs, as well as us hardware types.

Fig. 5-4 C128 prototype PCB with chip emulators.
Photo courtesy of Bil Herd.

C128 for Games

Our attitude at the engineering level (marketing didn't do planning that we could tell, just reactive talking) was that the C64 was *the* game machine. If you wanted to play a game (from what was probably the largest home computer game collection), either get a C64 or hey, a C128.

We actually thought that the C128 might be a good machine for developing games for the C64 since you could code on one screen and watch the results on the other. The inclusion of the ROM monitor was also in this vein, I believe. Our commitment to the C64 library was such that we made sure that we removed the advanced features in C64 mode as much as possible, so as not to corrupt in any way the definition of a C64. There were no "C64+" versions or any chance that someone would write a game for the C64 mode on the C128 that didn't run on the original C64 machine.

C64 Cartridges

As soon as the C128 had any C64 compatibility at all, we all started shoving cartridges into it at every opportunity. A cartridge left lying on the bench for any unknown reason would find its way into a C128, just to make sure it worked.

One day, I inserted the *Visible Solar System* cartridge, a game for the C64 that shows the different planets revolving around the Sun. Unfortunately, when it got to one spot in the rotation, the program would crash, freeze, and otherwise destroy the solar system. I slightly freaked out and tore into the machine immediately. Before getting too frustrated, however, I did try the cartridge in a normal Commodore 64 and found that it crashed at the same place in the rotation of the solar system where it had crashed on the C128, so I knew it wasn't the C128 outright.

This would be one of those times when we relied on intuition rather than the test equipment to tell us what was going on. I made my way to the chip designer who had been in charge of one of our early ROM products, the one that actually ended up in the cartridge for the *Visible Solar System*. I remembered having heard that there had been a bug, a glitch on one of the address lines, A10, which seemed to be the most common address line for bugs, as it turned out. It would appear that the flaw was at the chip level. I carefully asked the engineer if this could be the problem, as someone had told me that he was pretty touchy about the subject, this being the only bug I'd ever heard attributed to him. I was careful, I was smiling, and I wanted to know whether it was me or the chips. He confirmed that it was indeed one of the chips that had the bad, glitchy line.

I ended up carrying around a *Mach 5* cartridge. It was a speed loader program that made the serial bus go faster in C64 mode. I used the cartridge to do two things: 1) knock the computer into C64 mode; and 2) start loading the disk at hand at a higher speed than normal. I carried this cartridge around in my back pocket so much that my jeans all developed a wear spot from the cartridge to match the wear spot from my wallet in the other pocket.

KoalaPainter and Font ROM

I used to trade things to people in other departments in order to recruit them as assets. I had *somebody* in the downstairs QA Department on my payroll, so to speak. One day, I got a phone call from my "asset" that "they" were headed up to my office, claiming to have a show-stopping failure. So, I calmly got prepared for the attack.

The movie *Dirty Harry* was out back then, and there was a pretty famous scene where Dirty Harry kept chewing a sandwich while interacting with bank robbers. I hadn't actually seen the movie: I was much too busy at Commodore, but I did read the synopsis of it in *Mad Magazine*. I grabbed a sandwich out of the refrigerator that Greg and I kept--usually full of beer, but it was also useful for sandwiches--and I headed out into the hallway to meet the QA guys head-on.

This was a true rabble, as they had gathered steam as they came up from downstairs, through the hallway, and towards R&D. Our R&D QA manager had gotten hold of a C64 cartridge and was now holding it over his head as the proof that the C128 would fail, once and for all. Thanks to having been prepared for this, I was out in the hallway eating my sandwich. I relieved him of the cartridge before he realized what I was doing and now proceeded to the R&D lab, with the rabble following me instead of only him. I remember that he made a gutted fish noise when I did this.

I shoved the cartridge into a C128 and saw that it was *KoalaPainter,* one of my favorite programs on the C64, which honestly was ahead of its time. What became obvious to me was that the screen that I was looking at had our original Commodore 64 font (the shape of the letters), which we knew wasn't as clean of a font as it could have been. In fact, we had swiped it from Atari (we made their ROMs after all) and called it the "Atari Font." Now, I have to say that, in our C128 version of the font ROM, Terry and Fred had tried to clean up some of the nasty stuff that was in the original C64 font. They fixed the way the "j"s and "g"s descended, *and they moved the dot on the letter "i" one pixel over*, so that it was better centered.

What I saw that day on *KoalaPainter* was that it would first put up the letters of the words "KoalaPainter," and then paint the letter "K" one color, paint the letter "o" another color, and so on. When it went to paint the dot over the letter "i" as a foreground color, it missed the dot. The dot had moved (thanks to Terry and Fred's fix) from where it would have been in the C64. The program was now painting the background instead of the dot on the letter "i" (leaving the dot unpainted). As it turns out, the process of painting the background by accident rather than just the dot took almost two to three minutes back in the day. To the good folk from QA, they mistakenly thought that the program had crashed completely as they missed the significance of the dot.

So, it turned out that, in order for the C128 to be totally Commodore 64 compatible, we could not even move the dot on the "i" in our 128 font ROM!

This was an easy fix though. I grabbed an old Commodore 64 font ROM; soldered it directly on top of the new Commodore 128 font ROM (known as "bricklaying"); and used the signal that determines whether we are in 64 or 128 mode to select between the two (see Fig. 5-5). We showed a fix of the C128 system now working, in less than an hour--closer to 40 minutes actually. The rabble quietly slinked back downstairs.

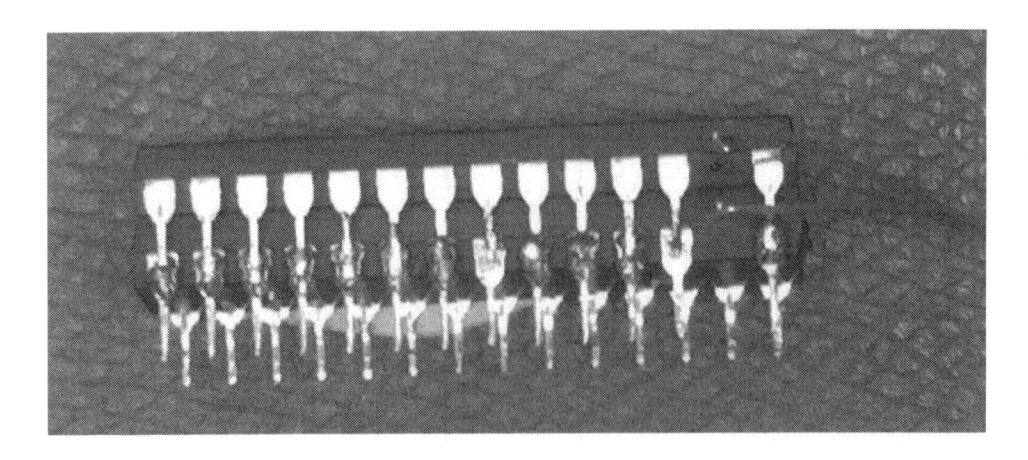

Fig. 5-5 Bricklaid font ROMs.
Photo courtesy of Bil Herd.

Phantom Key Problem

During this time, Terry Ryan came to me and said that we had the "phantom key problem." The phantom key problem is where there is a need to close three keys on the same keyboard matrix, a keyboard matrix being the way that the keys are scanned from the microprocessor. Simply put, if you have to close three keys at once, there is a fourth key that looks like it is also closed (see Fig. 5-6).

Normally, we don't close three keys at once, but with the caps lock key, the shift key, and a normal key all pressed simultaneously, that was three. It was the caps lock key that was causing the problem. What a great problem to have: there was no caps lock key on the C64.

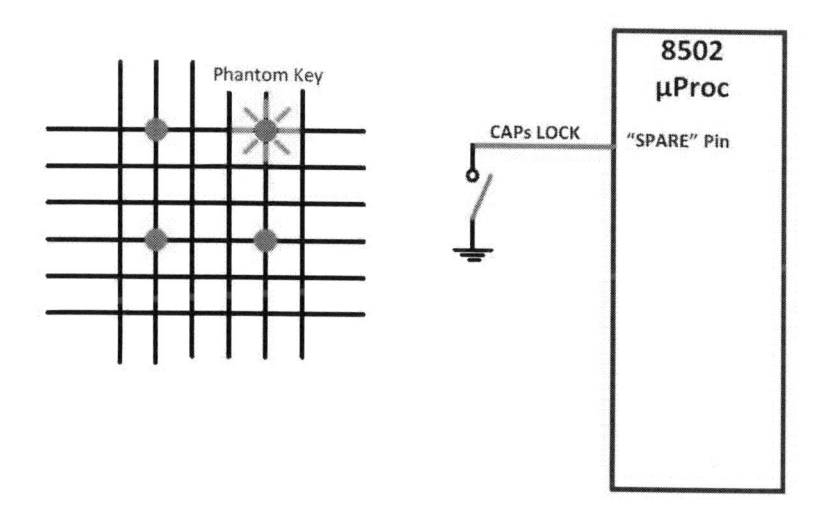

Fig. 5-6 Phantom key problem matrix.
Graphic courtesy of Bil Herd.

I grabbed Dave DiOrio, Fred Bowen, and Terry Ryan and we headed for Shiraz's old office. We grabbed the whiteboard there, and I started out by asking DiOrio if he had any room on the edge of the 6510 processor chip (on the inside), which was my way of asking if he could get the register wired out correctly. He said, "Yes." I smiled, knowing that we had just solved our problem: we would hook one of the keys directly to the processor to fix our dilemma. The problem later would be--after we added a Z80 to the design (something that we had not initially planned on doing)--that the register now had to ask the 6510 processor if the caps lock was pressed.

It was that simple--we had decided to do the caps lock via a dedicated pin on the big chip--and this problem was handled for now. What I never dreamed was that I had just made it so a future coprocessor, such as the Z80, would not be able to scan the caps lock itself. It would have to ask the processor connected directly to the caps lock if the key was pressed.

Sure, I made a long term architectural mistake, but the value of making a decision as a group in under five minutes was priceless. We didn't bother telling management, or the other supervisors wandering the halls, about our decision-making process. We knew they would want in on it, and we knew that they would want to leave their mark on anything, whether they understood it or not. This manager interference would plague us throughout the development, necessitating some strong-arm tactics on our end. We'll get into more of that later.

Commodore's 25th Anniversary

Speaking of decision-making, I finally did get to meet the lead designer behind the IBM PC, Bill Lowe, at the 25-year anniversary of the Commodore 64, back in 2007. I asked him about their decision-making process at IBM and volunteered that our theory was that they had big committees to make simple decisions. Mr. Lowe was gracious, laughed, and indicated that I may have been close to the mark. It wasn't surprising to me that I and the lead designer of the PC got along so well; we were competitors, but we knew what each other did for a living.

C128 Keyboard

When the time came to pick a keyboard layout for the C128, I looked down at my VT100 terminal that I had hooked to the VAX (what felt like ages ago) and couldn't think of anything better. I walked down to Fred and Terry's office and they agreed. That quick, the keyboard layout was selected (see Fig. 5-7).

I was prepared to explain to management, just in case they objected, that the usability issues would have been worked out by DEC when they made the VT100, but no one called me on the issue. I remember walking a VT100 keyboard down to the mechanical guys' area, as the physical example. I am less clear on whose system I got the keyboard from, but it had to be one of the other seven VAX users.

Fig. 5-7 C128 keyboard layout similar to DEC VT100.
Photo courtesy of Joel Herd.

I remember that the next time I had to interact with the mechanical guys regarding the keyboard was when they showed me working samples (apparently the vendor gave us a high priority). The keyboards were, for all intents and purposes, perfect--the only difference being that the legend was painted rather than injection molded as they would be in the production version. The keyboard was ultimately one of the things we didn't have to worry much about amongst the dozens of other sources of problems, and we already had the muscle memory to type on it!

Random Number Problem

During the C128 software development of BASIC 7.0, Terry Ryan went to examine how random the random function was. He ran a chi-squared test on it and found that it was not random. He discovered, for example, that if you made a dice program using the random number generation, the odds of rolling double-sixes would be less than in real life. The random numbers were incorrectly weighted near the upper limit of the random number range. Probably no user would have noticed, but when designing code for millions of people, a small thing can become a big thing very quickly.

1571 Disk Drive

While this was going on, a whole other computer had to be designed, this being the 1571 disk drive that would be compatible with the C128 (see Fig. 5-8). This was the work of Greg Berlin and Dave Siracusa, and their job was every bit as hard as ours. They had to make a 6502-based computer work in five months, and be sellable soon after that in quantities of millions. Again, this flew right through management who were probably looking for ways to justify their positions.

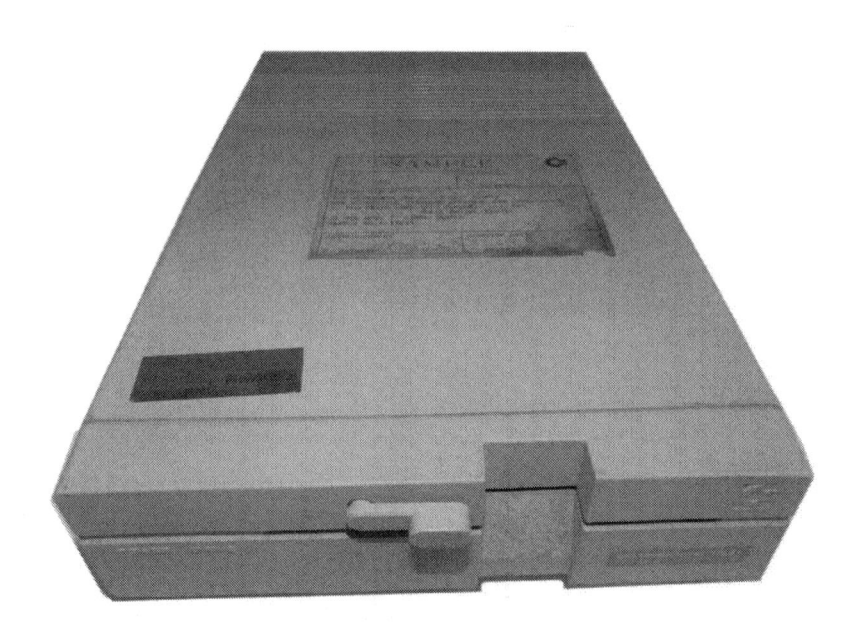

Fig. 5-8 Bil's prototype 1571 disk drive.
Photo courtesy of Joel Herd.

Designing a new disk drive for the C128 gave us a chance to fix the serial bus speed, which was really the only major complaint about the Commodore 64 family. Anyone that's ever loaded disks on the C64 will know what I mean. I remember a time when I showed an article to one of the Japanese engineers about the existing C64 drive and there was a comment that it was "slow as molasses." This led to me demonstrating--with an actual jar of molasses--what they meant by this jargon.

Anyway, having new products ready was always a good thing. So now we had a new disk drive to go along with the new C128. We started talking with Commodore Tokyo: could a new monitor be ready in time? We did after all need to have a monitor that supported both 40 and 80-column displays. Imagine working at a company that could turn on a dime and add a new monitor to its product line in response to adding an 80-column output to the computer.

This was a good time to be young engineers and working at Commodore!

5.5 Customized Chips

We needed to customize four chips to accomplish our goals.

Microprocessor

The first chip that needed to be customized for the C128 was the microprocessor. This was basically the same processor that was in the venerable C64, the MOS 6510, which was a modified 6502. Since we had added the caps lock key though, we knew we needed another pin out of the chip, and it was slated to be turned into HMOS II, meaning it would become an 8502 very shortly.

One story about the re-pin out of the C128 processor that comes to mind is this: I was walking through the hall and I heard Terry Hudson, one of the guys in charge of chip testing, say he couldn't get the zero page port register to work correctly. I stopped dead, backed up, and said, "Say that again?" He said, "I'm trying to rotate a bit through the 0 Port register and it's not working." Terry was talking about writing a program to use in the MOS Chip Production Department to probe the wafers and tell if the chip die were good or not, while still on the wafer. Terry was our favorite test engineer and was known for the Santa's hat he wore the week of Christmas. As it turns out, I had heard one of the chip designers say that normally they just remove the pad that we no longer needed, but in this case, DiOrio needed the extra room on the die, and so removed the register all together. I have to admit Terry didn't act surprised that I knew this, or that a chance passing in the hall addressed the issue, and I pointed him at Dave for a confirmation.

6510-HERD

One of the pins that we usually needed for debugging was not brought out on the 8502 and that was the "sync," which is used by the logic analyzer to tell if a fetch cycle is taking place or not. While we could still watch the signals without the sync pin, we couldn't do full analysis. I grabbed Mike

Angelina and Dave Esposito and said I could use a new chip: a 48-pin chip, temporarily with a custom pinout.

Mike grabbed a piece of paper that had been photocopied too many times, which showed a lead frame and the pads, and we hastily sketched in how we wanted this new chip to be pinned out, while standing at the photocopier. As luck would have it, we went too fast and we made a mistake; unfortunately the bond wires could not reach from every single pad to every single pin on the package. The industrious people over at MOS still made it work, by rotating the die by 45 degrees so that it looked like a little diamond tie tack. Well, this looked ridiculous, but it worked, and it turned out that the young Bil Herd had created his own version of the 6502, a chip he idolized, now called the 6510-HERD (see Fig. 5-9).

Fig. 5-9 6510-HERD "Tie Tack."
Photo courtesy of Bil Herd.

A 48-pin package was brand new for MOS in Commodore. I accidentally became the first user of the new package, which was good, as we would need several more for the production C128.

A couple of years later, after I had left, I stopped by the main plant to see somebody, and in the lobby was a selection of ICs made by MOS. Whoever put the display together didn't realize that the "tie tack," (due to its appearance) as I called it, was not a real chip, but there it was on display in the main lobby, a 6510-HERD.

"New" VIC-II

Since the C128 was mostly based on the C64 architecture, we would be using the venerable VIC-II chip, only augmented with some additional features, not the least being the ability to double the processor clock and run at 2 MHz in 80-column mode. We almost doubled the computer speed in one shot!

PLA

The Programmable Logic Array, PLA, is probably the second most important chip in the Commodore 64. It allows the VIC-II chip and the processor to access all the resources it needs, based on the special modes that it's in. It's a very busy chip. The PLA is made of gates and can be programmed to create various outputs, based on the inputs, or in other words the stimulus. Essentially, it takes the state of the core and translates it into lots of control signals for all the various parts of the system that need to be told when it's time to talk or listen.

In the C64, this was a 28-pin chip, known as the 82S100, and it was ultimately our own version of that chip. We had high failure rates of our version of the PLA in the C64. We would get holes in the seventh layer, called "passivation," and it would allow moisture in under the protective silicon nitride coating. This became visible as a creeping crud, as seen under the microscope. In fact, I called it the "purple creeping crud." I don't know that it was really purple, but by the time the physics of the layers could become involved, it tended to be purplish in hue when viewing it through the microscope. Yes, you could actually watch the chip rot in real time. Ultimately, this was traced to too much boron in the mix.

We needed something bigger and better for the C128's PLA. We needed many more outputs, and so we put it in a 48-pin package that had just become available, and even then, I ran low on pins. By putting so much logic into one device though, I could do almost anything I wanted, including fixing problems or issues or adding features that we hadn't thought of initially. I could have any logic I wanted, but I had to turn in the required logic equations about five weeks before I needed it, so that MOS had time to fabricate the chip.

Now, the PLA is basically a bunch of rows and columns of terms that hook to logic, resulting in a big row-column array. The problem with making something like this bigger is that the delays don't get twice as big when making the array twice as big. The delays get four times as big, due to a square term. So, we had to deal with that; just not yet.

DiOrio had the new PLA assigned to one of the TED designers. On my end, I assigned Haynie to be the main engineer on the PLA emulator, the wirewrapped PC board that would plug into the PLA socket in the meantime, while waiting for the chip to become available. This amounted to taking lots of PLAs and stacking them together in a way that still met the timing specifications. Since this wasn't for production, Dave could use otherwise noisy and troublesome parts, such as Schottky parts to accomplish the speed requirements.

MMU

In order to break the 64 kB barrier, I would need a memory management unit, called an MMU. The MMU was nothing more than a bunch of registers that were set up to control various aspects of the computer. While the processor can only talk to 64 kB at a time, the MMU created a window into the 128 kB, expandable to 512 kB initially, where the processor could work. The MMU also managed how to store and quickly pull up previous configurations of how the memory and I/O space was to be organized.

The one thing I did not add to the MMU was a "supervisor mode" since there was no supervisor mode in the microprocessor itself. A supervisor mode is where the operating system itself has the only access to certain resources. This means that the Kernal could make some assumptions about how things are set up and work better and faster on the fly. I should have discussed this with Fred ahead of time. As it turned out, Fred could never make the assumption that something was available since the user could write a program to change everything about the computer itself, with the exception of the read-only memory. So the best features that I tried to give to Fred to make his life better, he wasn't able to use. I only found this out during the last two months of the project. If I had asked about it sooner, who knows, maybe I could have slid in a supervisor mode in time. I've often said that the MMU in the C128 was *almost* the first MMU in the consumer computer, but the fact that it didn't have a supervisor mode, in my mind, makes it not a real MMU compared to today's MMUs.

I took on the design of the emulator MMU myself. Since this was the core of the computer, I needed to make sure it was behaving the way that I envisioned it working.

Breaking the 64 kB Barrier Problem

At some point in software development, Terry Ryan came and showed me something that we needed to address in the new MMU. Sometimes he showed me cool things, but as often as not, he was showing me something broken. He had just started using the full 128 kB of DRAM memory.

Basically, Terry was now actually breaking the pervasive 64 kB barrier that signified all previous 6502 machines. This is not as simple as it sounds. These days, we think that memory is just a big bunch of memory, and you just add more to the bunch to make it bigger. Back then, the question was, "How does a 64 kB-based processor access twice that amount of information in an efficient way?" Terry's answer was to store data in one of the 64 kB banks (these are the variables and whatnot), and then store the BASIC program itself in the other 64 kB bank. This was a good compromise for the 1980s.

Terry had stumbled across a problem with the MMU though. Apparently, information written to one of the 64 kB banks could sometimes show up in the other bank: data into program memory or vice versa. The original data was still intact in the original bank; it was only when we started using all 128 kB that we figured out that we had missed this.

Now, Dave DiOrio did a great job of bringing most of the IC design efforts together, so we brought this problem to him. Dave took a look at the issue and figured out what was wrong. Thankfully, he had the foresight to have saved half of the production lot of the MMU chip in case there was a problem. We called this a "1-2-3" in that he had asked MOS to save the bottom three layers of the chip run, typically in a quantity known as a "lot," a "lot" being a batch of wafers. So, Dave had one half of the production run set aside in storage after it was "half" fabricated with only the bottom three layers. Well, it turns out that he was really good at this kind of engineering, which was fixing something using only the top three layers of the chip, "4-5-6" (see Fig. 5-10). As engineers, we assumed that something that was half broken meant that it was also half working. So presumably, it was simply a matter of figuring out a way to make the rest of it work, in spite of itself.

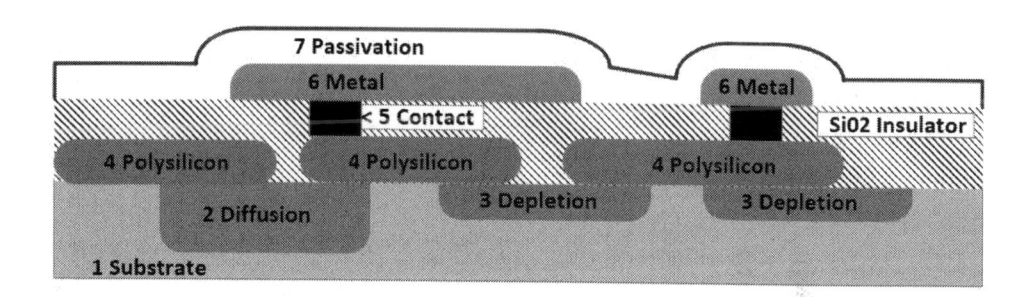

Fig. 5-10 Depiction of NMOS chip layers. Split lot "1-2-3" and "4-5-6." Graphic courtesy of Bil Herd.

But, a problem then happened when the next rev of the MMU came in. The chip had gotten worse, not better. In fact, it was pretty broken. Dave headed off immediately to try to figure out what had happened. I saw him at the end of the day, and he was in that particular type of Dave-being-quiet mode that told me he was thinking deeply about the problem, after having spent the day looking at the MMU chip through the microscope.

Michelob to the Rescue

I dragged Dave out to the local bar, grabbed one of the tables that we inhabited on a fairly frequent basis, and got our regular pitcher of Michelob, a classy and full-bodied beer for the 1980s. I remember we just sat drinking and not talking much. Dave and I were the kind of friends that didn't always have to talk. In fact, it felt good to just be quiet after the hustle and bustle of Commodore life.

As we were sitting there in the bar, I remember Dave slowly starting to smile, which made me start to smile, and he quietly said, "I know what's wrong." Dave had spent the afternoon looking at the bad MMU chip under a microscope and storing what he saw in his memory, like one might collect Polaroid pictures to look at later. Later that night, under the influence of a few Michelobs and some quiet, his brain developed the pictures his eyes had taken earlier; and he realized the fact that MOS had used one of the wrong masks, and an earlier layer had gotten into the design. This resulted in bad silicon for a chip because the old and new layers didn't line up with each other in a meaningful way. Dave informed MOS about this and they did a special production run to fix it.

This would not be the first time a problem would be addressed at this particular bar, the Courtyard. (If you ever saw the David Letterman episode where the guy stops the fan with his tongue, he was a bartender there.) I still marvel at the time frame that we used back then as our definition of a good day. Success basically meant that no major problems survived till the next day. There simply wasn't time.

5.6 80-Column Chip 8563

To review, I had originally planned to use the venerable 6845 CRT controller in the original C128. It was a tried and true part that I loved. All of us hardware engineers of the day loved seeing something actually appear on a CRT screen when we were done. But that changed early on when Bob Olah caught me in the hallway, along with the designer of one of the chips for the soon-to-be defunct Z8000 machine. They had been working on an 80-column chip, the 8563 VDC, for over a year and they were looking for a new home for it.

The 8563 was a holdover from the Z8000-based C900, the Z Machine, as we called it. The people who worked on it were called the Z People, the place they hung out was called the Z Lounge, and well, you get the idea. The most interesting thing that came out of that group, besides a disk controller that prompted you for what sector and cylinder you'd like to write to on every access, was that one day they stole the furniture out of the lobby and made their own lounge, called the Z Lounge, disguising it as a VAX repair depot. We were so amused by this that we stopped teasing them for a week.

So anyway, while it seemed to make sense to use the 8563 for what we needed, it turns out that there were some early miscommunications and assumptions that proved to be problematic as we progressed.

6845 Superset

Since the designer was standing next to me and it was his chip, I turned to him and asked, "Is it a 6845 superset?" (The 6845 was the definitive standard for the day.) He responded, "Yes," and I made a mistake in that moment. I realized years later, by looking back, that the designer did not know what a "6845 superset" meant, and I should have asked if he knew what I meant. It was such common knowledge to us hardware engineers, that I assumed that he knew what I meant with the question. Apparently he didn't, and I adopted the 8563 with this misunderstanding.

As it turns out, the 8563 was *not* a 6845 superset. It was what a chip designer thought a computer needed, without ever having designed a computer himself. Now this chip designer was brilliant; he owned some of the patents in the Motorola 68000 microprocessor, but he maybe didn't have experience with small-computing systems needs.

Looking back, I realize that the source of a lot of the problems with the 8563 is that it wasn't designed *for* the C128 and that the IC designers did not take part in the application of their chip the way the other designers did. The VIC-II and MMU designers took an active interest in how their chip was used and how the system design worked in relation to their chip. I had overlooked the ramifications of how the 8563 was spec'd to work, and that came back to haunt me later.

Scroll Register

For example, it was explained to me how there was this block transfer feature for transferring characters for things like scrolling--a scroll register. Cool. We needed that. I assumed it would scroll the *entire 80-column screen* by the amount in the register, but later it turned out that when this feature finally did work correctly, it only was good for 256 characters at a time. I never stopped to think to ask if the feature was semi-useless because it could only block move 3 and 1/3 lines in 80-columns at a time. Now if you had a car that would only drive thirty-three feet at a time, you would say it was a broken car. This was a broken scrolling mechanism. We almost didn't use it, but we figured a little bit faster was a little better than nothing at all, but barely.

Did I mention the block move was only good for 256 characters? Later, a bug in this feature would almost prove a show-stopper, with a serious problem showing up in Vegas the night of setup before the CES show. But I am getting ahead of myself. Stand by.

Timing Differences

It was also my understanding that this part, the 8563, had the same timing parameters as the 6845, a *very* common graphics adapter. Not scrutinizing the chip for timing differences the way I normally did any new chip was another mistake I made. The major timings indicated what speed class it was in, but I didn't check them *all*. I blame myself, as this really is the type of mistake an amateur makes. I wonder if I was in a hurry that day. Again, I had assumed incorrectly that the chip was a superset of the 6845.

Prototypes Occasionally Blew Up

There were many revs of the 8563, as we fixed and found more problems. It was sometime in October (or so memory serves) when we got 8563 silicon good enough to stick into a system. I can't remember all that was wrong with the chip, but one concern we had was that it occasionally blew up--big time: turn over, die, and then smell bad. But then all of the C128 prototypes did that on a semi-regular basis, as there wasn't really any custom silicon yet, just big circuit boards plugged in where custom chips would later go. But again, we couldn't wait for a system to be completed before starting software development. I don't think any of the Animals really gave it a thought until the next rev of the chip came out, and now with fewer other problems, the blowing up *seemed* more pronounced.

Cold Spray

Also, the prototypes got more solid *almost* every day. The programmers had found that spraying the board with cold spray would make it act differently, sometimes better, sometimes worse. I knew to go check on the programmers' prototype whenever I heard the sound of cold spray coming out of their office. Later, it turned out that they usually weren't spraying the boards, just using their hardware engineer call, much like a duck call. I would respond by trying to make the system work better in that moment, while silently praying that it was fixable. Sometimes, all I had to do was touch the board in a mystical way and then back out slowly, sometimes accompanied by rituals like chanting and humming. This became known as the "laying on of hands." This worked every time except one, and that time it turned out that I had stolen a badly needed component myself without telling them, which broke my own rules and was just rude. I apologized profusely afterwards, but I had to live with the ribbing for a few weeks.

If anybody else got caught messing with my guys like that, they'd get duct taped to a locker and then the box kicked out from under them, leaving them stuck until they could peel themselves down, but that's another story.

8563 Read/Write Timing Problem

It turns out that a major change from the real 6845 had been made to the way the read/write line was handled. A read/write line is the control line that tells the 8563 whether the cycle is a read cycle or a write cycle. In order for this to occur properly, the 8563 has to work with other chips in the system.

So, the problem was that I made an error in the *timing* of the read/write line: I missed the timing by three nanoseconds when taking into account all possible manufacturers and versions of one of the mundane "jelly bean" chips that help to make everything work. I ended up *fixing* the read/write timing violation by removing USSR-made parts from the list of vendors that were approved in Japan. I wouldn't have even known that we used chips from the USSR until this problem cropped up.

When I asked about this weird timing requirement very late in the design cycle, like *in production* when this problem turned up, I was told, "Remember, this was designed to work in the Z8000 machine." Shoulda seen the look on my face! Even though the Z8000 machine was long dead and we had been trying for months to use this dang thing in the C128, I was being told now that it wasn't designed to work the way we'd been using it for six months? Shoulda asked. It was my fault. Shoulda asked, "Is this meant to work the way we're using it?"

Don't get me wrong, remember, the 8563 designer was very smart. It's just that the chip had to work in conjunction with other chips, and that's where some of the problems lay.

5.7 Why the Z80

I didn't set out to add a Z80 to the C128. I don't think any of us thought about it at all. I had seen a memo about issues with the CP/M cartridge for the C64, and so it's fair to say I was apprehensive of the Z80 in general and the CP/M cartridge specifically. Before it was over, I would come to understand what the problem was with the CP/M cartridge--in production--but only after a painful realization of our own.

I have since come to the conclusion that we didn't choose the Z80; it chose us.

C64 CP/M Cartridge Not Working

We had two CP/M cartridges in the R&D lab and one did not work in a C128. This was a very poor sample size with very poor statistical results, and in my mind, it would be a problem until proven that it would not be.

I remember that I plugged the CP/M cartridge back into the C128 for another test and watched it fail to boot (again), which in my mind was the newest problem of the day--the problem of the entire computer really, if we were going to say we were C64-compatible. At this point, though, marketing had yet to throw down the glove declaring the C128 to be 100% compatible, something I never believed was possible. I spent the day trying to figure out how to fix this problem.

Power Supply Issue

Around the same time, I was looking down the road to the power supply design and how much extra current would be needed to provide for cartridges or the cassette recorder, assuming someone still used one. There was a major problem in my mind, as the Z80 CP/M cartridge drew well over an amp. In the C64, this would just mean the power supply would run a little lower voltage and get a little warmer, but on the C128, the switching supply might actually shut off, if the maximum current was exceeded.

For a consumer computer, we had the wonder of a switching power supply--a rather sophisticated technique of the day that used multiple transistors, coils, and other paraphernalia to create the output voltage without creating quite as much heat. The trade-off, however, was that switching supplies were more expensive per watt, but they were better. We couldn't just fudge the numbers; we had to get them right for the power supply to work correctly. Basically, in order to support the CP/M cartridge, I would have to carry an extra amp-plus on the power supply that probably would never be used for most installations. If done this way, I was essentially increasing the per unit cost for an accessory item.

Adding the Z80 to the C128 PCB

With the power supply issue on my mind, as well as the CP/M cartridge issue, I thought to add the Z80 directly to the main PC board. Doing so would increase the current consumption only by a couple of hundred milliamps and would make it irrelevant that the CP/M cartridge didn't always work, since the computer itself would have the Z80 CP/M functionality built in.

I again pulled the schematic of the Commodore C64 CP/M cartridge, and I found the folder from when I inherited the office of the engineer who had done the cartridge in the first place. Lo and behold, I found that the original schematic was that of a third-party cartridge for the Apple II computer. Well before my time, someone had modified the CP/M cartridge design to make it run on the C64. I looked at the schematic carefully and figured out what it was doing. Then, in my mind, I subtracted all of the extra parts that were not needed, if the cartridge could be moved onto the main board of the C128. It was deceptively simple, with only needing a few components, at least so far.

I walked around talking to people whose opinions I trusted on this matter, and then got with the programmers and floated the idea of moving the CP/M function to the main computer off of the cartridge. Essentially, the

C128 would become a dual processor computer if I were to pull this off. Meanwhile, I was mostly worried about the power supply cost: I lived and died by $0.10 increments to our bottom line. As an example, I once figured out a way to save a dollar and got very drunk that night.

I laid down a quick design on paper as an add-on to the fledgling C128 board. This would have been around Rev 2 of the PCB. I went to the R&D lab and got a technician assigned to build out this new version of the C128, adding a wirewrap section for the Z80 to the PCB. The next morning, when the same sun came up, there was now a version of the C128 that was a dual processor. In all honesty, the Z80 did little more than just jump back to 6502 mode. This proved that I could make it work; and I quickly added the circuitry to the schematic for the next C128 PCB, Rev 3, which was to be the first true, stand-alone C128 PCB, given the fact that we still had to plug "chip towers" into the sockets where custom chips would eventually go.

It should be noted that I hadn't yet told management that I was adding a Z80 to the design, something I did not tell them about until the new PC boards came in and we stuffed them with Z80s. At that point, they would see the Z80 already in as part of the core design.

Yanking Sinclair Z80s

When the new boards arrived, we had one problem: we didn't have any Z80s in stock! I got the first PCB working by taking my doorstop--in other words my Timex Sinclair Z80-based computer that had a nice wedge shape--tearing it open and taking the Z80 out of it. Surprisingly enough, the C128 *with* Z80 started right up after some pushing, probing, and wiring; but it worked!

I now proceeded to show management what we had done, with the rather lame attempt to make it sound like it was their idea in the first place. But really, I focused on the fact that I was saving money, both in the power supply and in the cost of even making a CP/M cartridge in the first place. The piece de resistance in defending the Z80 was the fact that the C64 CP/M cartridge didn't work in the C128, so it was common sense that we needed this modification. No manager pushed back on me, and I was given de facto permission to continue doing what I was doing.

In a true embrace of becoming a multiple operating system computer with multiple processors, management contracted Von Ertwine from a consulting company to repurpose CP/M to run natively on the C128. I assumed that we would start from the C64 cartridge so that we had working models almost right away; in fact, it almost seemed easy. But instead, now we would be working from the C128 PCB with the addition of the Z80.

We had only three or four working C128s, so that all the programmers could have one, as well as us in the R&D lab, but we needed more Z80s. It should be noted that the Z80 was hard-soldered into the C64 CP/M cartridges, so they were not really a viable source of Z80s. So, I went on a hunt for other doorstops, knowing that marketing had picked up on the whole idea after I started propping a door open with a Timex Sinclair. I would make a show of appearing at somebody's office asking to see their doorstop. Then, I'd tear open the doorstop with extreme vigor and tell them I needed the Z80 out of their now broken doorstop. At one point, I returned to the R&D lab bleeding from my hand where I had cut myself while tearing open a Timex Sinclair. I just grinned maniacally and replied that one had fought back. It really was a lot of blood for such a simple cut.

Enter Frank Palaia

We had been continuing to interview people throughout this process, just one of the necessary tasks of working at Commodore back then. One engineer I spoke to on the phone was Frank Palaia, and he sounded interesting enough that I asked him to swing by the plant in West Chester. He asked if it was right across the river and I replied basically yes, thinking he meant the Delaware River near Philadelphia.

The next day, Frank did not show up for his interview. This would have normally been a hard "no" for me, if somebody couldn't make it to an interview. Since we had to juggle many things as CBM employees, being in the right place at the right time was pretty much considered to be a good thing. Finally, I got a phone call from Frank. He thought I meant

Westchester, New York, and an entirely different river. He had spent the morning trying to find Commodore in a completely different state. Mind you, this is before the Internet or any of the mapping GPS functions that we enjoy today. In fact, GPS might not yet have been invented; certainly not for consumers.

I laughed at his openness and honesty, and gave him a second chance. He said he would be there on time this time and meant it, and I knew he did. His interview went well, but finally I asked how well he knew the Z80, and he said he knew it well. He had done so well in the interview that I knew that he meant that the Z80 was just another processor to him and that he also had valuable time on debugging Z80-based systems

Frank was hired and became my new Z80 guy, to take on the extra workload of adding a Z80 to the C128. To this day, I have never hired somebody that missed their interview other than Frank (see Fig. 5-11).

Fig. 5-11 Frank Palaia (center), Jeff Porter (left), Dave DiOrio (right) at Herd's CBM party.
Photo courtesy of Dave Haynie.

Z80 to the Rescue

During this time, my friend Tom Brightman stopped by from Commodore Texas, bringing the *Magic Voice* cartridge with him to demonstrate it for the C64, and hopefully the C128 in C64 mode. We plugged in the cartridge and nothing worked, nothing. It didn't try to do C64 mode; it didn't stay in C128 mode; it just crashed, rolled over, and smelled bad ... real bad.

To back up a bit, there are two selection lines on a standard C64 cartridge, called /EXROM and /GAME. Normally, one or both of these jumpers are soldered in a closed position on a standard cartridge, meaning that they would not change state: they were either shorted to ground by being soldered closed, or they were left in an open position. When I threw the cartridge on the logic analyzer, I found that the cartridge designers were manipulating these two control lines on the fly! They would literally wait until they saw the processor starting to reset and then toggle these master control signals, as if they were a C64 cartridge. The only problem was that it was a C128, not a C64, and the C128 did not understand those commands. They meant nothing to a C128, especially one that had not yet been initialized with all the parameters for the MMU and memory maps.

I got back with Tom and we had a good laugh, as I told him that that was an aggressive use of jumpers/signals and not something I had ever considered. I came across this problem early in the design cycle as, at the very least, I would need to make every Commodore-based cartridge work, let alone the thousands of third-party cartridges.

Booting the Z80 First

My desire was to fix this issue overnight, as I tried to fix every major problem overnight so that in the morning we could start with all new problems. I knew that the cartridge was watching for the 6502 reset vector, an address that the processor goes to as the very first thing it does. I also knew that the Z80 had its reset vector in a completely different location, in this case in $0000 instead of $FFFC. The Z80 also used a different polarity for its reset line: the Z80's line was high in reset, whereas the 6502 used a low reset.

My thought was to start the Z80 first, and to do so, I would need to invert the reset logic. We had this done in a couple of hours, and it appeared that it would work. But, I would need code to tell the Z80 to just jump to C64 mode, as this would be proof that it could be made to work with the cartridge.

I called Von Ertwine, our CP/M contractor, at his home; he was not available, but his wife was. I told her over the phone what I was trying to do and that I needed a handful of instructions that I could hand punch into the EPROM programmer to make the Z80 boot, set up the MMU, and then jump to C64 mode. Being a programmer in her own right, she looked up the commands and the actual opcodes that I would need to punch into the EPROM programmer.

It was a long night, but by the morning time, I could stick a Commodore brand *Magic Voice* cartridge into a C128, and the Z80 would properly boot it into C64 mode where the cartridge would grab the bus in the reset vector and do its thing (see Fig. 5-12). So far, we had kept our record of fixing every major problem overnight.

Reset Vectors

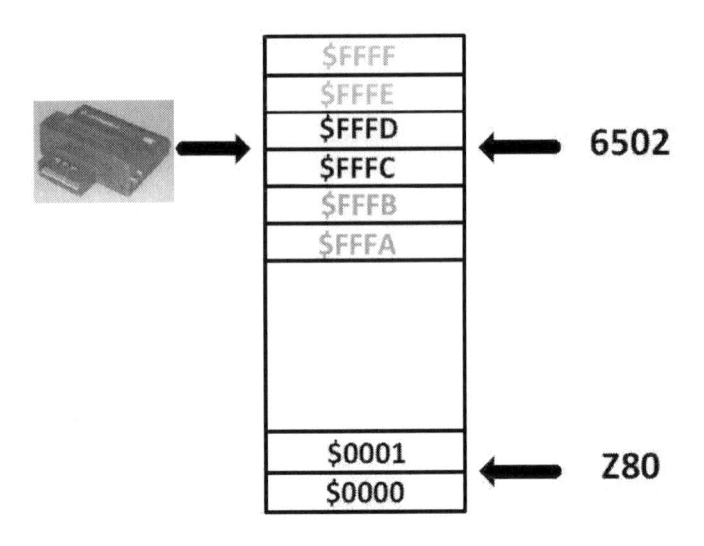

Fig. 5-12 Booting Z80 first for *Magic Voice*, other C64 cartridges, and the Commodore key.
Graphic courtesy of Bil Herd.

I liked the idea of doing this for all cartridges in general, and from that time on, the Z80 was the first processor to wake up from a reset on the C128. It would look to see if there was a *Magic Voice* cartridge sitting out on the bus, or any recognizable C64 cartridge, or optionally look for the Commodore key to be held down. If any of these things were true, the Z80 would set up Commodore 64 mode and then jump directly to C64 mode.

In talking with the programmers, we decided that the Commodore key would be perfect to use for this function, and that quickly, it became *the* key: no long meetings with management, no steering committees. We looked down at the keyboard, there was our logo sitting on a key, and we went with it.

Putting the Z80 chip on the main board had just saved our tail ends. I had no other way to make a *Magic Voice* cartridge work that I could see in a C128, which did not bode well. Even if we had changed the speech cartridge to do something special in a C128, it would have been a failure in my book using that route versus dual booting the C128. As far as hardware went, the only change was that I had to wire in a single inverter on the reset line so that now the Z80 would come out of reset first.

We received a Telex one day from Commodore Australia telling us that they would personally desolder each and every Z80 out of any C128 circuit boards sent to Australia. Knowing the head of Commodore Australia as we did, we considered this a good indication that we were on the right track by including a Z80 in the first place.

My Trusty Light Pen

While the new PC board did support a built-in Z80, it had a very serious problem. Under certain conditions, it would suddenly crash, badly, resulting in random, trash characters all over the screen.

As it turns out, this was not related to the Z80 being included on the PCB; this was happening in normal C128 mode as well as C64 mode, and I was convinced it wasn't the processor that was causing the problem. When I put the C128 on the analyzer, sure enough, it would crash at various places without regard to where it was in the software. In short, it was crashing pseudo-randomly. It didn't take long for me to figure out that this was corruption of the memory itself, not corruption due to the microprocessor writing bad information to the memory.

The only problem was how to catch the corruption right when it occurred. I couldn't trigger my analyzer on the software code, which would have been the usual method of catching this type of error, since it was happening randomly. Then the thought occurred to me that, more often than not, the crash resulted in certain locations on the monitor screen memory, where garbage was always getting written to them. I figured that, if I could trigger approximately when the garbage first appeared, then I could use the VIC-II chip as my memory analyzer since it scans memory repeatedly in order to display the contents on the monitor as the characters we know. Thirty times a second, the VIC-II chip would read the memory and display the contents. If I could trigger the analyzer as soon as the garbage appeared on the screen, then I stood a chance of catching the actual corruption, or so I thought.

The trick was how to determine immediately that corruption had occurred. My answer was to circle the location on the monitor screen where garbage appeared more often than not (it was actually an @ sign that appeared most of the time). Pulling out my handy Commodore brand light pen, I plugged it into the joystick port and held it up to the monitor. I ran the output from the light pen to my Tektronix 7D01 (hardware) analyzer, which I then used to trigger my 7D02 (software) analyzer, which could tell me what the processor was doing at the same time that everything else was happening (see Fig. 5-13).

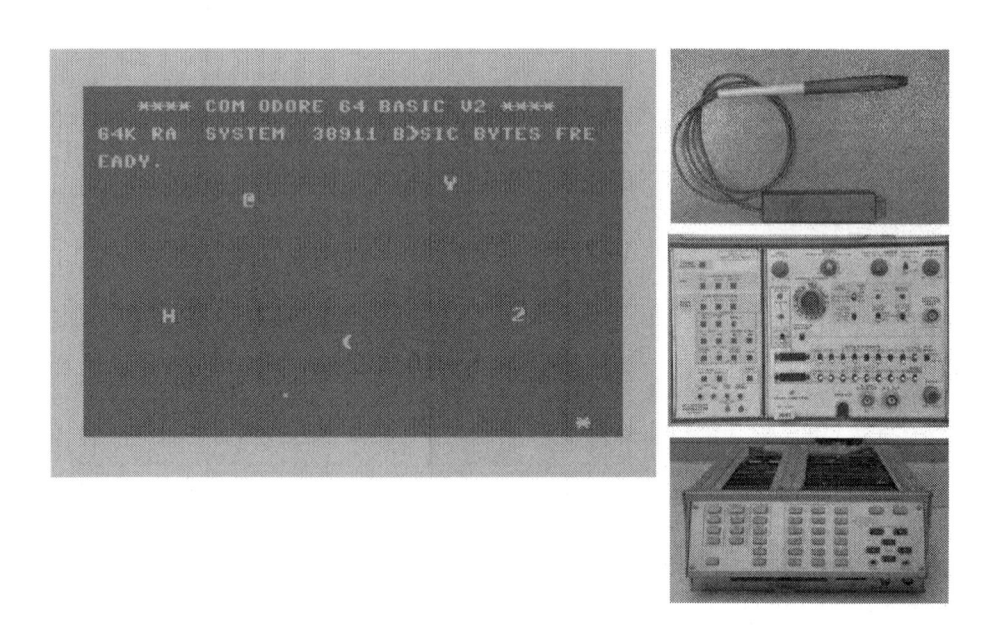

Fig. 5-13 Light pen fix.
Photo courtesy of Bil Herd.

Sure enough, after several reboots, the analyzer told me that the @ sign had appeared, and I captured the processor crashing at the same time.

I was able to determine the area in memory that was causing the problem and studied it carefully. Here's what I found: when the address bus went from mostly "0"s to all "1"s except for a single "0", that bit became a "1" also! It had gotten *dragged* along with all of the other "1"s and couldn't maintain the voltage needed to be seen as a "0".

I found that the issue was that a single ground trace on the PCB was too long by ⅛ of an inch, and it was causing the "noise" to get into the DRAM memory. I should have been scared that such a small thing could cause such a big problem, but for some reason I was confident that we could find and fix issues like this as they arose and called this a win, especially since it was found and fixed in a single afternoon.

Now, with this unexpected problem resolved, we could move onto other problems, which we naturally anticipated would be coming up.

Chapter 6

Middle C128

The next CES deadline was looming. We all knew it, even if we didn't express it. Problems continued to pile up and people became hotter, despite the cooler autumn temperatures in West Chester. While we had solved a lot of problems already, they just kept coming and, in some cases, it seemed like we were being sabotaged from within. This was a time when we had to dig deep and the true spirit of the C128 Animals shined through.

6.1 Other Problems That Plagued the 8563

As I mentioned at the very start of the C128 project, we knew that there would be problems. What we were doing was big: maybe not revolutionary, but certainly novel for an 8-bit computer. We didn't have the luxury of facing new problems, one at a time. The on-going challenge for us was to juggle multiple, unexpected snags simultaneously, without meltdown.

Back-bias Generator

Going into December, a couple of things happened. First, the design of the 8563 had been changed to support a back-bias generator, which the designers added late in development. This thing is generally used to reduce power consumption and speed up the chip. Well, something was not quite right somewhere in the design, because the chip got worse. Let me explain about back-bias generators and the problem.

NMOS gates can be made to reduce their power consumption if an artificial voltage is made that pinches off the gate completely. This is referred to as back-bias, meaning that the bias voltage is shoved in the backward direction even further than a logic zero would normally do. To pinch the logic gates completely off, the chip designers had to create a new voltage, called the back-bias voltage, typically 2 or 3 volts below ground. This extra negative voltage would clamp off parts, allowing very little extra current flow.

The problem is that they had to swing the additional voltage, so that 5 volts plus 2 to 3 volts of back-bias meant that they now had to swing 8 volts in the same amount of time that they used to swing 5 volts. So, they reduced the power consumption by doing this, but increased the delay of the chip.

A good chip designer would understand that the systems guys couldn't live with the slower chip just to make it use less power. We needed the chip to work properly at speed, first and foremost, and *then* worry about the power. This is probably why they were sneaking in this change, instead of telling us up front, hoping we wouldn't notice. But, I noticed. Every single chip design that had back-bias installed failed at least once before it got tweaked just right.

The second thing that happened was that both designers took vacation. Nothing against that from my point of view here many years in the future, but right then we couldn't understand what these people were doing while working on a critical and time-sensitive project.

Or maybe I was just getting too used to eating Thanksgiving dinner out of aluminum foil off of a lab bench (kept warm on a floppy drive). We also used to use the warm vibrating floppy drives to keep our coffee warm and to keep the sludge from hardening in the bottom of the cup. Christmas consisted of stopping at Greg Berlin's house, which was in the area, for a couple of hours on the way home from work.

Back-Bias Generator Fix

To make the 8563 chip work again, I had to short out the back-bias generator with a jumper wire. The chip designer looked like I had taken his kitten away from him, when I said I had shorted out the back-bias voltage. It was as if it personally affected him that it was no longer in use.

To accomplish this, I soldered a wire between the pin 1 indicator notch and the closest ground pin (see Fig. 6-1). Now, the back-bias generator connects to the substrate of the chip and, if you've ever seen the ceramic versions of any of the 40-pin and 48-pin chips of the day, you would notice that the pin 1 indicator notch is gold colored. That is actually a contact to the substrate. I have never heard of anyone ever soldering to the pin 1 indicator notch, but I had little to lose. At this point, all I did have to lose was a HUGE jar of bad 8563s. One night, a sign in my handwriting appeared on this jar asking, "Guess how many working 8563s there are in the jar and win a prize." Of course, if the number someone guessed was a positive real number, that would be wrong.

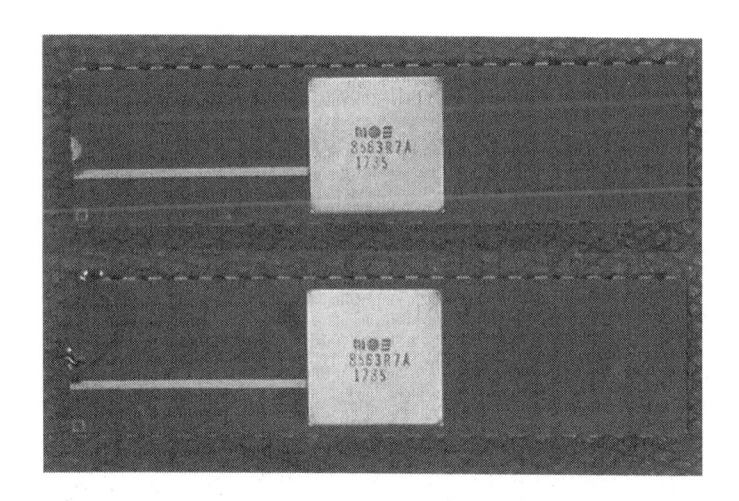

Fig. 6-1 Sample of soldered wire from Pin 1 Notch to Ground.
Photo courtesy of Bil Herd.

Once the wire was in place, the left column reappeared, though still a little broken up! The EADY prompt now proudly stated that the machine was READY and not really proclaiming its desire to be known as the shortened version of Edward.

The yield of chips that even worked this well fell to where we only got three or four working chips from the last run. A run was a half-lot at MOS and cost around $120,000. Pretty expensive chips.

To fix the remaining tearing, we put 330 ohm pull-ups on the outputs and adjusted the power supply to 5.3 volts. This is the equivalent of letting Tim "The Tool-Man" Taylor soup up your blender with a chainsaw motor, but it worked. The side effect was that it would limit the useful life of the part to days instead of weeks, as was the normal Commodore Quality Standard. I was afraid that this fix might be deemed worthy for production (said with the kind of sardonic, cynical smile that makes parole officers really hate their jobs).

Texans' Register Problem

Another problem takes a second to explain and some review. Back before TED (the Plus/4) had been mutilated, decimated, and defecated upon, management decided to kick the body one last time. "TED shall talk," came the decree from above, and the best minds in the industry were sought. As I mentioned earlier, we actually did have two of the most-noted consumer speech people at the time: the guys who designed the TI *Speak n' Spell*, who worked out of the Commodore Dallas office.

During the development of Talking TED, one of the engineers from Commodore Texas set up shop in our place in order to lay out a CMOS gate array for the speech chips that we were using, with the guidance of our chip folk. I remember they taught him that he couldn't use an inverter as a delay on a chip, because the inverter was so fast that the actual delays of the signals that do the routing may cause them to arrive *before* the signals it was racing, rather than after.

One of the things that sounded like a good idea to this young engineer was that if you wanted the command to be implemented immediately, you would write the same data twice to the same register. We thought that this was awkward and obtuse. This is actually a bad idea since, in reality, the processor has very little control over how fast it can do things, as it may get interrupted for a different task between the two writes. We referred to this as the "Do it, do it now register," or the "Come on, pretty please request," or my favorite, the "dang Texans' register." They had made registers that needed to be written to twice in a row, in order to be functional. We called this action a "Texan Write."

This was a problem that we had experienced back in the Talking TED days, and now we were seeing it again with the C128, coincidentally again from our Texas Division. We found out about this problem too late to really have any input, even though we tried to have a mini-intervention with the engineer. We ended up shaking our heads and just walking away.

Texans' Register Fix

The Texans' register problem was relatively easy to fix with this repeated action, providing you didn't give a hang about your own self-respect. When the 8563 engineer had mentioned that the block copy seemed to work better when you wrote the same command twice in a row, I made him explain this to me in public--in the hallway--mostly due to the mean streak I was starting to develop when it came to this particular subject. He calmly explained that you merely wrote to this register and then wrote to it again.

"You wouldn't be from Texas, would you?" I asked, my face the definition of sincerity. "Why, yes ... yes, I am," he replied. Mind you, a crowd had formed by this time. That poor guy never understood what was so funny about being from Texas or what a "dang Texans' register" was.

This odd fix actually did work somewhat. The only problem was that no one told Von Ertwine, who was developing CP/M at home as a consultant, and therefore was out of the loop. Von had wisely chosen not to try to follow all of the current revs of the 8563. Instead, he latched onto a somewhat working Rev 4 version chip and kept it for software development. Later, we would find out that Von, to make the 8563 work properly, was taking the little metal cup that came with his hot air popcorn popper (it was a Butter Cup brand popcorn popper to be exact), would put an ice cube in it, and set it on the 8563. He got about half an hour of operation per ice cube. On our side, there was talk of rigging cans of cold spray with foot switches for the CES show. Anyway, no one told Von, but don't worry, he would find out the day before CES during setup in Vegas.

No Interrupt?

I remember when we found out that there wasn't an interrupt capability built into the 8563. I remember how patient the designer was when he sat me down to explain that you don't need an interrupt from the 8563 indicating that an operation is complete, because you can check the status anytime merely by stopping what you're doing (over and over) and looking at the appropriate register.

Interrupts are an important feature in computers that have many things to do. They can start processes and then wait for an interrupt to tell them that the process is finished and that it's time to complete what was started. We thought the 8563 had interrupts built into it, since everything used this simple technology. Evidently it was unknown to the chip designers. Simply put, for example when scrolling, we want to set the scroll register to scroll the screen a certain number of rows and then tell us when it's done so that we can tell it to do more scrolling or whatever. The 8563 wouldn't tell us when the process was done, so we had to spend valuable processor time either waiting for the 8563 to finish so that we knew it was done, or lose time by only checking it every now and then, not immediately after it was finished. There is no excuse for not having an interrupt line, and there was no excuse for me missing this fact, despite having been assured that this was a superset of the 6845 which does have an interrupt line.

Unfortunately, this missing interrupt meant that the programmers had to manipulate the MMU and memory map to bank in the chip so that it was visible and could be checked, which was intrusive, if not inefficient. Or, you could just sit in a loop watching the register that indicates when an operation is done, which means absolutely nothing else gets done in the meantime. What else could be going on in the system besides talking to the 8563?

Our running gag became not needing a ringer on the telephone because you can simply pick it up anytime to check to see if someone's on it. Or better yet, sit at your desk all day picking up the phone. Even in the hottest discussions, someone would suddenly stop, excuse himself, and pick up the nearest phone just to see if there was someone on it. This utterly failed to get the point across to the chip engineers, but it provided hours of amusement. The owners at the local bar wondered what fixation the guys from Commodore had with the pay phone.

In other words, without feedback from any of the system design people--the engineers--the chip designers had defined the command registers. While not against the law, it's against common sense to design something this complex without feedback from the guys who will be stuck using it.

Scroll Register Problem

The scroll register was pretty much useless, as it transferred only 256 bytes. Between not telling us when it was done via the interrupt and the fact that it scrolled such a pitifully small amount, it was probably faster just to have the process reprint the screen manually every time.

Aside from the fact that the scroll register only held a measly 256 bytes, to pile on even more, the 8563 also had a problem where the 256 byte transfer didn't always take place properly. Sometimes, it left a character behind. This ended up having the effect of characters scrolling upwards randomly.

We found out about this right before CES: just another feature of a chip where the designer thought he knew how we used it, but never bothered to ask us until it was too late. The CP/M programmer, Von Ertwine, our outside consultant who met us at the show, would come to the rescue the very night of CES show setup.

6.2 Things Heating Up

And to pile on ...

Finger Pointing

Finger pointing was in high swing over this one chip with one department pitted against the other in spite of my efforts, which was sad because the other hardworking chip designers had performed small miracles in getting their stuff done on time. Managers started getting that look that rabbits get in the headlights of onrushing vehicular traffic. Some started drinking, some started reading poetry aloud, and the worst were commonly seen doing both. Our favorite behavior was when they hid in their offices. It was rumored that the potted plant in the lobby was in line for one of the key middle management positions. Programmer beatings had hit a new high only to fall off to almost nothing overnight, as even this no longer quelled the growing tension.

Non-technical Problems

I would say that half of the obstacles in developing a computer at CBM, especially at the speeds we were going, were not technical. In fact, the 8563 only represented a string of the most visible challenges. We averaged a couple of challenges a day in November and December. Every chip had problems, the chip emulators had problems, the board layout was hard, and the programmers (both of them) were working round the clock. We were finding out things hitherto unknown about true compatibility, and yet that was only half of the challenge.

The other half was obstacles that were created by management. These were the middle managers who couldn't or didn't embrace what we were truly trying to do. They either wanted to stake out their own territory, were mortified that the rules were being broken, or simply wanted to be noticed.

One of the ways that we got revenge on these middle managers was what we called the "Middle Manager Intelligence Test" where we would leave a permanent marker lying in proximity to a whiteboard and see how long it took for a manager to ruin the whiteboard.

R&D QA Manager

One of the new departments that was created near the beginning of the C128, and that we sorely needed, was that of an R&D QA Department: somebody who could cure our own work before it got released to the Production QA people. I thought this was a great idea as we needed to know everything that was possibly wrong with our machine before it was too late to fix. In the quantities that we made machines, even the smallest error could end up affecting hundreds of thousands of machines, if not more.

But alas, something went amiss when the head of QA did the equivalent of standing on a chair declaring that the C128 would not work. This would be fine, if he was only testing it to see if it would not work, but he became an active impediment to it working. Once again, a middle manager was trying to justify his existence.

One day, strangely enough, a report came in right at 5:00 pm, the end of the normal work day, saying that the C128 no longer worked in the QA test jig; and therefore, the C128 would not work, as the head of QA *had predicted*. The status meeting was scheduled for early the next morning, so I felt that the timing of this report, stating that the C128 was broken, was a little suspicious. The timing allowed enough time for a rumor to start before there was supposedly time to do anything to fix the problem--that is, for people who only worked one shift.

I got a copy of the EPROM that QA was using to *prove* that the C128 would not work from Kim Henry, in QA. Kim was one of my friends, and she was the best person in the entire QA Department in my opinion. I had her watch as I plugged the EPROM into the data I/O EPROM burner, and I read the raw machine code innately by scanning through the contents of the EPROM. What I saw, as I looked through those opcodes, was nothing more than hexadecimal characters in pairs, but these translated directly to the opcodes in my mind as I read them. The capability, which Bob had noticed during my interview, of my being able to memorize and read machine code, was now front and center. I noticed that whoever had written the code had started writing to the MMU incorrectly. I know it was incorrect because I was the one who wrote the spec telling them how to do it. They had to write the high byte first, and then the low byte. They had clearly not done that.

I stood at the EPROM burner now writing corrected code based upon my memory of opcodes, making sure I had a witness in Kim as to how I fixed the issue. While this might have seemed like a superpower--the ability to edit machine code on the fly--I will say that any one of the other Animals could have done the same thing, as we were all at the level that we understood how the processor "thought."

Speaking of Kim … One time, she and I went to the bar (the same bar where the bartender stopped a fan with his tongue) with a databook. She sat and listened to me ramble, over a beer, while I occasionally patted the databook lying on the table. Suddenly, it hit me how to use an existing chip to do something that wouldn't impact FCC or production. She smiled and replied that she knew I would figure it out, given time. I credit her with taking my mind out of the problem enough to solve it.

How do you tell someone that one of the most meaningful contributions the QA Department made to the C128 was that Kim knew how to be a friend, how to be supportive, and when it was time to get my ass to a bar? (None of these things were in her job description.)

Back to the story …

Bear in mind that I got my opportunity at Commodore because I knew opcodes in their native form really, really well. I stood at the data I/O and reprogrammed their EPROM from my memory of the opcodes. I dropped a new EPROM in, programmed it, inserted it into the test jig, and once again, the C128 operated correctly.

The next morning, at the status meeting, I reported that there had been a QA report that said that the C128 no longer worked, but that I had already fixed it by reprogramming the EPROM. The QA manager started to state loudly that the code had been locked up, implying that I must have broken into the QA cabinet. I just smiled a sardonic grin, and looked at him as he realized that he had just implicated himself. But, this would not be the first time he actively gunned for me.

International Soccer Cartridge

We were always shoving cartridges in the C128, even if it was a half-wirewrapped monstrosity sitting on the workbench. A handful of times, we would find some kind of problem that would need to be fixed, but better on our workbench than out in real life. So, I encouraged anybody and everybody to come and tell us the moment that a cartridge was found to be problematic or just plain crapped out.

One day, they came to me with *International Soccer*. I think somebody actually went to play the game for fun, and it didn't run. What made it worse was that it was one of our own CBM cartridges. Now, this game already had some notoriety within CBM, as we had to name it *International Soccer*, whereas its original name was *Football*. You figure it out from there.

I have to say that, at some point during development, I required my guys to make mistakes. If we weren't making mistakes, we weren't going fast enough: simple as that. I would rather have something done on schedule, with the slight chance of mistakes, than three weeks late with no mistakes. It just became a running gag, as I would walk up to one of the guys and ask him if he had made his mistake for the day. I was serious to know what they were doing and if they were toeing the line as close as they could.

As it turns out, when this cartridge was plugged in, all we got was this weird zebra-staircase pattern. I quickly looked at the original C64 PLA table and found the problem with the C128 version. It was trying to use multicolored character mode in C64 mode, and something was wrong. I compared the PLA terms of the original C64 to our new terms, which were four times bigger. I found the problem: there was a single "X" where a "1" belonged.

Whereas the C64 terms fit on a single 8 and 1/2 by 11 piece of paper, ours for the C128 had grown to the point where you held one of the old computer green and white paper listings out straight in front of you at shoulder height, and the paper would almost touch the floor. There were four to five pages now, as everything goes up at a square term, meaning something doesn't get twice as big; it gets four times as big.

Luckily, we had held back half of the PLAs (a half-lot) and had them stored as 1-2-3s (remember our earlier Michelob to the rescue discussion about the bottom three layers versus the top three layers?). Well, the bottom three layers had been completed and then they were put into storage for emergencies such as this. I got with Dave DiOrio, his boss, and some of the chip layout guys; and we figured out that we could use some of my spare terms that we built in for emergencies--terms being the combination of equations that ultimately produced the correct output for a set of inputs. The PLA could be fixed, using just the top three layers, 4-5-6. This problem was literally solved in about an hour and a half; however, we had to wait another week for the updated PLAs, but that wasn't a critical item at the time.

QA Managers Ganging Up

While all this was heating up, there is still another QA manager story to tell, but this time it's about *both* QA managers (Production and R&D) who tried to work together to get me fired. This was the first and only time they got together about *anything*.

At the next status meeting, the R&D QA manager couldn't even sit on his hands long enough, as he kept nervously waiting for his turn to do something. Finally, when it was his turn to speak, he started with the words, "Bil Herd screwed up, and *we have proof.*" He said this while nudging a pile of papers to the center of the conference table at the meeting. Let me say that the C128 was a team effort, which meant that, regardless of how the error occurred, I was dead set on taking the blame myself. I immediately addressed the situation with the statement, "Yeah, I f***ed up. Here's how we are going to fix it." He then nudged the papers again stating that he had *proof*, and I repeated my statement, in slower baby talk.

When he tried a third time, the VP of MOS cleared his throat, which caused the room to fall silent, and he calmly said, "I think Bil is trying to tell you how to fix the problem, if you will listen." At that point, the Production QA manager's body language changed completely, and he physically leaned away from the R&D QA manager as if abandoning him. Meanwhile, the R&D QA manager made a sound not unlike the flopping of a fish out of water.

True to form, we ran a quick half-lot, the half of the chips saved in case there was an error such as this, and found a way to fix the issue using just the top three layers of the chip. What we did was quick, and it was clever, in true CBM fashion; but it seemed more like an anticlimax after the fun of having QA gunning for my job and failing at that.

A "New" Sparkle Problem

A new problem cropped up with sparkle in multicolored character mode when used for one of the C64 game modes. We were all getting all too used to this type of crisis. I tried a few things, including adjusting the power supply to 4.75 volts which made the display clear up completely. Total time to remedy was 2 minutes, 18 seconds. Of course, now the 80-column display was tearing again. Machines were marked as to whether they could do 40-column mode, 80-column mode, or both, for their use at the CES booth.

The day of CES, this problem required me doing last minute hand-tweaking to the adjustable power supplies to make sure that certain software demos worked properly. This amounted to carrying a "tweak tool," a type of plastic screwdriver that fit the adjustable control inside the supply better than a fingernail. I had to open the cabinet under the kiosk display, and I would adjust the power supply right there in front of people. We turned the whole process into a demonstration of Commodore's new attitude towards power supplies, while my motivation was really making the dang station work correctly.

Power Supply

The C128 power supply was unique for Commodore at the time. It was an external switching supply which was our way of making sure we didn't just build bigger, hotter C64 power supplies. Those had very poor load regulation. When you hooked up more load, the voltage would drop. If you overloaded the C64 power supply, it would just produce lower and lower voltages until the computer stopped working. On the C128 though, if you exceeded the maximum power, it would actually shut off intelligently. This was good and bad, depending on your point of view.

I remember my boss telling the Japanese vendors how much he wanted to pay per watt. At one point, he said $0.15 per watt, and everybody in the room started laughing, except for one person who heard him differently. He asked him to repeat himself, and this time when my boss said $0.15 per watt, nobody was laughing. They thought that he had said $0.50 per watt. $0.15 was very aggressive, but we hit it.

The C128 power supply was also our first supply to have an externally accessible fuse in it. The way I got away with this was that the fuse had to be only accessible through the use of a tool, to comply with UL regulations, so we picked a fuse holder that could be unscrewed using a U.S. dime. Literally, a dime became the tool needed to change the fuse in the C128 power supply.

VIC-II 2 MHz

One of the features of the C128 is that the microprocessor can actually run at twice the frequency, or 2 megahertz. This feature wasn't really compatible with C64 mode and was supposed to not be available in that mode. I remember clearly the three seconds that it took me to decide whether to make the 2-megahertz mode register disappear completely in C64 mode, or whether to leave the register available, but in an obscure place. This was the only C128 mode register that was present in C64 mode, and the reason was simple: I was afraid that the register might not come back after a reset, if it were truly removed.

That is, what if there were a bad reset, and when the C128 woke up, the register was still missing from when it had last been disabled? The register was in the VIC-II chip and my concern came from the VIC-II chip having had a history of strange reset behavior. I would figure out later that some of the strange behavior came from the fact that, when the VIC-II chip was doing a DMA for sprite pointer fetches, it pretty much ignored everything else. If the reset pulse occurred during this time, it could be missed.

I also thought about the option of making it so that you had to write a complex pattern like $55 (01010101) and then an $AA (10101010), in that order, but I worried that the additional logic this late in the game might actually create a chip bug. We were a little outside the window of comfort for adding new functionality to the chips, as we only had time for one more rev of the chip at this point, so this would have been a risky option.

So, I remember those three seconds when I opted for safety, which was leaving the register in, but in a place that *shouldn't* be written to.

Unfortunately, within a month of release of the C128, we discovered our first cartridge that had mucked with the 2-megahertz register. The game, *Rescue on Fractalus,* was unplayable, as the 2-megahertz bit got turned on in the game, causing garbage on the C64 screen.

With all of that said, I'm not sure that the decision to leave the register in place was a mistake, even though it wasn't 100% compatible. For all I know, the big story of the C128 could have been that the 2-megahertz register kept disappearing. I will never know if I made the right choice or not, as maybe the alternative was to have machines that didn't reset correctly. I just have to live with the choice that I made.

Living In My Office

Probably the biggest thing about the C128 wasn't that we got the technology to work, which was a handful at the time, especially in the 1980s, but that we also had to deal with the recurring theme of a middle management crowd that had to justify their existence; and the only way they could do that was by walking around messing with things. We were used to this, but there were ways where the environment also messed with us. Since we were working two and three shifts a day, minus the time it took to take a shower and get a beer, we lived in the office for all three shifts.

I was known for having an air mattress in my office under one of my desks, on which I would sleep pretty much anytime I was too tired to work. At one point, the pace got so hectic that we started "hot bunking" ("hot racking" for you Squids) on my air mattress. I would stay up working till about 2:00 or 3:00 am, go wake up the technician asleep on my air mattress, and show that person what work needed to be done, while I sacked out for a couple hours. Then, I'd wake up at about 4:00 or 5:00 am, in time to understand what was going on before management arrived. My record was 11 days without leaving the office at all. I would shower out of the sink, eat out of the vending machine, and sleep under my desk.

This was part of the nightly magic that allowed us to say that we fixed every problem overnight, that and the fact that management went home every evening.

My air mattress was also somewhat therapeutic for other groups. All were welcome. It was not uncommon to walk into my office only to find someone else asleep under my desk. I would come into my office to find somebody either asleep on my air mattress or relaxing, and I would just say "Hi" or be very quiet. I remember one day, Ferenc Vadovszki, from the Business Computing Group, was lying there, talking about something as he worked through a problem. I got up, left, and came back a few minutes later, to find that he was still talking to me as if I was in the room. I quietly came and went without disturbing him, so that he would get the full therapeutic benefit of having a quiet listener.

It Was So Hot

As you may recall, my West Chester office had a wall that was all window. It was a great office. The only problem was that my office would get up to over 90 degrees during the day, even though there was that mirrored reflective coating on the window, which was popular in the '80s. They would turn off the air conditioner after hours, so the room that I did my debugging in would get so hot that I would drip sweat on whatever board I was working on, causing it to stop working. It should be noted that my attire, especially on weekends and late at night, consisted of no shirt and an olive drab headband that I kept from my time in the service; shoes were optional. Even then, I would eventually drip enough sweat onto the board that I would have to stop and spray the whole board off with flux remover, and then start whatever problem-solving I was doing again.

I also had at least four sets of chips at any one moment, and if the system I was working on died unexpectedly, I would swap out the whole set of chips as a starting place. Usually, I'd only leave them in for about 15 minutes if the system was still broken, and swap in yet a new set in case my replacement set had a problem. There realistically wasn't enough time to troubleshoot things that actually broke. I needed to troubleshoot design issues, so I did the quickest method I knew, which was swapping out parts in batches. The downside to this was that whole sets of batches would then end up in the trash, as I would not reuse something that I suspected of being bad. Again, I quite simply didn't have time to pick through chips, determining if they were good or not.

Deciding to Not Decide

Elton Southard was the president of MOS and the vice president of CBM when I started. He was someone I admired, and not just because he signed my offer letter for employment. One time in a meeting, he stated in so many words that he liked to make decisions, and that stuck with me, as I hadn't realized that I, too, liked to make decisions and liked the decision-making process. In fact, I would rather have made a decision and been wrong than to have left the decision to someone else. The C128 Animals were a powerful decision-making team unto itself, as we were nimble and non-political in how we approached technological decisions. Our goal was simple: to get done on time, with the best product that we could make.

The middle management layer, however, was not so gifted in the realm of decision-making. I remember sitting at the same conference room table where I heard Elton exclaim about making decisions, when I took note as a software middle manager said that we should put off deciding when to meet to decide something, which pretty much needed to be decided just then.

I pointed out that that ridiculous statement was basically resolving to *not* be able to decide to decide something, which we didn't have time for. I no longer remember what the issue was, so trivial was it, but I know that we at the team level proceeded with a plan and no one stopped us. Deciding to not decide was simply not in our DNA. Bear in mind that this was long before there were cartoons depicting this kind of managerial dysfunction, unless you count the Gary Larson comics that were already hanging outside my office.

Technicians Hijack Me

Did I mention, the technicians were great? They were there 100% when we needed them, though they did get to go home, leaving the problems behind. One time, the technicians felt I needed a break. They jumped me. After some wrestling around, they said, "Yer comin' with us." Two of them took me for a ride, just to get me out of the place. For over two hours, we rode around with me stretched out in the back seat just relaxing and drinking a beer--okay, multiple beers. The techs drove bigger cars than we did, so I remember actually stretching all the way out. They wouldn't even let me take a databook. I still remember that afternoon; I got a full head of steam just from a few hours off. I apologized for being an ass, which is what set off the hijacking in the first place.

Unsung Hero

It was during this time that Commodore did what I considered to be one of the smartest things they could have done in getting the C128 done on time. They hired my girlfriend, Kim Constein, a fellow alumni from Pennsylvania Scale Company where Hedley and Terry Fisher also originated. Kim listed being a NASA certified solderer among her many qualifications.

As it turns out though, management had been against hiring her due to nepotism, and rumor had it that the head of the R&D lab waited until the boss was out of the country before hiring her. So the irony is that, while it was one of the best things they could have done, it's not what they wanted to do: it's what happened in spite of management.

Kim would often do a full shift in the R&D lab as an assembly technician and then spend a second and third shift attending to whatever needs the C128 had that night. She would often spend the entire night, and she was one of the primary technicians who I could give work to at three o'clock in the morning.

More than that, she believed in me and us, and did everything she could to make sure that we would be successful. Whereas I might not go home for several days at a time, Kim would drive the hour home and the hour back, bringing with her a fresh change of clothes for me and food--real food, not that stuff out of the vending machine.

Kim also drove when I was too tired to stay awake. Driving had become a real hazard for me, as I was severely sleep-deprived and would fall asleep within minutes of getting behind the wheel of a car. One night on my way home, I drifted to sleep and went off into a ditch, knocking the bumper off of my car. On a different occasion, I remember waking up to a weird slapping sensation only to find out that my hands had fallen off the steering wheel and had landed on top of my knees, which was what woke me up.

If there was an unsung hero who nobody's heard about, who was as much responsible for us getting the C128 done as anybody on the team, it was Kim.

6.3 Comic Relief

We averaged one to three crises a day for the last month before CES. Several of us suffered withdrawal symptoms, if the pressure let up for even a few minutes. The stress level was off the charts, but we didn't buckle. After all, we worked at Commodore. We knew how to keep cool and roll with most of the punches. That's not to say we didn't find dark places to hide and cry in upon occasion, but we made sure to not do so publicly.

Hole in the Wall

One morning, I went to go into the room that was now dedicated to the C128, just off the hardware lab, and found it locked. I attributed this to a mistake by the security guards, as they did like to lock doors for no reason other than that the door had a lock on it. I guess this made a type of sense, if you're a security guard. I didn't think much more of it and crawled over the ceiling through the ceiling tiles (getting that white powder all over me), and I dropped down and unlocked the door. To prevent a recurrence, I put a sign up asking them please--in my most polite terms--*not* to lock the door, as there was no key for the door (at least no one knew where the key was; no one).

The next day, the door was locked again.

I repeated the actions of the day before: climbing up over the ceiling, getting covered with white powder, dropping down, and unlocking the door. I left another message, this one a little more tense, saying, "Look. There is no key to this door. Please don't lock it."

The next day happened to be a weekend day, and sure enough, the door to my room (which was probably already over 95 degrees) was locked again. The rumors that circulated after that day said that I punched completely through the wall in one punch, so that I could reach the doorknob and unlock the door. This rumor was mostly untrue as it took me *two* punches to get through both layers of the wall so that I could reach through and unlock the door.

They continued to lock the door, even though the gaping hole stood silent witness to the ineffectiveness of trying to lock us out of our own lab during a critical design phase. We admired this singleness of purpose and considered changing professions.

The story didn't end there though. The next day, the door was locked again, in spite of the raging hole right beside the doorknob. Well, it was actually more at shoulder height, right above the doorknob, as that was the height that I'd punched at. I had to reach through the hole, getting that white powder all over my arm again, to unlock the door. This time, my sign on the door wasn't nearly as gracious as my past attempts at communication. The sign said, "Look, a**holes. There's a f***ing hole in the wall. Stop locking the door!"

The hole in the wall story lived on as the head of QA was given the task of repairing the hole in the wall. Oh, and I had to sit through many meetings where that was the highlight of his weekly status report--how he had gotten hold of a contractor's quotes and eventually got the hole in the wall fixed.

Of course, this wasn't the only hole in the wall, I'm sad to say, that was formed during my tenure at Commodore.

Fake Punch Game

As I mentioned earlier, we used to play games to relieve stress. Another game that we played--and Jeff, the technician, was among those who played it with relish--was the "throw a fake punch at Herd" game. It was as if they knew that I had really oversensitive reflexes, being young and full of testosterone. The game evolved into "see if you can get Herd to spill his coffee." This game was short-lived though, as I learned to throw the coffee outwards whenever somebody would fake a punch at me, usually resulting in them getting soaked with coffee, not me.

One time, Jeff threw a fake punch at me, and I counted footsteps--one, two--and turned suddenly. I caught him in mid-step and shoved him into the wall so hard that the entire drywall gave way underneath him. I remember the surprised look on Jeff's face as his shoulder was now sunken into the wall all the way up to his neck. I could see the urinals of the men's room through the broken hole in the wall. I believe this became known as Herd's Hole. It seemed I was getting blamed for all the holes in the wall by now.

Waterworks

We had these frightfully expensive timeshare terminals that we no longer needed; they were actually being stored in the hallway, of all places. One day, one of the workers hit the sprinkler over them with the ladder. The sprinkler burst open and proceeded to soak all of the equipment that did not belong to us. It belonged to whatever supercomputer company we were leasing time on. Claude, one of the technicians in the R&D lab who later transferred to the PCB layout section, came running into the lab screaming about the water, only to slip on the water that was on his shoes and go sliding across the room into the wall.

We were torn as to whether to go help Claude or whether to go look at the equipment being soaked by water, and figured we had time to do both. So, Engineering gathered as a whole and watched as $100,000 worth of equipment became waterlogged, their expressions much like the bystanders at a grisly accident who can't tear their attention away from the ensuing carnage. Then, we checked out Claude. (He was mostly okay.)

Later, after the water had been shut off, we walked over to these now not-so-expensive keyboards and noted that every time we pressed a key, water would squirt out from the keyboard in various directions. We were typing on what had been a keyboard, which was no longer a keyboard.

Blood Spurting Everywhere

Back then, the chip guys would almost manually lay out each and every device on a chip. They would draw polygons and then, to check them, they would need to print them. When I first got there, we had a big pen plotter, which had ink pens that ran back and forth. Inevitably, one of the pens would run out of ink during the night when they would run these plots, but that would be okay as it left a line pressed into the vellum. Unfortunately, if more than one pen ran out of ink, they would have to run the plot again since now the multiple uncolored lines on the plot would be too confusing.

Later, they got their big electrostatic plotter, and they were like kids on Christmas morning. This was a cool piece of technology that we had needed for a long time. Not only could they now print our plots in a fraction of the time, but we could also use the huge rolls of paper to print our PC boards on for checking purposes.

Now, I was known for telling people not to mess with things that they didn't understand and to keep their fingers out of other people's machinery. One night, I broke my own rule. We had run out of red ink in the electrostatic plotter. This was around two o'clock in the morning, by the way, and I went to change the red ink, confident that I could figure it out. Well, at some point, the tubing came off an ink reservoir, and it pulsed red ink, almost like you would picture an artery pulsing blood.

Well, it turns out that this ink was really, really good quality, and it stained my jeans, my hands, my shoes, and the carpet. As I headed to the bathroom to clean up, I left a trail of what looked like bloody tennis shoe prints leading to the sink that was now also stained red. When everybody arrived the next morning, they assumed that there had been a major injury on the premises. Once again, I had to apologize to Mike Angelina for something I had done wrong in the area, but this time he laughed and appreciated my honesty. His response was basically that everybody figured I was somehow involved; they just didn't know what had happened. I promised to not try to change things again in the electrostatic plotter, provided I could call somebody at 2:00 am. We left it at that.

My Shoes

Unfortunately, my tennis shoes had about as much of a bad reputation as I did. What would you expect for shoes that have been worn 20 hours a day? The shoes did become nasty enough that I preferred walking around barefoot, but knew that I couldn't all the time. For example, stepping on an integrated circuit with bare feet hurt an awful lot. One time, I went to take a nap on the vice president's couch, and I kicked off my shoes. I quickly fell asleep, a trick I learned in the Army, only to be awakened by the smell of my tennis shoes wafting throughout the entire office. I got up, went back to my office, threw my shoes in the corner, and lay down on my air mattress to try and go back to sleep. A few minutes later, one of the security guards stopped by, a guy that I liked and usually chatted with. He asked if I had just been in Adam's office to which I replied, "Yes." I asked how he knew; he grinned and said, "It smells like your shoes in there."

This is a true story. Note that he didn't say he could smell my shoes at this moment in *my* office, or he was too polite to say so, but he had hit it right on the head. I had just been in Adam's office with my shoes off.

Commodore Mouse

Later, my girlfriend bought me a new pair of shoes, and I just left the other shoes sitting in my office. One day, I noticed that a mouse had chewed through the tip of the toe and had taken up residence in my shoe. I nestled the shoe deeper into the corner so that he was protected, and I would leave little Fritos for him (I detested Fritos myself). I called him my "Commodore Mouse." At night, I would even see him exploring around. He wasn't your ragged, street mouse; this was a mouse with more going for it than half of the middle managers in the place. He had my respect.

One night, my mouse explored a little too far and disturbed some programmers down near Hedley Davis's office. It was decided by all present to gather pitchforks and torches and go chasing my mouse. I tell the story that Hedley exclaimed, "Let's get it!" which was met by a rabble of "Yeahs." I can picture the mouse running headlong down the hallway, quickly turning the corner into my office area, and running into it. I saw it heading for the safety of my shoe in the corner, only to look up to see programmers carrying pitchforks and torches (might have been pencils and some paper; it was late). Being a hardware engineer, I was not afraid of a bunch of programmers with pitchforks and torches, though the guy with the pencil bore watching. Because of the threat to my mouse, whom I respected more than most managers, I explained that the next programmer to endanger my mouse would quickly have a pitchfork shoved somewhere, possibly followed by a pencil. (I was still watching the guy with the pencil.) I remember the apologies: "We didn't know this was your mouse." What's ironic is that Hedley went on to design the true Commodore brand mouse for a whole range of future products.

Fun with Programmers

All the playful interaction with technicians and hardware engineers was mostly physical: not so with the programmers, who we made a point to protect. This didn't mean that we couldn't do practical jokes with each other; they just couldn't result in injury.

We used to joke about Terry Ryan being programmable, and that he would get stuck in a loop while coming down the stairway. If nobody could find Terry, they would go check the bottom of the stairwell in case he never got off at the floor that he was supposed to.

One day, I tested how programmable Terry might be. He was just about to go into the men's room, and I got his attention with some odd topic, talking to him while making eye contact. As we discussed the random issue, I was slowly stepping down the hall, luring him to follow me in order to keep eye contact. Once I got in front of the women's bathroom, I stopped walking, talked a bit more, and then motioned for him to continue. I said, "Well, go ahead and go to the bathroom. We'll talk when you get back." He turned and walked into the door that was right next to him, thinking it was the men's room, but it was actually now the women's room. I stood waiting the 5 to 10 seconds that it took Terry to figure out that the men's room did not get a couch in it overnight. Suddenly, he came out, his cheeks bright red-- and me with a smile on my face, meaning that I had gotten him. One must know, however, that to be on the retribution list of Terry Ryan or Fred Bowen was not a good thing, especially since I slept in the place.

Adrenaline Pump

I was working late one night and was very engrossed in what I was doing at my desk. Two members of the Z8000 team had snuck into my office behind me, which is still hard for me to believe they did without me noticing. I must have been really engrossed in what I was doing.

One of them bent down next to my right ear and yelled "Boo!" inches away from my ear, which caused an electrical current to flow in my head that was probably measurable on an oscilloscope. In response, I heard one word in my head: "Go!" I jumped to my feet in one motion, striking both knees on the bottom of my desk as I had not pushed away from the desk. I had merely jumped straight to my feet, the chair flying behind me.

I pivoted to my left a full 270 degrees, grabbing the culprit by the shirt and with my left hand slamming him against the wall, while cocking back my right arm to deliver a blow as I pinned him against the wall. At this point, my eyes delivered a rather late interrupt, and I developed the picture they had seen as I pivoted. What I saw was the other of the two with his eyes as big as dinner plates. My soon-to-be blow screeched to a halt, with inches to spare, and I now developed the picture of the culprit being held by my left hand; and he had the same expression on his face as the onlooker had.

My reputation grew that day; certainly, no one else would be trying to surprise me while I worked. What they didn't see was that, after they left my office, I shook for five minutes as the adrenaline left me.

"Get Out," She Said

Nancy Rahn was the executive secretary of whoever filled the VP slot at the time, starting with Lloyd Taylor and ending with Adam Chowaniec. Nancy was the classiest woman I knew and was always quick to smile, like it was always just there waiting to get out. In times of stress, she was one of the people I would go and talk to, as being in her presence would calm me down.

To back up a moment, one of the ways someone would find out that they had been laid off was that their Commodore entry card would stop working in the middle of the day. Obviously, this was less than ideal, but it was a humorous artifact, as you would see people lined up at the door, who all had in common the fact that they had been laid off and just didn't know it, yet.

One day, in the middle of the C128, with just a month to go, my card stopped working at the R&D lab entrance. On this particular day, I was not amused as I was busy, I had work to do, and I couldn't get into the R&D Department. Somebody let me in, and, unfortunately, Nancy's office was the first door I encountered. I stopped there, threw my card on the floor with disgust, and was beside myself with just being so irritated that I didn't know what to do. Nancy looked at me, staring, and said, "Get out," pointing at the door.

I took this to mean to not only get out of her office, but also to take a break, and I did. I went home, took a shower, and went to sleep. I slept till the very next morning, and so must have needed it. When I walked into her office the next morning, I thanked her for throwing me out of the building. Her relief was immediate, as she was so worried about how I would react the very next day. I thanked her again, and said I needed to hear that: I needed some moment of normalcy before stepping back into the storm again.

6.4 Lingering Problems

So to recap, going into December, we had a chip, the 8563, with .001% yield. The left columns didn't work--anytime. There was one pixel that couldn't be seen. The semi-useless block transfer didn't work correctly. The power supply had to be adjusted for each VIC-II chip, based on which game was being run. And, the 8563 blew up before you loaded all of the fonts, unless you took 10 seconds to load the fonts, in which case it blew up only sometimes. The MMU had a problem where data was bleeding through from the upper 64 kB bank into the lower. This was the only problem that I didn't really have to worry about as DiOrio undertook straightening out the *snafu* in time for CES.

8563 Synchronicity Problem

When the major problems that kept the chip from being anywhere usable still existed on Rev 4, we got concerned. It was at this time that the single scariest statement came out of the IC design section in charge of the 8563. This statement amounted to, "You'll always have some chance statistically that any read or write cycle will fail due to synchronicity."

Synchronicity problems occur when two devices run off of two separate clocks: the VIC-II chip, hence the rest of the system, runs off of a 14.318 MHz crystal and the 8563 runs off of a 16 MHz oscillator. Now picture walking towards a revolving door with your arms full of packages and not looking up before launching yourself into the doorway. You may get through unscathed if your timing is accidentally just right, or you may fumble through losing some packages (synonymous to losing data) in the process. Or, if things really foul up, some of the packages may make it through and you're left stranded on the other side of the door (synonymous to a completely blown write cycle).

What I didn't realize that he meant was this: since there's always a chance for a bad cycle to slip through, he didn't take even the most rudimentary protection against bad synchronization. It was my fault that I didn't ask

"What do you mean *fully* by that statement?" because, if I had, I would have found out early that there was no protection whatsoever.

As it turns out, the 8563, instead of failing every three years or so (very livable by Commodore standards), it failed about three times a second. In other words, if you tried to load the font all in one shot, it would blow up every time!

The IC designers refused to believe this up until mid-December (CES in two to three weeks!) because their unit in the lab didn't do it. Finally, I said, "Show us," and they led the whole rabble (pitchforks, torches, ugly scene) down to the lab. It turns out that they weren't even testing the current rev of the chip! Also, they were testing the chip from BASIC, which was much slower and *appeared* more stable, because the 8563 blew up every time they ran it at faster system speeds.

"That's what we're trying to tell you!" we said rationally, with neck veins bulging. And even then, it screwed up once more--before our very eyes--and the designer reached for the reset switch, saying that something does occasionally go wrong. Being one of the Animals, with my reflexes highly tuned by programmer-abusing, I was able to snatch his arm in midair before he got to the reset switch, with blatant evidence of the error right there on the test screen.

One of the rabble was their boss. The word finally came: "Fix it!" Hollow victory as there were only two weeks until we packed for the show, and there were four or five other major problems (I'll say more later) with the chip and *no* time to do another rev. It was obvious that, if we were going to make CES, something had to give. As Josey Wales said in the movie *The Outlaw Josey Wales*, "That's when ya gotta get mean. I mean downright plumb crazy, loco mean." And we knew we had to.

Synchronicity Fix--Phase Lock Loop

In order to synchronize the VIC-II with the 8563, we built a tower for the 8563 chip that had something called a Phase Lock Loop on it, which basically acted as a frequency doubler (see Fig. 6-2). This took the 8.18

MHz dot clock (I think it was 8.18 MHz ... been too long and too many other dot clock frequencies since then) and doubled it. We then ran a wire over to the 8563 and used this new frequency in place of its own 16 MHz clock.

As I mentioned earlier, synchronicity is equivalent to putting a revolving door at the other end of the room from the first door and synchronizing them. This tower working amounted to a true miracle and was accompanied by the sound of hell freezing over, the rabbit getting the Trix, and several instances of cats and dogs sleeping together. This was the first time that making CES became a near possibility.

Fig. 6-2 C128 8563 Phase Lock Loop tower.
Photo courtesy of Bil Herd.

We laughed, we cried, we drank. So much in a hurry were we that the little 3" x 3" PCB was produced in 12 hours (a new record) and cost us about $1000 each. We stood in a huddle around the coffee pot in the hardware lab making up versions of bad things that might befall Curt as he rode to get the boards on his Harley. We actually turned on the radio for the traffic news, in case there was a report of a motorcycle and PCBs splashed all over Route 202.

The boards worked better than I could have hoped. I also had left in an adjustment capability by allowing a jumper to be moved to various delays to account for what we didn't know yet about the 8563. I equated this to being able to adjust the dwell angle in your car engine's ignition circuit. I was able to adjust the phase delay of the 8563 clock, based on each chip.

A couple of days later, Paul, the head of Commodore Software at the time, shook my hand and said he had heard that I'd saved CES. I hadn't really thought that way about it. I was actually shocked that news had gotten outside of Engineering about what we were doing. I appreciated him shaking my hand as he had been in LRRP (long-range reconnaissance patrol) in Vietnam and had my respect at a level that I can't express here.

PLA Problem

As mentioned earlier, the PLA had a problem where my group had made a typo in specifying the hundred-some terms that comprised the different operating parameters, so this rev would need to be changed. Well, the designer in charge of the PLA took this rev as an opportunity to sneak a change into the chip without really going public with the fact that he was making a change.

During the third week of December, we got back what was supposed to be the final rev of the PLA. The only problem was that when I inserted it in the circuit, nothing worked at all, nothing. I don't even think I blinked. I just reached for a scope probe and started trying to figure out what was wrong.

Quick enough, I found that there was a 200-ohms short between each pin on the left side of the chip, which happened to be the input pins mostly. I'd learned from DiOrio about back-bias generators and about the resistance of polysilicon (poly), one of the layers in a chip. As it turns out, poly has a resistance of approximately 200 ohms (per square), which means that it would appear as a 200-ohm short between the input pins, if they were shorted by poly and not aluminum or copper. I knew that the back-bias generator worked by having a ring of poly around the outside edge, and I knew that the chip designers were trying to slip them in without telling us, as they had done to the 8563, completely ruining the chip for at least two or three revisions.

When the change went through, it caused one of the layers to shift towards one side and effectively shorted the input pins together, resulting in no signal being able to get in or out of the chip! You should have seen the scene where the designer's boss was loudly proclaiming that the Hardware Department must have screwed up, because his guy didn't make any changes (that would've been like admitting that something had been broken). You could tell by the way the designer's face was slowly turning red that he hadn't yet found a way to tell his boss that he had made a change. Talk about giving someone enough rope to hang themselves; we just kept paying it out yard by yard.

Well, I went to the chip designer and his boss, and said, "Your back-bias shorted out the pins with poly, down the left side of the chip." They told me that I was wrong, and said that I didn't know what I was talking about. Then they asked how I even knew what poly was. I simply restated my claim, "You shorted out the input pins with poly. Down the left side, there's a 200-ohm short between each pin." They denied reality. Finally, Dave Esposito, one of the chip layout guys, slid his chair back and yelled across the room, "They reset the database origin, except they didn't have the poly selected when they did it." He slipped back into his office. I just looked at the engineer and his boss, and as Fred Bowen said, "That's when you just reach up and give the noose a tap and set it to swinging."

Fixing the Phone

One day, my old beat-up desk gave up the ghost. In trying to move it out of the office, the entire leg came off of the desk, which was part of the problem--the desk wobbled. I started carrying this desk leg around on my shoulder, like Bam Bam did with his wooden club on the *Flintstones*.

Another day, while I was *trying* to sleep, there was a gathering of people right outside my office, near one of Dave Haynie's spare offices that we used to house one of the VT100 terminals. The spare office held this communal terminal, which freaked out the in-house VAX guys. They said there weren't enough terminals, and they thought we would not want to share our access to the computer. But, we felt that everybody should have access, so we shared ours.

The problem was that there was a phone in this office (without a phone answering machine on it). As there also was no paging system, it was not unusual to just let the phone ring until somebody picked it up. That incessant ringing was happening on this day: the phone was ringing and ringing and nobody was answering it because it was a shared office. They knew the phone call wasn't for them, so they let it ring. But, it was keeping me awake.

Finally, I couldn't take it anymore. I came out of my office with the club over my shoulder and started to beat the phone to death while it was still ringing. The people clustered around the terminal, including both Dave Haynie and Dave DiOrio, as well as Terry Ryan, as witnesses. They all just watched while I pulverized this phone. Of course, the phone stopped ringing, and I went back to my office to go to sleep, nobody having said a word during this time. I'm sure they just turned back to the terminal and went back to work. There was no more phone in that office from then on.

TV Problem

Around mid-development of the C128, something bad happened to C64 computers, or more specifically the TVs of the day that they were meant to run on. Up until now, there was always a vertical hold control on the TV, and it was common to adjust a set so that the picture would not roll vertically. As it turned out, the VIC-II chip had an error in it: the frequency wasn't exact. So, on a TV set that had a vertical adjustment, it was easy to adjust; but when TVs started coming out without a vertical hold, it was somewhat disastrous as the picture would continuously roll and would be unusable.

I remember Dave DiOrio stopping by my office with the RS-170A spec. Basically, it was right there in silicon. We had the frequency wrong, so in the middle of the C128 effort, Dave stopped and fixed the big chip for all new Commodore 64s.

This problem led to us getting 10 or 12 different brands of TV sets shipped to us, which we placed in the small conference room so that we could test various TVs with various computers. Two weeks later, after the initial excitement had died down, the TVs started disappearing into managers' offices. We worker bees did not care, and in fact, we actually liked having managers in their offices watching TVs and away from the hallways where they might run into us and ask for a status report.

This reminds me. When I would go to visit my boss, I would take a piece of paper with me. This was because it was often that, when I would talk to him, he would be watching TV instead of listening to me. So, I would take the paper and stick it on the screen of the TV where static electricity would hold the paper, blocking his view and forcing him to listen to me. I would then take the paper with me when I left, so he could go back to his TV watching.

Knife-Throwing and Ball Peen Hammer

Not long after, we had a meeting in that small conference room which was still full of packing material, as nobody had removed the packing that the TVs had come in. I came up with an idea to make a knife-throwing course inside the conference room. I went and gathered every letter opener in Commodore's R&D Department, and I would throw them like knives at a block of styrofoam on a chair. Then, I'd walk to that block, pull the knives out, and throw them in the opposite direction to another styrofoam block sitting on another chair.

This particular meeting was a design review with some of the silicon managers, and the MMU was the topic of the conversation. Now I *like* design reviews. My belief is that if you can't explain what you're talking about to people who don't like you or who don't understand what you're talking about, then you have no business producing something for millions of people. This isn't an easy bar to clear--explaining the design and listening to their feedback--and I do mean listening, regardless of whether they're talking about the color it should be or how the manager used to produce silicon-on-sapphire or some other inane fact.

However, in this one meeting, I was starting to get annoyed at one of the silicon managers whose questions about the MMU's functionality were tedious at best. Finally, he started a sentence with the word "Duh." I'm not kidding. He actually said, "Duh. I guess I don't really know what an MMU does." Now, this did piss me off, as I'd spent a lot of time explaining myself. All the while, I was throwing knives, and the blows to the styrofoam were getting harder and harder. My accuracy improved, the angrier I got. Finally, with one last hard blow that went through the styrofoam, I turned to him and said, "Look, I'm going to go get a ball peen hammer, and I'm going to hit you in the head with it, and it's going to hurt, the next time you ask a question like that."

Not only did the conference room get quiet, but also the Calma (chip layout) area, just over the wall, had suddenly fallen quiet, too, as they huddled near the wall listening to Herd's recent tantrum. From that day on, I called that manager "Ball Peen Hammer."

Font ROM Problem

Fred and Terry came to me and said we needed to revise the font ROM. The reverse "V" had a bar over it, which meant a single byte was wrong. This is not unlike where a single term was wrong in the PLA. This was absolutely no problem, if this was the *only* thing wrong with the font ROM. Later, I would learn that they found this while producing the Easter egg (hidden message) that they hadn't yet told me about. If Von's name didn't start with a "V", this would have been another error that would get through QA.

I consulted my schedule, which turned out later to be a PERT chart--similar to what I had done back in the TED days. I knew the schedule to get a font ROM made. We had about a week and a half before we needed to submit it to MOS. At that point, MOS would need five weeks to get it done. So, our department was in a time crunch, based on MOS's time requirements and the available windows in their schedule.

When I announced this at the weekly status meeting--that I was about to release the corrected font ROM to MOS--the manager of Software said that the font ROM was clearly software, not hardware, and therefore should come under his responsibility. I remember looking at him very strangely and asking why it mattered. We needed to release this font ROM. It needed to be done quickly. I had a small window now, down to about a week, to do this. The software manager insisted and said he would have it looked over and he would release it. I said, "Fine," and told him the drop-dead date.

Breaking into the Manager's Office

Now, after I'd had to break into my own work area, there had been a rash of other break-ins. It turns out that the security guards were doing it, but at this time, we didn't know that. Often, it was just things like foodstuffs that were taken. Steve Finkel had written a great story about how his bag of peanuts that he was savoring had been taken from him all too early in life and how his enjoyment of life would be much less without that bag of peanuts. Steve was the designer of our "Jack Busters" t-shirts that drew a parallel between the popular *Ghostbusters* movie and the fact that our old boss was now the competition. We walked around singing "Who ya gonna call?" during CES setup.

Management's answer to the break-ins was to produce a memo, of course. The memo said that anybody caught breaking into offices, or otherwise damaging walls, or doing anything like that would be fired. It all but said: "This means you, Bil Herd." You could tell it was targeted at me, in part at least. I was fine with the memo, provided they never gave me a reason to break into an office to continue my working. I was neither a thief nor a vandal; however, I was focused on getting the job done and was not going to let the excuse of anybody else slow down my project.

A couple of days before the font ROM drop-dead date, I kept asking the software manager how it was going, and he kept making vague noises that told me that he hadn't done anything at all. In my opinion, there was now no time for him to do whatever he had planned in order for the font ROM to go to MOS.

That night, I broke into his office by climbing over the ceiling--my old trick that got that white powder all over my hair, my clothes, and everything. I took the font ROM out of his desk drawer. It was still sitting there in the same position he had set it when I originally gave it to him, which is how I knew exactly where to look for it. I released the EPROM to MOS so that they could verify the code against an actual EPROM.

At the next status meeting, the software manager was trying to explain about how he was still working hard on the EPROM, in spite of having missed his deadline. I pointed at him and said in a voice that let everybody know I was not kidding, "You're lying. I broke into your office, stole the font ROM, and released it to MOS several days ago. You're lying." I had learned from Bob Russell to point my finger at a manager when I spoke to him, as Bob had learned that doing this in front of Jack Tramiel got everybody's attention. I used it now to get everybody's attention, and instead of me being guilty of breaking into his office, I accused this manager of being guilty of almost costing us the entire program. Nobody ever said a word to me about breaking into the office, and nobody at his level ever tried to get between me and a milestone again.

Middle Managers' Low Expectations

Through this experience, along with others that got in our way leading up to CES, it became clear to me that the middle-of-the-road middle managers weren't expecting us to succeed or to have a chance of succeeding. Their comfort zone appeared to be more about meddling and trying to look important. In short, they really weren't in the gear and in the mindset that we were. That we had only five months to produce something, by itself, was a heavy lift. It got even heavier with people trying to dogpile on us, but we were familiar with their tactics and had come to expect it.

At some point, we had pulled off enough small miracles that other people began to believe that we would actually make it. This worked to our advantage as now nobody wanted to be the person who actually interfered with us achieving the goal--in a visible way, that is, where the blame would land on them. This meant that their meddling would have to be more insidious and subtle, which was more difficult for them in hindsight, given that they had no real subtlety that we could detect.

Unfortunately, this newfound freedom from having to constantly watch our backs, running up to CES, quickly dispelled after CES. But, more on that later.

What Would Have Been Helpful

Here are some things that the QA Department didn't find that would have helped and would have been a minimal performance level, if they had achieved it:

The reverse V character was broken (we found it when we added the Easter egg with our names).

The Shift-Lock-Q didn't shift lock (it came out as lowercase). This was found by a user group within three days of the release, as was the Easter egg.

The LED didn't work on the disk drive: "We just assumed it was burnt out." The reality is that the code was bigger than the EPROM and the LED blink routine fell off the end of the device, but it was easily remedied once noticed.

This is just a sample of the challenges that we faced pretty much day after day. We didn't mind. We thought that it was fairly normal that half of our daily challenges would be technical or related to the laws of physics, and the other half contrived by other employees. Sometimes we felt sorry for them; sometimes we hung remorse on a peg as we steamed over the obstacle.

CBM had always been an environment where the strong survived and where you had to fight for the resources that would allow you to fight for the resources. Just getting your project to where it would be reviewed by upper management for consideration as a product meant that you had walked through fiery coals. So, with all of that, the 8563 was just another chip that had a string of problems exacerbated by circumstances and interaction (plus some unwillingness to deal with reality by some people).

Sanity

We did not have status meetings as the C128 team. We simply didn't need them. With only five to six people in the group, we would meet whenever we needed to and for longer than we needed to. I would meet with management in order to keep my guys from getting bogged down in meetings. I don't know if Fred and Terry met with their management, or if my meeting with the director on up was good enough to keep them from being bothered. It was in these higher up meetings that I was able to schedule the chip runs in things like housings, power supplies, and other accessories.

For my own personal sanity, I carried a legal pad in a leather holder. Every day, I would transfer the tasks that were still outstanding from the day before to a brand new sheet of paper. By the end of the day, I would have filled in one and a half columns of legal pad with tasks, started and completed, leaving only a few for the next day.

On the run-up to the CES show, I commandeered a huge whiteboard in the R&D lab, and I would spend about a half an hour a day standing on the desk in front of it, updating all the statuses of every single unit, every single chip, every rev of every single chip, and their build status. It was like manning an old-fashioned scoreboard, as I was standing there hand tallying the status of the various chips and components crammed onto this board. In addition to the revision numbers of each chip, we also had little colored dots that went onto each chip, based on what kind of testing had occurred, so it might not be unusual to require the VIC-II chip to be an R3 chip with a white dot and two green dots on it: meaning that it had been tested at a certain voltage, and also tested and retested for sparkle.

The Respected Middle Manager

Less than a month away from CES, I got a new immediate boss named Ed Parks, though I still also answered to the director, VP, and others, depending on the day. I remember his first week. Ed asked questions when he needed to, but otherwise stayed out of the way, a talent that we respected as lowly engineers. Ed went on to become the one middle manager who we had respect for.

This was the week when I found out that the PLA had been broken by the engineer moving the back-bias ring (same feature that broke the 8563), and thus shorting out the pins all down one side (found a new way to break the chip). I then made the chip work by driving it with a small PC board that overrode the problem, but resulting in a very hot IC that would not be usable in production. But, at least I could test that the function was correct, even if I was testing it destructively. I released an action report--I mean memo--describing the problem with the PLA, how to fix it, and what the impact would be. It would not cause us to miss the CES show. We just would not be able to play every game there, but that was never the goal.

That Friday evening, as we were walking down the hall, Ed said to me, "You worked hard this week." In response, I told him that Greg Berlin had just returned from Mexico with some real tequila in our office and that he was welcome to come and have a shot with us. Ed replied, "Sure, I'd like to have a belt." I stopped and said that the offer for tequila was still on: he just couldn't ever call it "a belt" again. It was a hard week, we had done a good job, and it was good tequila. I still have the empty bottle somewhere in my house today.

6.5 Winter CES Las Vegas 1985

No single custom chip was working completely as we went into December, with the possible exception of the 8502 CPU. I can honestly say that it didn't seriously occur to me that we wouldn't be ready for CES, for if it had, I might have succumbed to the temptation to go hide in my office (checking the telephone). There were just too many problems to stop and think, "What if?"

Late Change Removing 512 kB Expansion

Now, before we proceed to the CES show, I'll tell you a story about a late change, made by one of my bosses (I had several bosses, depending on the time of day). There's something in a manager that makes him want to add some little part of himself to the end product, regardless of whether the end product benefits from it or not. Some managers were smarter than others at this. For example, my boss knew to wait until we had the airfield made. In other words, we knew that we could get the product done on time, and it was just a matter of finishing. We called this little addition, the act of a manager hiking a leg on the project, as a way of marking his territory.

And so one day, my boss told me that we would *not* be doing the 512 kB MMU for the C128. He stated that it was just too risky, and that we could expand it later, in case next year's computer needed the expandability as the *new* reason to buy a Commodore computer. That's similar to not putting brakes on this year's model of car so that next year, you can tout the *new* model as reducing those annoying head-on crashes.

I was tired and worn out from having actually accomplished everything we had, so far, and his statement in no way jeopardized making CES on time. I knew that the C128 was a sound machine at 128 kB, and that would have to be good enough. This would come back to bite us.

A Good Omen

My theme song throughout the hectic days was *Solsbury Hill* by Peter Gabriel. We were running hard, were extremely focused, and the song sung in a wispy voice far away somehow felt right. The other song we liked was *And We Danced* by The Hooters, because it made us dance when we needed to dance.

We finished getting ready for CES at about 1:00 in the morning of the day we were to leave at 5:00 am. I had jetted over to Greg Berlin's house and caught a nap, a beer, and a shower. On the 10-minute ride from Greg's to CBM where we would catch a shuttle to the airport, I heard the live version of *Solsbury Hill* for the first time, which was an amazing coincidence--almost providence--and I took this as a good omen. Once we were standing in the dark morning waiting for the shuttle to arrive, I reached into my pocket, pulled out an ever-present beer, and popped the tab. I was rewarded by the sound of chuckles as people realized that the only person likely to be drinking a beer at 5:00 am was one of the Animals.

512 kB Expansion Ads

Not that I totally expected smooth sailing at CES, but, right off the bat, we encountered the unexpected. When we got to CES, the Las Vegas airport to be exact, that was when I spotted the first flyer announcing that the Commodore C128 would be expandable to 512 kB (yes, the 512 kB that one of my managers had nixed before the CES show). I was highly amused and held it up over my head so that Greg Berlin could see it across a swath of people at the airport baggage claim. Greg grinned in a maniacal fashion and also held up one. These flyers were everywhere--lying on the floor and also stacked in neat piles on chairs and elsewhere.

If that wasn't enough, on the cab ride to our hotel, we passed a huge billboard. Well, I guess it was a normal-sized billboard, but to me it looked huge, once again pronouncing that the Commodore C128 was expandable to 512 kB. It was a great advertisement: it showed an apple with an arrow in it sitting on top of a derby hat, and at that time, a derby was one of the props used in IBM commercials. I liked the ad because this is how we felt about the competition at the time. We simply felt we had a better product.

Now, the C128 had been designed to be expandable up to 512 kB *originally*, but later, as a result of management cocking a leg, it had been respecified *not* to be expandable, and now we had to deal with what marketing had done. For now, since we knew that this did indeed need to be dealt with, the programmers would later put hooks into BASIC that would work with an external RAM expansion cartridge, even though we didn't yet know what that really meant.

Reservations Cancelled

We arrived at the MGM Grand Hotel to find that our hotel reservations had been cancelled for the CES show. Those of us who had been at the previous year's hotel were actually relieved as no reservations seemed better than reservations, at least at last year's hotel. Everybody was standing in line, I guess waiting to argue with the hotel desk person. I did what came naturally to me at the time, which was problem-solving. I went over to the executive secretary of Commodore's president, and asked her if she had a credit card, as I wasn't worthy of credit myself in those days.

She replied, "Yes," and I immediately escorted her up to the desk with her credit card in hand, and me holding her arm so that the credit card was plainly visible. We rented rooms for the nights that were available, as they were already sold out for one night. So now, I had hotel reservations for all but one night in Vegas. I could definitely pull an all-nighter in Vegas. That was not a problem for me.

As I stood commiserating with everybody else, I was making sure that everybody in line knew that they could stay in my room if they had to, on the available nights we had. So, we were wheeling and dealing on how to split up the available rooms. We were talking six and seven people to a room at this point. It was at this time that David Rogers brought out a Commodore SX-64, set it on the reception desk at the MGM Grand Hotel, and started bargaining in earnest. He basically gave away an SX-64 in exchange for rooms, so that everybody who needed one had one for the nights that were available.

It was about then that I noticed somebody on the phone, and it became apparent that we were trying to cancel Atari's reservations in the hotel they were staying at, as we had it on good word that it was Atari that had cancelled our reservations. Business was war after all, as we had been taught by our mentor, Jack Tramiel. I didn't feel good about it, but I was at the point where I didnt feel bad about it either.

So real quickly, and in Commodore fashion, we had adapted to the lack of hotel rooms. This was just another problem to be solved for CES, in my view. We had visited revenge upon the people responsible--in our opinion--and we had adapted and coerced our way into having hotel rooms in the course of about 10 minutes.

Tackled at the MGM

It was after this that we were standing and milling about in the MGM Grand Hotel lobby, when I noticed a stillness in the air. Time slowed and my Spidey Sense tingled. I saw people turning in slow motion to behold what was coming towards me. I must have heard the rumbling, because I closed my eyes as Von Ertwine, being in a playful mood, hit me at a full dead run and tackled me to the floor.

Now, Von was a stocky guy, a natural wrestler, whereas I had years of Judo training. But, he knew that to get an advantage on me, he had to get me off the ground as my balance was really well-tuned back then. Well, he did get me off the ground, by hitting me with such force that we flew a good 6-10 feet into the center of the room, with him on top of me and both of us sliding on my face. I had a rug burn on the right side of my face on my cheekbone for the rest of that CES show, but I didn't care as now our CES team was complete. The fact that Von was at the CES show, in person, would turn out to be a show saver as he would have to recompile CP/M later that night to make it showable the next day.

Setting Up

Setting up at CES was relatively uneventful, compared to the insanity that led up to it. We were old hands at unboxing and setting up stations (see Fig. 6-3).

Fig. 6-3 Unpacking and CBM booth set-up at Vegas CES 1985.
Fred, Yash, Gale, Arlo, Claude, Hedley, Porter.
Photo courtesy of Terry Ryan.

We didn't even need to be told in general where to do what, as we could look at the layout of the booth and figure out what was needed where (see Fig. 6-4).

224

Fig. 6-4 Setting up our Commodore booth at CES Vegas 1985.
Photo courtesy of Terry Ryan.

Anybody who arrived at the booth during setup was checked to see if they had been carrying an 8563 from West Chester with them. We joked about satin pillows to protect the chips when we carried them around: they were so vital at this point.

CP/M Fix

It was on this day that Von showed up with his last version of code and we found a problem, a big problem. Someone forgot to tell him about the silly little ramifications of the "scrolling character left behind bug" in the 8563, where fixing it meant writing to the same register twice in a row. Yup, a Texan Write was required (for those of you keeping count). His development computer didn't duplicate the bug, as he had stopped upgrading 8563s on his machine somewhere around Rev 4, and the problem appeared somewhere around Rev 6 of the chip.

As Von didn't carry all the machinery to do a CP/M rebuild to fix the bug in software, it looked like CP/M might not be showable. One third of the booth's design and advertising was based on showing CP/M. In *true* Animal fashion, he sat down with a disk editor, found every occurrence of bad writes to the 8563, and hand-patched them. Bear in mind that CP/M is stored with the bytes backwards in sectors that are stored themselves in reverse order on the floppy disk. Also bear in mind that he could neither increase nor decrease the number of instructions; he could only exchange them for different ones. Did I mention hand calculating the new checksums for the sectors? All this with a disk editor. I was truly impressed.

Von was a true hero of CES that year.

Our Battleship Booth

We took over one of the marketing rooms on the second floor of our booth. Yes, our booth was two stories and shaped like a battleship in "attractive battleship yellow and gray," to quote Steve Finkel. We ran every single C128 through that room as we prepped it for its final usage, either tweaking 40 columns or installing a working 80-column chip, complete with a tower that actually made it work (see Fig. 6-5).

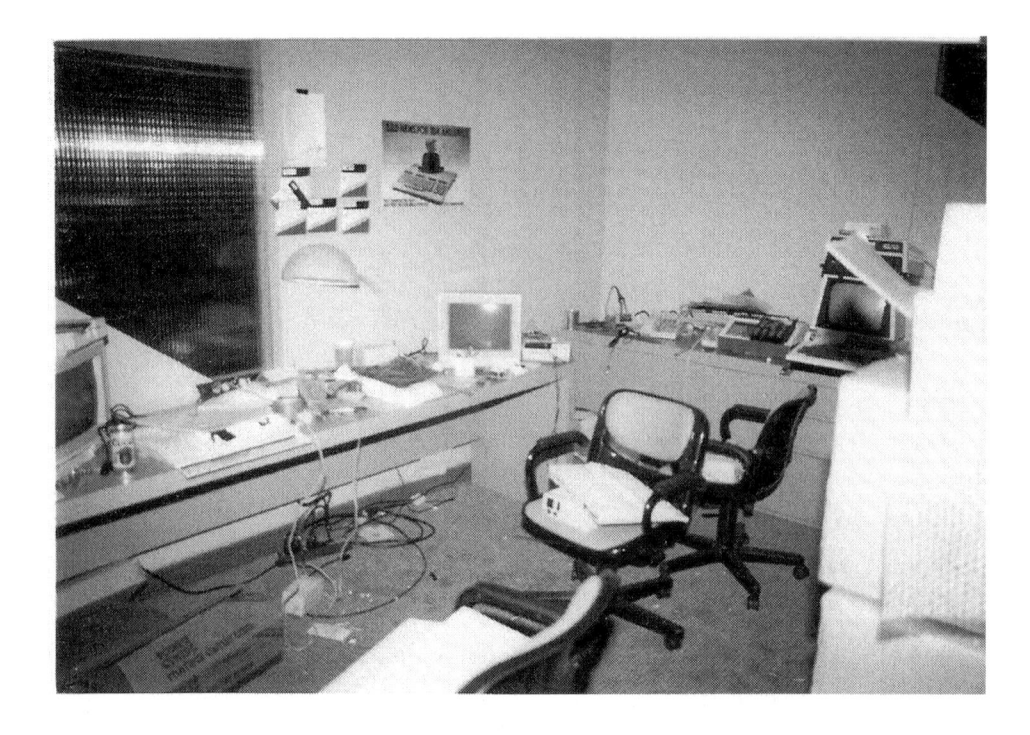

Fig. 6-5 Second floor prep room at Vegas CES 1985.
Notice the 512 kB expansion poster on the wall.
Photo courtesy of Terry Ryan.

This is the same room where Von performed the CP/M fix miracle.

As a form of pressure relief, we created the Commodore death list. We taped it right behind the door in the room so that you had to shut the door to see it, making it usually only seen by us working folk. The people on the death list often didn't realize that they were on it since they were never in the room with the door shut. The death list was interesting in that it also specified the manner of death chosen. I remember Gale, the lead technician, storming in and adding somebody to the death list because they had been mean to one of the programmers, Judy, in an unprofessional way. We all agreed that the person deserved death by being thrown off the second floor balcony.

227

When the CES show opened the next day, the booth was ready (see Fig. 6-6). As was our norm, we had fun at the CES, as well as displayed our workmanship (see Fig. 6-7).

Fig. 6-6 Commodore's Battleship Booth at Winter CES Vegas 1985. Photo courtesy of Terry Ryan.

228

Fred Bowen setting up at CES Vegas 1985.

Claude Guay and Terry Ryan at CES Vegas 1985 with C128s.

C128 Animal kicking a Commodore disk drive, held by designer, Greg Berlin.

Fig. 6-7 Work and fun at CES Vegas 1985.
Photos courtesy of Terry Ryan.

LCD Makes Debut

Jeff Porter was far better at doing something that I couldn't do, and that was acting like a decent, real human being in front of customers, while wearing a tie no less, whereas I had this long hair and tended to bite people. Jeff knew how to tie a tie and how to be respectable, and his role at CES gave the LCD some prospects for success (see Fig 6-8).

Fig. 6-8 Jeff Porter (with tie) demonstrating LCD at CES in Vegas 1985. Photo courtesy of Terry Ryan.

A third of the Commodore booth at the 1985 CES show was dedicated to the LCD machine, and Jeff and his team put their hearts into cutting all new CBM territory for this system. What he did at the CES show was to go around and get commitments of sales from people to buy the LCD. I couldn't have done that, but he did it. I believe he had 10-15,000 sales by the end of the show.

The Atari Booth

The first day of the show was rather uneventful. I got several reports in the morning about 80 columns not working, but these inevitably were caused by the 40/80 column switch being in the wrong position. By the afternoon, I had nothing to do and was standing around getting ready to go lose myself in Las Vegas when the phone rang. Yes, a single hard line telephone. There were no cell phones back then and very few answering machines.

The person on the phone asked me to go to the Atari booth and check out the interface for their newest printer. I reminded the person that we Commodore employees had been threatened with being fired if we went to the Atari booth, because the assumption would be that we would be looking for jobs. We secretly hoped that maybe some middle managers might wander on over there.

The person on the phone got irate with me when I reminded him about the moratorium on Atari visits and he asked point-blank: "Do you know who I am?" I didn't know exactly who he was, but I figured he was in our Marketing Department by his attitude, and he wanted me to scope out the competition. My response was that my visiting the Atari booth might actually draw some attention--the opposite of what we wanted--to which his response was "I don't think it's too much to ask." Feeling frisky at this point, I replied, "Fine. I'll go over there." Though he never did tell me who he was, I assumed that he worked in what we called the Marketing Fishbowl, and he never asked who I was.

A short walk brought me to the Atari booth and I wasn't there but a minute when down the steps from their second story booth came Jack Tramiel, surrounded by a bunch of people I knew, as they were *all* ex-CBM. I had never spoken with Jack personally and took this as an opportunity to introduce myself and shake his hand. Jack said a few kind words. I also shook hands with some of those *Speak & Spell* guys who had changed companies, as well as some of the old CBM management including a couple of my old bosses.

That quick, the conversation was over, but immediately Sig Hartmann, the ex-head of Commodore Software, threw his arm over my shoulder and led me to the side to tell me that Jack had been serious about what was offered to me. I hadn't realized it, but I must have had an employment offer and missed it.

Later, when relating this to Fred and Terry, Fred mentioned that when surrounded by the upper echelons of Atari, I should have reached into my jacket and pulled the pin on the grenade as a 5:1 ratio was acceptable.

I checked the printer before leaving the booth and noted a bunch of colored ribbon cables, so I figured it was a parallel interface. I also noted that the guy from marketing, who had phoned me and just *had* to know this, never did call back to find out what I had learned about their printer.

Electronic Arts

At one point, Greg Berlin and I did part of the show and then hit the suites in one of the hotels known for having open-door suites for people in the industry. Well, having a CES badge that said Commodore on it was a ticket into every single door we approached. We were in the Electronic Arts (EA) suite, and they were loading us up with software which ended up being played in the Commodore booth, so good marketing for them. They asked if there was anything else that they could get for us, and I pointed towards the full case of Michelob bottles. Without any additional thought, they grabbed the case and loaded it up on my shoulder as Greg and I walked out the door, now with a full case of beer to go do Vegas. Our first stop was that ride where you can ride in a column of air as if you're skydiving. Amazing as it seems all these years later, I have an old photo of me from that day on that ride (see Fig. 6-9).

232

Fig. 6-9 Bil skydiving at Winter CES 1985 in Vegas.
Photo courtesy of Bil Herd. Photo restoration by Elizabeth Fryer.

We had even prearranged for our beers to be kept in a small refrigerator while we were doing this, which made us happy.

On a subsequent visit to the EA CES booth, I ended up speaking with the president of EA. Years later, I had to call EA for support on a game for a PC, and I actually laughed at one point when I told the tech on the phone that I had met the EA president, which he didn't believe. I had to point him to their own web page to show what their top games were back in the '80s and who CBM was.

Adjusting C128 Power Supplies

Everything else went pretty smoothly at the CES show. Every C128 power supply was adjusted at the last moment for best performance for the particular software demo. One application had reverse green (black on green), and the 330-ohm pull-up resistors wouldn't allow the monitor to turn off fast enough for the black characters. I had had alternate pull-up resistor packs made back in West Chester, and now put them into service depending on whether we were doing green characters on black or black on green. On the average, two to three almost-working 8563s would appear each day, hand-carried by people coming to Vegas.

Another crisis, no problem. This was getting too easy. If a machine started to sparkle during a demo, I would pull out my ever-present tweak tool and give a little demonstration as to the adjustability of the new Commodore power supplies. People were amazed by Commodore supplies that worked, much less that had a voltage adjustment and an externally accessible fuse. I explained (and meant it) that really bad power supplies with inaccessible fuses were a thing of Commodore's past and that the new design philosophy meant increased quality and common sense.

I'm told that removing the fuse from the production units was one of the first things done the month after I left Commodore. When I heard this, it didn't make me feel bad; it just made me feel gone.

Chapter 7

Late C128

This is one jam-packed chapter, as I enter the end time for me at Commodore. It's exciting, dangerous, fun, exhausting, irritating, redemptive, and commemorative. Here goes.

7.1 Finishing the C128

One would think that, with the CES show behind us, things would get easier, but that was not the case. In fact, it got a little harder now that middle management was no longer in fear of being spotlighted as the holdup before a CES show. It got so obnoxious when they would try to trip me while merely walking down the hall, just to say they did something for the day.

Fixing a Manager Problem

It was about this time when Nancy came and took me to Adam's office, the VP. He had a list of people in the department in front of him with some names scratched off. I recognized those names as being people who didn't really move the ball, or in some cases didn't believe there was an actual ball to be moved. The list was clearly a list of people that were about to be let go.

One name had been scratched out, indicating being fired, and then the scratch had been erased. The name was still legible, as if someone had decided to keep him after all. Without saying anything, I reached down and tapped that name, a couple of times. Also, without saying anything, Adam reapplied the scratch to the name.

I had just gotten a middle manager fired. It was nothing personal; I still had work to do and this person had a history of impeding the team on a near daily basis.

Expandable to 512 kB ... Really?

One of the items that we had to deal with was the nagging question of expandability. One of my bosses had nixed the 512 kB function of the MMU, but we had seen billboards and brochures proclaiming the expandability up to 512 kB. To top it off, at some point, a dog and pony show had been done with the CEO of CBM, who asked where the 512 kB expansion plugged in, to which our boss replied, "In the back."

We left the dog and pony show before it was over and huddled up as a team to work on a solution. We decided to approach this using direct memory access (DMA), where we would make a cartridge actually push the information into memory so fast that it would act like it was expandable to 512 kB. Since we made our own chips, it was a given that we could use a custom chip to pull this off; and because it was right after CES, we knew that we had a small window when we could modify the operating system and BASIC. It was during this time that the STASH and FETCH commands were installed in BASIC 7.0, even though there was not yet any kind of cartridge that supported their use.

The cartridge and custom chip management fell to Frank Palaia to follow through with, and it became known as the RAM expansion unit (REU). The way it worked was that there was an entire 256 kB or 512 kB of memory in the cartridge. When the user or a program needed some of that memory, they would ask for it with a FETCH command in BASIC, or would use a STASH command to store the information. There is also SWAP, which combines both operations and makes the computer swap information in and out of the REU. These commands would go on to be the basis for an impressive demo at the next CES show when we used it to display a spinning globe in real time--animation from BASIC!

I don't think any of us dwelled on the fact that we had already had this expanded memory capability and had designed it out. We just concentrated on getting it to work again, now that we were all in agreement, this time including management.

BASIC 7.0 Advanced Commands

I ran into Terry Ryan who had just gotten his review. He had not gotten a good review, in spite of the fact that he had performed miracles with BASIC 7.0. Terry had created a whole new aspect to Commodore BASIC, something that we now call structured BASIC. In short, there would have been no DO, LOOP, WHILE, and UNTIL instructions, except for Terry's desire to include them. These were initially included in BASIC 3.5 by Terry and he added them to BASIC 7.0, despite his manager's attempt to block them.

Unfortunately, Terry's review criticism included the point that he had been told specifically *not* to include those commands or structure. Terry related that the manager had said to him, "While it appears to be the correct decision to include structured BASIC commands, it goes against what you were told to do," and therefore, there was no big raise for Terry.

In short, Terry was punished for doing something good.

FCC

So now, we had to actually produce the computer that we had just shown at CES. I had already submitted it to the FCC so that it could be produced in time. This had the effect that I could no longer move or add any ICs or major parts. I could only add jumpers and transistors.

FCC submission is where the Federal Communications Commission certifies that your computer won't interfere with your neighbor's electronic appliances. Strangely enough, the FCC wasn't worried about you interfering with yourself, just your neighbor. To that end, we supplied them with a sample computer, and they pointed a radio antenna at it to check it for interference. Yes, it's more complicated than that, and we did our own scanning so we knew what the results would be, but that's the gist of it.

From here on out, any changes I would make to the board would have to be documented as a "permissive change," and it basically meant that I had only one more revision of the PC board before I had to wrap it up. (Our deadline was June to be in full production, and we wouldn't have time for more than one rev.)

Before locking the design, I made sure there were some spare gates--the little electronic usable blocks that we designed the hardware with. In this case, we had spare 7406 inverters and 7407 open collector gates. What that means is that they could be anything from an inverter to an exclusive nor-gate by having their outputs combined into complex functions, kind of like some basic Lego building blocks, only we called them jelly beans. Almost every problem that was fixed post-CES was fixed using a combination of 7406 and 7407, or with a transistor, or just with plain old cuts and jumpers.

Monochrome Output

It was during this time that we decided to add a monochrome output to the video output connector, which I did using open collector gates and a transistor (see Fig. 7-1). When I was finalizing the 80-column output, my boss had a negative suggestion. He told me to invert one of the sync signals for the RGBI, either the vertical or the horizontal synchronization signals, which would make it so you couldn't use a non-Commodore brand monochrome monitor (of which there were several back then). In other words, he wanted me to muck it up so that C128 users had to buy a new Commodore brand monitor (such as the then non-existent 1902) if they wanted to use 80 columns.

Fig 7-1 Last minute addition for C128 monochrome output for FCC submission.
Photo courtesy of Bil Herd.

This was the one time I lied to my boss, and I lied to him by omission. I nodded vaguely and made noises like I would do what he wanted, but I knew in my heart I could not deliberately sabotage the computer-- especially not screw the end user, and especially not rely on a monitor that we didn't believe would exist in time.

Later, my boss would ask how it was going, and I said it was almost done and would use other euphemisms for not answering his question directly. This was the only time I ever didn't give my boss the straight dope. In the end, the C128 was still compatible with all the monitors of the day, as I never made the change; and true to form, the new Commodore brand monitor was months late. Again, if I had made the change that I had been told to make, that would mean that people would not have been able to even use 80-column mode. Disobeying my boss did not make me feel good, but messing up the computer simply wasn't a choice in my book.

Z80 Fixes

During this time, Frank Palaia found and fixed one or two other problems in the Z80 circuit. These were things like when it would not stop exactly on the cycle we needed it to, and would do an extra cycle. This could raise havoc and could be very hard to find, but Frank found them. True to form, we used 7406 and 7407 gates to fix the problems most of the time, and the area between the two processors on the schematic became known as Z80ville, as it became complicated.

It was during this time that we also found out why the Commodore brand CP/M cartridge didn't always work on the C64. It had nothing to do with the speed of the components, like everyone assumed; it was that the Z80 could be halted in an illegal mode and the chips that were connected to it would go into an illegal state. We fixed this on the C128 with more jellybeans and made sure that the Z80 couldn't get into the illegal state to begin with. The C64 CP/M cartridge remained broken in this aspect, unfortunately.

Reset Circuit

One issue I had seen was that the computer didn't always reset cleanly. If one remembers, the C64 had no reset circuit, so we knew that we had no history of how well the VIC-II chip interacted with a reset cycle. I wasn't all that surprised that we had a reset problem and that the problem was VIC-II related. I put the computer on the analyzer, and sure enough, I caught a botched reset cycle when the reset happened during the VIC-II chip doing a sprite DMA pointer fetch: fancy words for meaning it was busy doing all the fancy graphics and ignored the reset line during that time.

I was able to fix the problem by adding a single gate, and I did it in a strange way. I wired it backwards to an existing gate, so that it fed back, creating a latch. Now, when a reset occurred, it would not continue to reset if the VIC-II chip was busy, but it would wait till it was available. Then, and only then, would it allow the reset to occur. Once again, a 7406 inverter had fit the bill.

During this time, I also had to figure out how to put in the seven or eight jumpers and changes that we had accumulated since CES. Again, only jumpers and transistors could be used due to FCC requirements; I could not move or add any other components. I actually just disappeared into my office for a week. Very few people saw me, which was not really my style, but I had to focus. It took me all week to figure out how we would get those jumpers to become traces on the real board, and to do it in a mostly hidden way by placing many of the jumpers underneath chips.

True C64 Mode

I came to Fred Bowen and said that I'd had a request to leave all of the C128 super features in the C64 mode, or create another mode, called Super C64. The theory was that in this mode, the MMU and all the high-speed clocking would be made available, but would still be in C64 mode. Obviously, this would not have been compatible for all C64 software, but it would have been a very cool mode.

Fred responded immediately and said, "We will not be corrupting the definition of a C64." I immediately agreed when I heard it stated like that. It made so much sense coming from somebody as wise as Fred that I didn't argue. It became my new mantra, as well.

To have been able to include a true C64 mode was a gift. We were uniquely positioned to be able to include a C64 mode, being the only people in the entire world who could do that. We would not repay the favor by creating confusion about what a C64 was in the Commodore community.

Screeching Halt

About a month after CES, it was time to put all of the known changes and everything we learned into the final rev of the PC board. This would be the one that would go to production and the one that would hopefully pass the final FCC submission.

When we went to do the finalization, we came to a screeching halt because of a middle manager who didn't care so much about the actual status of the product, as we lowly engineers did. The bosses were away on a trip to Italy, and control of the office had been given to the head of the Drafting Department. He wasted no time in telling me that the C128 would be demoted in priority: "It's just been going on far too long." He somehow felt that he now could stop the C128 with impunity or at least show his sway over the progress of it.

For an entire week, the C128 PC board layout went nowhere, and the manager felt pretty proud of himself, I would imagine. I have never understood the mentality where derailing something else would give somebody a sense of satisfaction, but I couldn't argue with the evidence that this mindset must exist for some people.

7.2 The Weekend of Tears

After that week when the C128 wasn't getting any PCB layout time at all, the bosses got back. They literally asked what the hell had happened during the week they were gone, as we no longer were on schedule. The middle manager who had issued the halt nimbly spoke, expounding the virtues of getting right on the job immediately and that someone else--*his* boss perhaps--had made such an ill-suited decision.

So, we were back in action. The PCB layout guys agreed to work 24/7 throughout the weekend to get us back on track.

Three Days and Nights

It was cool watching the PC board guys work when we got down to 20 to 30 remaining copper traces to be routed. We were doing the layout on a now ancient system called a Scicards that had a $40,000 terminal. It took its own dedicated DEC VAX to run, in addition to a very expensive VM bus graphics card that fit directly inside the VAX mainframe computer. This was a $100,000 system back in the day.

However, there was no autorouting the traces by machine. It was all figured out by hand, using the Scicards as an expensive Etch a Sketch. Near the end, it would take more than an hour to route a single trace, as many other traces would have to be bumped, moved, and sometimes rerouted. And, if all else failed, the circuit ground area would have to be reduced to make room (unfortunately). The amount of ground was vital for maintaining the logic levels, hence the operation of the chips, as well as affecting the FCC results. The three guys who worked so hard that 72 hours were Terry Fisher ("Fish"), Claude Guay (the "crazy Canadian"), and Paul Rubino (no nickname; just Paul Rubino or PAR for short).

The PCB layout guys worked in 8-hour shifts, around the clock. Near the end of an 8-hour shift, the next layout guy would come in and sit next to the active designer. You could tell that the person who just finished 8 hours was beat. Slowly, the new guy would start to point out places to move vias (holes) and traces, gradually taking over the job himself until finally he had the control in his hand. I believe this is what air traffic controllers do when they hand off to each other; they kind of warm hand off and that's what I witnessed.

Now, I have to say that I witnessed all the handoffs, since the only way the guys were going to be able to work 24/7 for a couple of days was to have me there with them. I brought in my old Army sleeping bag and my ever-present air mattress, and I set up shop right there in the CAD Department. I needed the sleeping bag and my big thick Army coat, as it was cold in that room. In fact, it was so cold that I had brought in Burger King breakfast biscuits on Friday morning, set them on a shelf next to my sleeping bag, and they were still edible on Sunday.

I told the guys to just tap me on the foot and I would get up to answer their questions, though I may not wake up completely. I think I surprised them when that's pretty much what happened. Monday morning came and we were done. It had been three long days and nights, but we were back on schedule.

Given what had happened, we decided that now was a good time to start leaving more than just our initials on the PCBs. We opted for little messages instead. On the bottom of every C128 and the original C128Ds is printed: "RIP: HERD/FISH/GUAY/PAR" (see Fig. 7-2).

The syntax refers to an inside joke where we supposedly gave our lives in an effort to get the production board done in time.

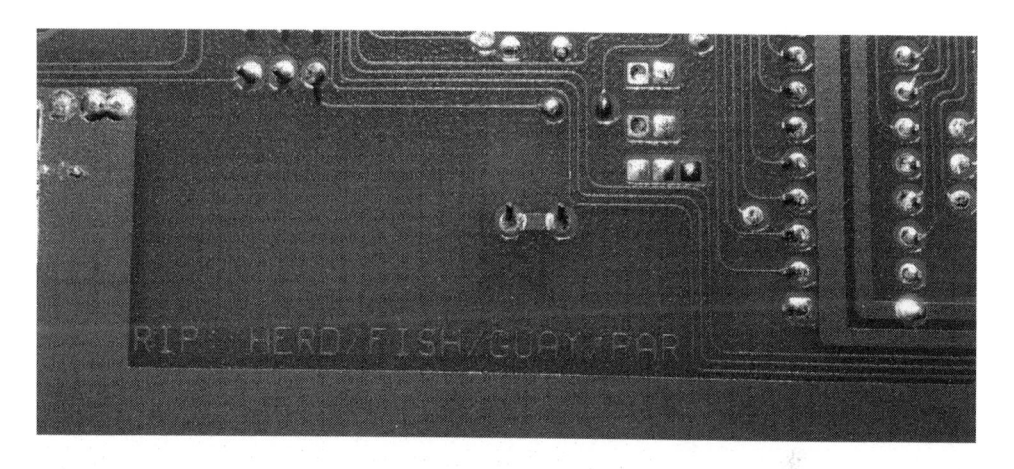

Fig. 7-2 Bottom of C128 PCB showing RIP.
Photo courtesy of Margaret Morabito.

Towing My Car

It was also during this time that I had to have my Datsun 260Z, that I had bought just to work at CBM, towed from the parking lot. I had parked it sometime in November and hadn't moved it since then. It had been under a snow drift for most of the winter and was suffering from that. I now needed to go places again and would need a new car, which started with me holding a funeral service for the old car. I have to say that when the car was towed, it left behind a sad little pile of rust and odd parts. I actually saw several nuts and bolts in the pile. All was not lost, however, as I used my bonus money from finishing the C128 on time for CES to purchase a used Datsun 280Z.

Easter Egg

Around this time we also finalized the EPROMS which would become ROMs, their mass production cousins, for release to production.

Not long after they were released, the guys called me in and showed me an Easter egg they had put in the computer. I figured that they knew not to show it to me until the ROMs were finalized, as I might have objected the next time that they said they didn't have room in the ROM to add something. In other words, I would sell them out in a heartbeat if it endangered the computer getting done in time.

Terry showed me the keyboard and said, "Take half of 64 kB (32,768 for you non-geeks) and round up; then 123,45,6." Terry had just shown me the command "SYS 32800,123,45,6". It would clear the screen and put up a little message about the creators of the C128 (see Fig. 7-3).

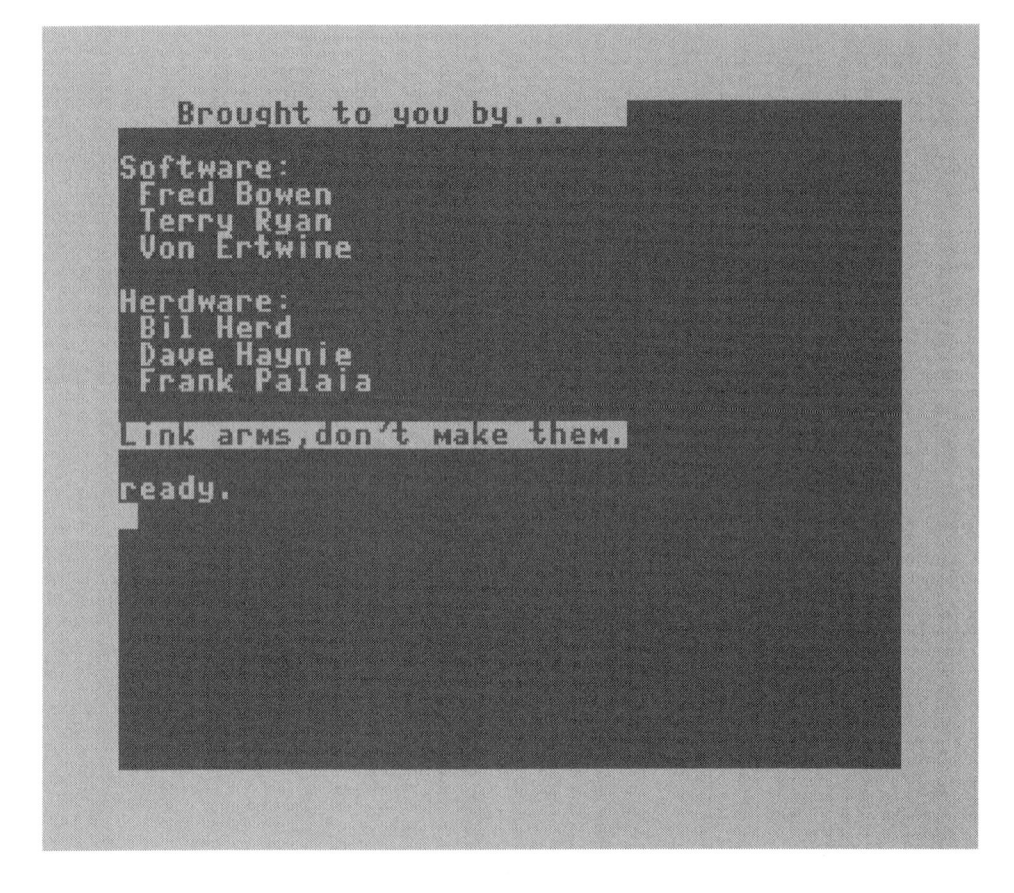

Fig. 7-3 C128 Easter egg. SYS 32800,123,45,6.
Note Herdware instead of Hardware.
Photo courtesy of June Tate-Gans (https://nybblesandbytes.net/) using VICE.

At no time were we worried about the QA Department actually finding the Easter egg as that would tend to make us believe that they were testing the computer in earnest, of which we had yet to see proof. Actually, the Commodore community was a much better tester, and we should have listed them as a QA alternative since they found the Easter egg the very next day after production release. Speaking of that user group, they were also the first people to tell us about the fact that the caps lock-Q did not result in an uppercase Q letter. In other words, the QA Department, which has "Q" in their own name, had not even tested all of the upper case "Q" options on the Commodore 128.

Rev 7 Show Stopper

In no time at all, we had Rev 7 PCBs in hand, or "Rev Nana" as we said in the Japanese office. This was the first time that I expected a PC board to work the first time. Normally, I liked it when the boards didn't power right up because they forced me to troubleshoot at a very intricate level, which gave me confidence in the board. But this time, it was time to act like it was a real production board and it needed to work. It needed to work the first time, no matter how many we built, and it did. We built up a bunch of C128s and a bunch of C128Ds, and started handing them out. I still shoved a cartridge in one every chance I got, just to make sure it still acted like a C64, as well.

Things were going good and I sort of didn't like it, but I was slowly coming to terms that the project might actually be over and that the board might actually be in its final rev.

Then we got the news that not every board booted up CP/M correctly.

Turns out that 20% of the new boards could not load CP/M--a real show stopper. It would be ironic that the thing, that when broken could give the C128 such a bad name, was something that wasn't even supposed to be included in the computer in the first place; but it *was* included and it *had* to work.

Off the Project

Negotiations between my boss and me broke down that day, as we say, and he felt that maybe somebody else should take over the project now that it was almost done. My response was "Fine!" and I immediately took it out of gear and relaxed. I spent the week sleeping, practicing personal hygiene, and eating; I needed no practice drinking oddly enough. I did a few other things also, being young and in love, but we won't talk about those here.

My boss walked into my office that Friday morning and gave me a mandate, as apparently the engineer he had put in charge of the C128 in my place, the original engineer on the D128 as it turns out, could not figure out what the problem was. I have to say that this was an unfair thing to have asked of him in the first place. I'm sure he didn't even know where to look at this point, whereas I knew every signal like the back of my hand; they were old friends and I knew who was finicky and who was not.

My boss's ultimatum was simple, "Fix it, or you're fired." I had heard that exactly once before. I grinned in anticipation, as I kind of knew this day would happen on the day he took me off my own project. I had kept my powder dry and got well rested in anticipation of when it would be our time to go back on stage.

I Saw Something Suspicious

I got lucky. Within an hour of probing around the computer, though I will say it helps a lot to know exactly where to look, I saw something suspicious. I saw an electrical reflection of a signal at exactly the wrong time, and only when the Z80 processor was active. This was not a problem caused by the main 8502 processor, and that meant that I only had to look at the artifacts when using the Z80 coprocessor.

The problem was that we didn't have anything that could capture a single glitch on an oscilloscope, and when we turned up the oscilloscope bright enough to see the glitches, they were lost in the glare of the strong signals.

Mind you, I was looking for a wispy little ghost of a line amongst really well-pronounced, bright signals that otherwise overwhelmed the human eye.

The Wire

A trick that I had taught myself was to move most of the signal off of the screen of the scope, so that only a little bit of it was still visible. And then, I would stare at it with my hands cupped around my face and burn my retinas while looking at the signal--like staring at the sun and then looking away. I stared at these white traces on a green scope and then would suddenly look up at a blank wall where I would see the reverse image in black on white. Sure enough, I could see this wispy little glitch on the white wall next to the oscilloscope.

I called Frank over and showed him the trick. I remember him pointing at the wall, saying, "I see it!" I showed this to several people and not everyone saw the glitch. Hedley declared one time that I must have lost my marbles, though it was hard to argue that point on a good day.

It turns out that address line 10 (A10) was the exact wrong shape and length when measured from the Z80, though it was okay when measured from the 8502. I liken this to blowing a flute. When you blow into the end that you're supposed to, you get a nice melodic tone. This is the equivalent of the 8502 driving the bus, but when I needed to inject a second processor, it was like blowing into one of the holes on the flute instead of into the mouthpiece. We got noise instead of a melodic tone. In other words, it wasn't tuned to have two processors driving the same line, and this was due to the lack of space on the PC board.

This problem had been created during the "Weekend of Tears," as we called it--the three days and nights where we laid out the board 24/7 until it was done. It was a win that we got all the traces on the board, so I never regretted the fact that we had one issue left.

To prove that this was indeed the problem, I added a jumper wire to the PC board, so that when the glitch got to the end of the trace, it could keep going and circle back around (see Fig. 7-4).

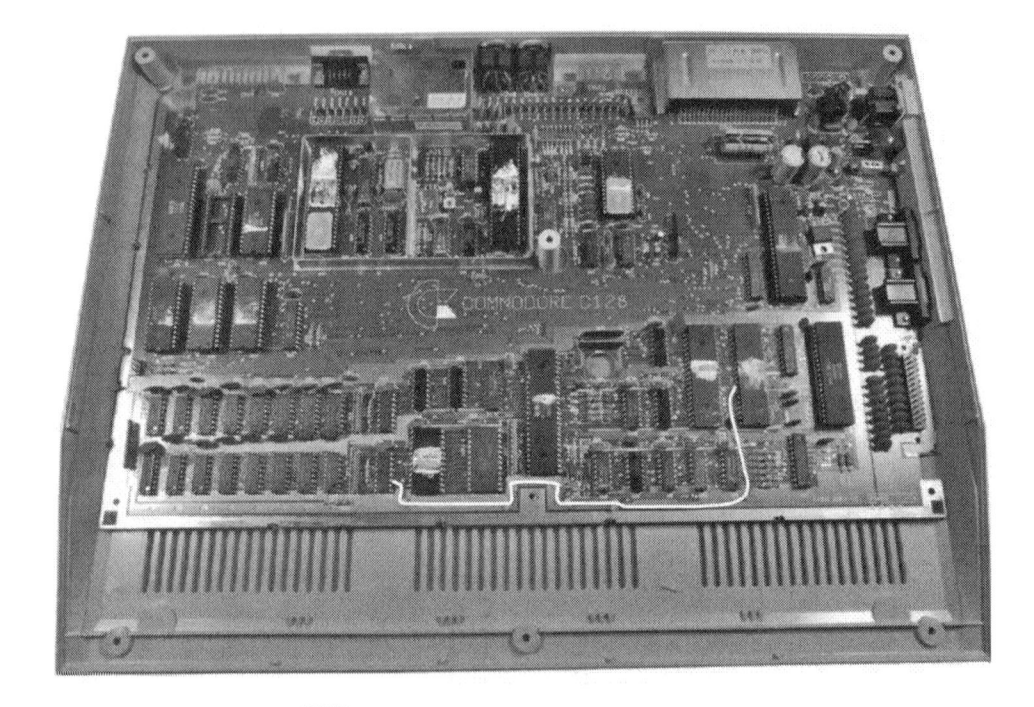

Fig. 7-4 C128 PCB with "The Wire" (bottom center).
Photo courtesy of Bil Herd.

In other words, I added a jumper to an existing trace and made it into a loop. Now, there would be no reflection off the end of the jumper, and it was that reflection that was causing the glitch. This wire was on every production C128 thereafter.

It Worked!

It worked, or I should say it *appeared* to work. It appeared to work, based on the one or two that we tried, but this was the big time. We needed to *know* that it would work on *all* C128s, *all* the time. My boss arranged for a special run of 10,000 units to be done over the weekend. They would take the boards, open them on "the super line," as it was called in the Production

Department downstairs, and add the jumper wire to each machine. They would then test it to see if it booted CP/M.

While I did not participate in the testing of these 10,000 computers, pretty much the entire Engineering Department had to give up their weekend for this emergency test procedure. I showed up, walking the super line with a case of beer on my shoulders, handing them out to my fellow engineers and technicians who had to test to make sure that I wasn't full of crap. It was agreed that I probably still was full of crap, but that the fix worked. Only a place like Commodore would have done a run of 10,000 units like this, which was really nothing more than a simple test of whether an engineer had his head up his posterior or not.

That was the last big problem of the C128 and it was time to go fishing, but since it was still cold outside, we went to the bar instead.

False Alarm

We began ramping down the stress after that, and there were no design problems that we had to respond to, just production and component related issues. I had become addicted to the stress to the point that years later I would work as a trauma technician at Cooper Trauma Center in Camden, New Jersey, just to get some added stress in my life.

I had taken to sleeping in a little more during the day, as I recuperated. I started the trick of putting one of three signs on my office door that stated the requirements before waking me up on a particular day. For example, if I *really* needed my sleep, I would put up a sign, signed by Adam, the vice president, saying that someone had to be a VP or higher rank to wake me up. I also had signs, signed by my director, saying that one had to be a director or higher, and finally one by my direct manager for times when I was mostly just resting.

One day, they awoke me from sleeping on my air mattress, saying that CP/M had started failing to load again during an important demonstration and would I come and look at it. By now, people had chilled and, instead of a demand for my presence to explain myself or my misbehaving child as it were, it was a request to understand and fix the problem.

We were getting better at believing that we could pull this off as a group. I never doubted that, not because I was egotistical, but because I knew that *we, the team,* would do everything in our power to succeed. Looking back, I think that it was this drive that was responsible for the fact that we did succeed.

This time, when I showed up, they had the case off of the disk drive, and it was sitting near a monitor that didn't have a case on it either. Sure enough, it was stuck loading CP/M from disk. As this was a demonstration of the drive for something, Greg Berlin was there, which explained why the case was off of the drive. I noticed that the shielded cable that went to the read/write head of the drive was sticking up in the air. This is not unusual in itself in an R&D environment, but it looked to me that this very sensitive "antenna" (very strong amplifiers are hooked to the read/write head) was in the electric field of the monitor itself (okay, some of us can see electric fields). I tucked the wire back into the frame, and CP/M went back to loading.

This time, everyone was very happy that it was easily fixable. Greg thanked me, and I went back to sleep in my office. I am not sure if I even said anything during the process, though I am sure that I was barefoot. I do admit that I was tempted to freak out before I spotted the wire. (Move a wire and software works; go figure.) Anyway, this turned out to be a false alarm, not a new problem, and now we were nearing the end of this C128 marathon.

The Last 8-Bit Computer

I once said that I thought of the C128 as the last of the 8-bit computers, and then people responded about lots of other 8-bit systems that sold a few thousand. So, I have to rephrase it as the "last of the mass-produced, *sold in the millions*, 8-bit computers." I once heard from a good source that all C128 models combined had sold between 4 and 6.8 million worldwide, depending on who you asked.

To totally misquote J.R.R. Tolkien, the time of the elves had come to an end, and it was truly the dawn of the 16/32-bit machines. Not saying that something couldn't be made cheaper by using only 8 data lines, but the era had shifted to 16+ bits. That was the same year that the unicorn that Chuck Peddle and company had left behind died. It was an ominous sign, but we really thought the Amiga would be the next revolution. It was also during this time that Yash left Commodore, and with him gone, the last of the C64 warriors was gone.

7.3 What Didn't Happen

Amidst all the happiness and joy and quasi-sadness of finalizing the C128, there were a couple of more lost items during my tenure, which actually went on to live in Commodore posterity.

C128D

Sadly, Commodore decided not to sell the C128D in its original form, except for some systems overseas, Europe in particular. After I left Commodore, the cost-reduced version would come out in the USA, called the C128DCR. I had no hand in the C128DCR and have no real opinion about it--at least none that I can print here.

Years later, when I saw my first C128DCR, the first thing I noticed was that they had a ground issue that resulted in more video noise than we had in the main C128 unit. Seeing the noise was very sad for me, but also bolstered my opinion of why we had worked so hard to get the video noise and ground effects addressed in the original C128.

Today, we see that the C128D and the C128DCR actually have an enthusiastic following, although there are fewer of them out there, compared to the original flat C128. I often refer to the flat C128 as a "Barn Door Stop" due to its shape and as a play off of what we had done with Sinclairs.

Tandy's Advice on the LCD

Not to forget the LCD, here's the endgame on that noteworthy, groundbreaking transportable. After we got back from CES, the rumor internally was that our then CEO had been told by the president of Tandy that there was no money in portable computing, as proven by their LCD. Despite already having thousands of pre-production orders for our LCD, the then CEO of Commodore still wasn't interested in producing it, and so another innovative engineering feat died on the vine.

I used to have an article hanging outside my office about how the Tandy LCD was their single highest-selling product at Radio Shack that year. The moral of this story: "Don't listen to the competition." The insult on top of the injury was that their portable computer didn't hold a candle compared to ours. With everything from the quality of the LCD screen to the software to the cool case, we had left our competitor in the dust ... at least until we started taking advice from said competitor.

LCD Kaput

Anyway, eventually the LCD got canned, in spite of Jeff Porter's efforts, and it never even went into production. It was cancelled after the 1985 Summer CES show in Chicago. Discontinuing the LCD didn't result from any lack of trying, and at this point in time, I would say if Commodore had to choose between the LCD and the C128, *they should have chosen the LCD* because the C128 really was just the last of the 8-bit machines and was not revolutionary in any way. We were throwing everything in there that we could. We were ready to turn off the lights and walk out of the 8-bit arena and into the 16-bit. But, CBM shouldn't have had to choose; we could easily have done *both*: finish the 8-bit family and start the LCD market for the masses.

Being Osborned

The LCD would have been the thing that wasn't just more of the same. I love a computer that you can carry with you. That just wasn't done in the 1980s. Even the Osborne-1, a successful portable computer back then, would just basically hit you right in the ankle and knock you off your feet, if you didn't balance the hinge right. It weighed 24 pounds after all. We called those machines "transportable" at that time, or "luggables."

Which reminds me, we had a term, "being Osborned," named after the famous Osborne computer company of the day. Lee Felsenstein worked for Osborne and designed the Osborne-1. I had the honor of meeting Lee at the 25th anniversary of the C64 held at the Computer History Museum in Sunnyvale, California in 2007.

The Osborne-1 was a good computer and was selling well back then. I had used it at my previous company. Then, Osborne became their own worst enemy when they started telling everybody about their next great computer, the Osborne-2. They promoted how good it would be, to the extent where sales of the Osborne-1 dropped off almost completely. They ran out of money and could never produce the Osborne-2, all because they had promised everybody how good the Osborne-2 would be. We called this "being Osborned."

Douglas Adams

As you recall, we had all started reading *Hitchhiker's Guide to the Galaxy* back in the TED days, after I brought it in one day, and it ended up being our theme book. Well, it turned out that Douglas Adams, the book's author, was at the CES show when we introduced the LCD. He stopped by the booth one day, though I was not there at the time. I won't tell you where I was--it was Las Vegas. He got into a conversation with Pat McAllister, one of my friends who was working the Commodore booth. While they were talking, while viewing our LCD computers, Douglas started scratching at one of the LCD screens, saying there was something on it. My friend quipped, "Use your towel," which actually made Douglas Adams laugh. To find out why this is so freaking funny, you will have to read *Hitchhiker's Guide to the Galaxy* yourself. Any explanation I could give simply would not do it justice; it's one of the best books I've ever read.

We had many themes that went along with the time we worked so hectically at Commodore. They make me think of those days, as if I was still there. One of those was Gary Larson's *The Far Side* comics. I had them all over the place: out in the hall, at the entry to my office, and on the walls of my office.

Scant Marketing

One of the things that we had noticed about the C128 marketing was that it was minimal, for the most part. It was a "build it and they shall come" attitude, left over from the Commodore 64 when the sheer number of C64s out there created a marketing base all its own.

I did see a couple of commercials at some point for the C128, as opposed to the Plus/4 series which I never saw advertised. The commercial that struck me the most featured the voice of Burgess Meredith, aka the Penguin on the *Batman* TV series, espousing the benefits of a C128 over the Apple IIc, talking about all of the things one would need to add to the Apple to make it equal to a Commodore. My favorite shot was that of a large drill, drilling a hole in the side of the IIc, making lots of plastic shavings.

While our team had been totally focused on the C128, at the same time, Commodore had come out with the more powerful Amiga family. I wasn't involved much with the Amiga, but I did notice some of what was, or was not, going on with that new computer.

We figured that Amiga's Marketing Department would show up since this was such a new and noteworthy computer line. We were waiting for marketing to kick the Amiga advertisements into high gear, and we felt like we just kept waiting. Finally, at one point, they put up some pictures, just outside of our office area, of them shooting the newest commercial. It was supposed to be a takeoff of the movie *2001: A Space Odyssey* where they showed the old and the new. The only problem was that the commercial was very hard to understand. Very hard. The ending of the commercial featured an unborn infant slowly rotating; no controversial subject there. When we saw the pictures of the commercial production, they literally had the fetus model propped up on a stick for it to be shot by the cameras, something we promptly called fetus-on-a-stick. It was creepy and awful at the same time. The marketing never got better than that, and for the next couple of years, I watched TV for any Amiga commercials and only ever saw two in my life.

7.4 On a Lighter Note

But wait! There's more.

Sword Fighting

One morning, I was just about to drink my morning cup of coffee when a middle manager in charge of the VAX system came into my office, accusing me of having bad-mouthed him in a meeting. I set the coffee down untouched and replied to him that I had indeed bad-mouthed him, and that I had a real issue with one of his decisions that was slowing us down. Mind you, the VAX team was great. I just had a specific issue with what was a bad decision in my opinion. I kept to myself the fact that almost everybody else in the meeting had brought up or agreed with the same point that I had made. In fact, I felt honored that it was only my name that was dropped as being the accuser.

The manager and I had it out, right there, and I made sure he knew that I had but one goal, which was to complete my project on time. I wasn't necessarily worried about making friends or about people's feelings; I just wanted to get done and succeed. I told him how he could help instead of hinder. Surprisingly, we came to an agreement and he departed my office. I remember that my coffee had gone cold by this point, but I drank it anyway. Having been in the Army, something as trivial as the temperature of the coffee mattered not.

Later, I related this as having a sword fight, even before my morning coffee, in the halls of Commodore; though in reality, it was in my office, not the halls.

CES Elevator

Terry Ryan and I were at the Chicago Summer CES show in 1985. It was after hours and we had had a few cocktails. When we got into the old relay-driven elevator, it did something funny, and we responded by trying to understand the operating system of the elevator. We learned quickly, through a series of button pushes, as well as opening and closing the door, that we could confuse it into believing that no one was inside the elevator. So consequently, the buttons on the elevator didn't work properly anymore. We laughed, though we had trapped ourselves in the elevator. About 10 minutes later, the elevator doors opened. We started to explain to somebody that we had tricked the elevator into locking us in. When we realized that we were talking to the house detective, we thanked him for freeing us and went about our way.

Coffee in the Floor Holes

One morning, I went to the VP's office to start a pot of coffee. This would have been about 6 o'clock in the morning, before anybody from the normal shifts had started to arrive, meaning that only us late-nighters and overnighters were left in the building. I left for a short while and returned to the VP's office to find out that I had not put the coffee pot in far enough: the entire pot of coffee had leaked all over the floor. Adam would literally have to walk through a puddle of coffee to get into his office, if I didn't clean this up. The problem was that we weren't trusted with mops or brooms or any implements that could be turned into pitchforks or torches, as we had a habit of rabble-rousing, or at least the reputation of rousing rabble.

I looked down and noticed some small holes in the floor where a wall had previously been removed, leaving just the anchor holes. I started to push the coffee on the floor down these holes using some napkins, when George Robbins, the other longhair of our motley crew, happened by. George (aka "GRR") had a passion for databooks that matched my own, and he had a habit of putting his initials on his books and anything else that belonged to him. Unfortunately, at one point, this meant *my* books, since George didn't realize that the big "H" on the book meant "Herd" and not "Hughes" who had already left Commodore. I gathered my books up with no hard feelings, just letting him know that the big "H" was mine and that I didn't mind that there was a "GRR" written on some of my books.

George also had the reputation of living at Commodore, something I can attest to since he was always there when I was. Unlike me with my air mattress, George would often sleep in a pile of bubble wrap. You would look under a desk and see an arm sticking out from a big pile of the stuff, something I called "nesting." One could tell if George had just woken up, as he had little bubble wrap impressions--circles--all over one side of his face. George was working on the Amiga 500. At this point, we didn't know what it would be called, or at least I didn't.

So anyway, George stopped and helped me push this entire pot of coffee through these little holes in the floor that early morning. Anytime I was downstairs in the Production management offices, I spent my time looking up at the ceiling, looking for big coffee stains on their ceiling tiles.

Bob's Juggling Programmers

It's not correct to say that I was entirely self-taught. I was self-taught enough to get in the door, but then it was working around brilliant people from whom I came to learn my trade craft of engineering. There was also another effect that I called "intellectual testosterone." It seemed that hanging around really smart people could cause a momentary rise in my own intelligence, and so I sought out really smart people. When I had any moment of downtime, I would just listen to the really smart people and whatever they were talking about.

Bob Welland was one of these people, a brilliant engineer who invariably had a bag of really interesting books that he lugged around. He was one of those guys who made you smarter just by hanging around him. Bob was leaving Commodore around 1985 to join Apple; turns out the secret project he was working on was the Newton, a handheld personal digital assistant device. He went on to become an architect and partner at Microsoft.

A couple of us were slowly walking him down the main corridor as he was saying goodbye, when we got to Programmerville, which is where we kept the programmers and lepers. A guy named Pete Bowman stepped up to Bob while juggling small bean bags, and handed them off to him, so now Bob was juggling. Pete went into the nearest office and disassembled the phone; so now he was juggling the phone, the handset, and something like a stapler.

Two or three more people--okay, they were programmers--stepped out of their offices and they were also juggling. Turns out that Bob had taught the programmers to juggle, in addition to advanced caching theory.

I stood there watching what amounted to a Juggling Programmer Send-off. As Bob got to the last goodbyes, he handed the juggling back to Pete, and everyone went back to their offices. It was both cool and sad.

Amiga Genlock

It was around this time that Cary Sagady had adapted the Amiga design to do what was called "genlock," which allowed computer graphics to be superimposed on NTSC video. It was amazing stuff and was breaking new ground. Cary was one of the most respected engineers I've met. He was part of a team that had won an Oscar award for work they had done on broadcast cameras, while working for RCA. Basically, they taught a camera how to learn to self-calibrate and store the results in ROM. In short, he knew his stuff.

The key to genlock is that the master clock of the entire Amiga computer had to change its frequency to exactly line up with the frequencies found in the television signal that it was trying to adapt to. Simply put, if using a VCR for playback, the main clock in the Amiga would fluctuate in response to the imperfections that may have occurred in the tape recording process, which still blows my mind to this day.

On the day that Cary first got it working, we were amazed as we gathered around the blinking pixels where we could see a television show underneath, literally from a local broadcast received through an old rabbit ears antenna. This was the basis of the future Video Toaster (a plug-in expansion card for editing and producing NTSC standard-definition video) and other popular editing capabilities that the Amiga became known for.

True to form, a middle manager stopped by, looked carefully at what was on the screen, and then turned to Cary and asked what he was seeing. This was probably the only time I've ever seen Cary hesitate for even a moment to come up with a fast quip, as it kind of blew all of our minds that it wasn't self-evident to this manager that a *major* event had just been accomplished. Dare I say, history was made and we witnessed it that day.

7.5 Nearing the End

After the C128 had been introduced, we continued working for the next several months doing long days getting ready for C128 production. My world was filled with purchasing issues, QA feedback from early builds, and all the things required to make computers in the millions.

The C128 passed FCC which was a predicted anticlimax, but it was still good to have it out of the way. Then we got ready for the Summer 1985 CES show in Chicago, when we would show the REU and the C128 expandable to a full 512 kB.

Worn Out

I made my last trip to Japan during this time, and sadly, it was much different than my first. The Commodore office had changed with most of the old-timers now gone, but I too had changed. I was no longer the wide-eyed engineer who had walked around Tokyo with my mouth hanging open a couple of years earlier. I realized that I had become addicted to the pressure and stress of working at Commodore, and it was hard for me to let go of the heady days of pre-CES show excitement. I was worn out and tired to the bone and yet still was driven. I realized that I had used up a lot of me in a short period of time.

I Left

I began to worry that Commodore was actually going to go out of business, as the direction without Jack turned out to be directionless, or so it felt to us grunts in the trenches. I was afraid I would be on the street looking for a job, along with my friends who were ultimately more qualified than I was--at least on paper, if not through the sheer education that I did not have. So, I started looking for another job. During this time, some of the people who had protected me left CBM, either on their own or through more *brilliant* management decisions. I figured I would be fair game now for all the middle managers whose toes I'd stepped on in order to succeed with our project.

By late 1985, I came to realize that my whirlwind tour of Commodore was coming to an end, and it made me sad. But, I was also excited about what might be next. I needed a way to get my fix of adrenaline and stress that I so enjoyed while working at Commodore. Ultimately, I left to become the Director of Engineering for a start-up in the machine vision field.

Commodore began firing their best people as well. The people who had made them a billion dollars were being let go, and I was scooping them up from my new position outside of Commodore. But, this would never be a substitute for working at CBM during the exciting days of home computer design in the 1980s.

There was a time when I wished that I had worked at Commodore again, but after hearing the stories about how bad middle and upper management had become, I knew that I never would have survived at the new Commodore. I would have been fired, or fired for cause--one of the two.

Finding Self-Redemption

Post-Commodore, I found it hard not to be in high gear all of the time. I hit the wall and had to deal with my drinking and the behaviors that went along with it. I made a decision and got sober, but it turned out that I was still addicted to stress and I sought out stressful situations for many years after I left Commodore in order to get my adrenaline fix.

More than that, I felt like I had made a hole in my life that needed to be filled, and I ended up working second jobs in my spare time in places like a trauma center unloading medivac helicopters, or in rescue squads. I worked as a Trauma Technician at a Level I trauma center and also did thousands of ambulance calls, eventually rising to the rank of Captain of a rescue squad.

One day, I smiled and felt a moment of peace as I found some small amount of self-redemption, realizing that somewhere in those thousands of ambulance calls, and with the help of others, that I myself had been rescued.

7.6 People with a Lasting Effect

Before I leave, I want to once again recognize important people in my life and in my work.

My Dad

I am not sure if I correctly stated the importance of the role my dad played in my being my own person and being equipped to teach myself technical stuff. As I mentioned earlier, he bought me an electronics kit; he let me take apart his strobe light (I figured out that the big blue things must store electrical energy, based on the burn on my finger); and he paid me for fixing his light organ when I was still in the fifth grade.

Later, when I was working on designing and building a musical synthesizer (inspired by my love of Emerson, Lake, and Palmer, and the intersection between music and electronics), he subsidized the build, a few bucks at a time. He didn't hassle me when I took off from school to work on it, nor when I dropped out, nor when I joined the National Guard in lieu of high school.

Similarly, as a dad myself, *the* thought that went through my head when I first saw my newborn son (I was 40 by then) was that this little guy is going to be free to be whoever he wants. As a child, my son had his own computer since the age of two, and his favorite toy was the garage door opener. I have a picture of him showing the remote to Santa Claus and explaining that you can have two doors up, two doors down, or one up and the other down, or one down and the other up (see Fig. 7-5). With a tear in my eye, I realized that the next generation of engineers had just explained a Boolean logic table at the age of four.

Fair to say, there may not have been a C128 as we know it without my dad's gift ever so long ago.

Fig. 7-5 Young Joel Herd teaching Santa about Boolean logic.
Photo courtesy of Bil Herd.

C128 Design Team

Here are the members of the C128 Animals (see Fig. 7-6) and their roles in the design team:

Fred Bowen: Kernal and all system-like things; dangerous when cornered; has been known to brandish common sense when trapped.

Terry Ryan: Brought structure to BASIC and got in trouble for it; was threatened with the loss of his job if he ever did anything that made as much sense again; has been known to use cynicism in ways that violate most nuclear ban treaties.

Von Ertwine: CP/M. Sacrificed his family's popcorn maker in the search of a better machine.

Bil Herd: Original design and hardware team leader.

Dave Haynie: Integration, timing analysis, and all those dirty jobs involving computer analysis which was something totally new for CBM.

Frank Palaia: One of three people in the world who honestly knows how to make a Z80 and a 6502 live peacefully with each other in a synchronous, dual video controller, time sliced, DRAM based system.

Dave DiOrio: VIC-II chip mods and IC team leader; ruined the theory that most chip designers were from Pluto, which was still a planet back then.

Greg Berlin: 1571 disk drive design; originator of Berlin-Speak. I think of Greg every night. He separated my shoulder in a friendly brawl in a bar parking lot, and I still can't sleep on that side.

Dave Siracusa: 1571 software.

As mentioned earlier, the names of the people who worked on the PCB layout can be found on the bottom of the PCB of production units: HERD/FISH/GUAY/PAR.

Fig. 7-6 Dave Haynie wearing C128 Animals shirt with disk drive and beer on head. 1985 CES.
Photo courtesy of Terry Ryan.

7.7 Back into the Storm

One day, unexpectedly, I knew that I wanted to write these stories down, and in that moment, I found the phrase that described my story arc for this book, though it came to me in a very sad way.

DiOrio's Memory

Not so long ago, I went to visit my onetime best friend, Dave DiOrio, who would pass away from cancer in a couple of weeks. The time window was narrow when I would be able to see him, and I drove to Pennsylvania between severe winter storms. When I arrived, I told his wife, Nancy, that I was "dragging a storm" behind me, and we kind of grinned at the fact that, at least *that* had not changed from our Commodore days.

When I went to leave after my visit, knowing that I would not see Dave again, I told him I loved him, and--suspending all belief for a moment--I told him with full intent that I would see him around. He raised his voice and also said he would see me around. When I hugged Nancy one last time at the door, I mentioned that I had to drive "back into the storm," and we looked at each other again.

At that moment, I realized that I had described my life in those four words.

That phrase may not belong anywhere near a published piece, but it is now my mental subtitle for who and what we were.

Fig. 7-7 Dave DiOrio and Bil Herd at Bil's CBM party. 1985. Photo courtesy of Dave Haynie.

The End of the Story

Glossary of Terms

1-2-3: slang for an NMOS chip that only has the bottom three layers fabricated.

4-5-6: slang for fabricating the top layers of an NMOS chip.

555: popular timer IC that lends itself to functions such as reset circuits.

6502: the predominant microprocessor of the 1980s, designed by MOS Semiconductor.

6502 reset vector: contained at address $FFFC, where the processor first fetches from after a reset.

6509: CBM version of the 6502 that can access up to 1Mbyte of RAM.

6510-HERD: a version of the 6502 pinned out in 48 pins for logic analyzer connectivity.

6522: VIA, Versatile Interface Adapter, a very popular I/O chip.

6529: I/O chip supporting 8 I/O lines, used to scan the keyboard on the TED series.

6551: a UART, universal asynchronous receiver-transmitter.

65C02: CMOS version of the 6502.

65C22: CMOS version of the 6522.

6845: popular graphics controller.

7501: HMOS version of 6502 with additional controls.

7406 gate: an open collector inverter.

7407 gate: an open collector buffer.

74LS257: a bus multiplexor, used in the DRAM circuit.

7D02 logic analyzer: a logic analyzer made by Tektronix. See "logic analyzer."

82S100: a Programmable Logic Array. See "PLA."

8501: HMOS II version of 6502 with additional controls; can run at 2 MHz; TED CPU.

8502: HMOS II version of 6510; can run at 2 MHz; C128 CPU.

8563 VDC: Custom Graphics Controller made by CBM.

/CAS: DRAM Control Signal, Column Address Strobe.

/EXROM: Control signal on C64 cartridges, EXternal ROM.

/GAME: Control signal on C64 cartridges, GAMEl ROM.

/RAS: DRAM Control Signal, Row Address Strobe.

address bus: an internal computer communications channel carrying addresses from the CPU to components under the unit's control.

alpha unit: units that are more than proof of concept yet not representative of the final units in any way but basic function.

Amiga: CBM series of 16/32-bit computers. The Amiga 1000 was introduced at the Winter '85 CES, 1985-86; Amiga 500 was more popular, released in 1987; mouse-based GUI, known for high quality graphics and audio, 256 kB RAM, color display, 1985-96.

amp: short version of ampere, the base unit of electric current in the International System of Units (SI). SI defines the ampere in terms of other base units by measuring the electromagnetic force between electrical conductors carrying electric current.

analyzer: a multifunction test meter, measuring volts, ohms, and amperes.

Animals: nickname of the engineers on the C128 project.

ANSI B tabloid: American National Standards Institute graph paper size 11 x 17.

architecture: the manner in which the components of a computer or computer system are organized and integrated.

assembly code: a human-readable version of machine language; a symbolic nonbinary format for instructions that allows mnemonic names to be used for instructions and data.

B128: CBM business computer, 128 kB RAM, BASIC 4.0, 80-column display, 1982-83.

back-bias generator: chip voltage generator for early NMOS integrated circuits.

back-bias voltage: a negative voltage source used to reduce power consumption. Unfortunately, it can also slow down the operations of an integrated circuit.

ball peen hammer: a type of peening hammer used in metalworking. It has two heads: one is flat and the other, called the peen, is rounded.

bandwidth: a measure of the amount of data that can travel on an electronic communications system, usually expressed as thousands or millions of bits per second.

barn door stop: useful purpose for the C128 since it is a large wedge-shaped object.

being Osborned: to announce a new system so early that sales stop of the existing system.

Berlin-Speak: a baritone mumbling, devoid of recognizable English context; sometimes mistaken for a fully loaded gravel truck shifting gears.

beta unit: representing the final unit in fit and function to a high degree; not perfect, but should fit the case and act like the final unit.

block diagram: a graphic representation of any operational circuit or system with each functional element presented as a box or a block and the relationship of each element to other elements being depicted by connected lines.

block transfer: the movement of data in blocks instead of by individual records.

bus master: the device that controls the current bus transaction in a bus structure in which control of data transfers is shared between the central processor and associated peripheral devices.

C16: CBM home computer, TED series, 16 kB RAM, BASIC 3.5, 40-column color display, 1984-85.

C116: CBM home computer, TED series, 16 kB RAM, BASIC 3.5, 40-column color display, rubber chiclet keyboard, 1984.

C64: highest-selling CBM home computer, 64 kB RAM, BASIC 2.0, 40-column color display, 1982-1993.

C128: CBM home/personal computer, 128 kB RAM, BASIC 7.0 and BASIC 2.0, CP/M, 40 and 80-column color displays, 1985-1989.

C232: CBM prototype, home computer, TED series, 32 kB RAM, BASIC 3.5, 40-column color display, 1984.

C264: CBM home computer, TED series, prototype that became the Plus/4 with built-in software, 64 kB RAM, BASIC 3.5, 40-column color display, 1984.

C364: CBM prototype, home computer, TED series, 64 kB RAM, BASIC 3.5, 40-column color display, built-in Magic Voice speech synthesizer, 1984.

C900: CBM prototype business computer, 512 kB RAM, Zilog Z8001, UNIX-compatible, built-in 20 mB hard disk drive and floppy drive, 80-column display, 1985.

CBM 1541: disk drive of the C64.

CBM 1551: disk drive of the TED series.

CBM 1571: disk drive of the C128 series.

CBM PET 8032: PET (Personal Electronic Transactor) business computer, 32 kB RAM, BASIC 4.0, 80-column monochrome display, 1980.

CES: Consumer Electronics Show held semiannually; the Super Bowl for the consumer computer industry.

checksum: a sum of digits used to check the validity of data to verify the integrity of a file or a data transfer, comparing two sets of data to make sure they are the same.

Cheez Whiz: a cheesy substance not to be confused with actual cheese.

Chiclets: a brand of candy-coated chewing gum formed in small, flat rectangular shapes. The CBM C116 had a "chiclet keyboard," the keys being similar in size and shape to the popular Chiclet gum and made of rubber. See also "C116."

chip die: a small block of semiconducting material on which discrete electronic components are embedded and interconnected.

chip selects (Q outputs): outputs from a storage latch circuit.

chi-squared test: a test used to determine whether there is a statistically significant difference between the expected results and the measured results.

clock: method of generating periodic timing signals for synchronization in electronic equipment and computers.

CMOS: Complementary Metal-Oxide-Semiconductor, a chip-making process that drives positive and negative voltages equally.

CMOS standard cell gate array: a hybrid design approach that allows some of the benefits of full custom, but also allowing some shortcuts of having a tested library of standard building blocks.

cold spray: a spray that quickly chills a device; usually used diagnostically, but can also be used to summon the nearest hardware engineer when used by a programmer.

Commodore Mouse: Bil's mouse (a small rodent) that lived in his shoe in his office and was fed Fritos; was hunted by the CBM mouse (input device) developer, Hedley Davis.

Commodore Paging System: walking through the halls bothering everyone, looking for someone since there was no actual intercom.

control signal: a set of pulses or frequencies of electricity or light used to identify a control command as it travels over a computer channel.

CP/M: Control Program for Microcomputers, developed by Gary Kildall of Digital Research, Inc.; popular operating system for computers in the '70s and early '80s.

CPU: Central Processing Unit, the primary unit of a computer system that controls the interpretation and execution of instructions.

D128: CBM development model business computer, 128 kB RAM, 40 and 80-column display, re-engineered into the C128, 1984.

data bus: the data lines of a computer-based system.

design rule check (DRC): a computer program that automatically checks the schematic against the actual layout in either chip making or PCB layout.

diddlebop: to walk with excited energy.

diode: an electrical device, such as a semiconductor or electron tube, that permits the flow of current in one direction while inhibiting the flow in the other direction.

disk editor: a computer program that allows the user to read, edit, and write raw data (at character or hexadecimal, byte-levels) on hard disks, USB flash disks, floppy disks, or other removable storage media.

DMA: Direct Memory Access, a way of accessing the main memory without involving the CPU. It allows for faster transfer speeds.

DO/LOOP/WHILE/UNTIL/EXIT: BASIC 7.0 statements; looping technique similar to FOR/NEXT. All statements between the DO and the LOOP in a program are continuously executed unless WHILE, UNTIL, or EXIT are encountered. If EXIT is encountered, program execution passes to the statement following LOOP. If UNTIL is encountered, the program loops until a condition is met. WHILE is the opposite of UNTIL in that a program continues while a certain condition is true. When the condition becomes false, program execution passes to the statement following the LOOP statement.

Doobutsu: Japanese for "Animal," Bil Herd's nickname.

dot clock: the clock that pertains to the size of a pixel as displayed on a monitor.

DRAM: Dynamic Random-Access Memory, a type of random-access semiconductor memory that stores each bit of data in a memory cell consisting of a tiny capacitor and a transistor, both typically based on metal-oxide-semiconductor (MOS) technology.

dwell angle: the number of degrees through which a distributor cam (on a car) rotates, from the time that the contact points close to the time that they open again.

Easter egg: an undocumented feature in a program that the makers added for fun and credits, not destructive to the software or hardware in the computer. C128 Easter egg is SYS 32800,123,45,6.

electromotive force: the force that causes electricity to flow when there is a difference of potential between two points.

EMS: Emergency Medical Services.

emulation: the imitation of one computer system by another, enabling the other to function in exactly the same way and use the same software and peripheral hardware.

emulator: hardware or software that allows one computer system to act like another, enabling the emulator to use software or peripherals designed for the other system.

EPROM: Electrically Programmable Read-Only Memory, the devices used to contain the operating system during development.

EPROM programmer: the system used to translate binary code in file form and allows programming of an actual EPROM device.

FCC: Federal Communications Commission, a federal body that enforces electrical interference limits.

FCC Part 68 Subpart J: the part of the FCC regulations that pertains to home computers and specifically about connecting to the phone lines.

FETCH: BASIC 7.0 statement used for getting data from the RAM expansion unit (REU) on the C128.

fetch cycle: the part of a computer cycle from which the location of the next instruction is retrieved.

flapper: slang for the liftable metal door of Herman Miller brand office furniture.

floating node: a dangerous situation where nothing is driving a specific node of the design, allowing it to float to illegal logic values.

font ROM: Read-Only Memory that holds the built-in font, which is a set of digital characters in a single style and scalable to different sizes.

function key software: software that is built into ROM and accessed through function keys.

gaijin: Japanese word for foreigner.

gate: a circuit or device that has one output and one or more inputs. The output state is determined by the previous and present states of the inputs.

germanium diode: a type of rectifier or detector made from germanium crystal, having the advantage of an intrinsically low forward voltage drop, typically of 0.3 volts.

glass plant: liquid crystal display (LCD) glass substrate manufacturing facility.

hand tape: to lay out a PCB using opaque tape on a frosty white mylar; a manual process for designing PCBs.

heat variable resistor: a resistor that when cold eliminates a large current rush when first turned on.

Herd's Hole: broken hole in the wall of the men's room at CBM, made by Herd while playing the Fake Punch Game.

hex inverter: an integrated circuit that contains six inverters. See also "inverter."

HMOS/HMOS II: high density, short channel MOS, an advanced form of NMOS.

hot bunking/hot racking: within the military, the sequential use of the same bed when sleeping quarters are limited, such as on submarines. Since the bed is warm from the prior occupant, the term "hot" is used.

I/O chip: Input/Output; how a computer senses and communicates to the world around it.

IC: Integrated Circuit, an electronic, self-contained assembly fabricated on a single chip of semiconductor material.

ikizukuri: a Japanese method of serving fresh fish while still moving.

interface adapter: a device that connects a terminal or computer to a network.

interrupt: a signal that indicates that something has occurred, such as a key press, or a timer has expired.

inverter: a circuit or device that takes in a positive signal and outputs a negative signal, or vice versa.

jelly bean chip: common logic chips that cost more for the effort to insert them into a circuit than the actual cost of the chip.

jumper: a short piece of conductor, such as wire or cable, used to close a circuit between two electrical terminals.

kB: kilobyte, in reference to digital memory capacity; kB denotes 1024 (2^{10}) bytes.

Kernal: Commodore Business Machines name for the utility routines that do most of the housekeeping and supervision in a computer. Misspelled by Bob Russell in the early days and the spelling stuck.

Lake Herd: the huge body of rain water that would collect on the flat roof above the CBM West Chester Production Department, which Bil Herd's office overlooked through a wall of windows. Herd drew a beach and palm trees on the window overlooking Lake Herd.

lead frame: part of an integrated circuit assembly that physically holds the chip die and is responsible for removing a good portion of heat.

light organ: slang for a piece of equipment used in the '70s and '80s to flash in time to music.

light pen: a computer input device in the form of a light-sensitive wand used in conjunction with a computer's cathode-ray tube (CRT) display.

logic analyzer: a piece of test equipment that displays electrical information as a series of highs and lows or ones and zeros.

logic equation: an equation consisting of logic highs and lows used to determine the resulting value.

lot: a batch of chips as produced by MOS.

LRRP: Long-Range Reconnaissance Patrol, a small well-armed team that patrols deep in enemy-held territory.

luggable: early term used to describe modern day laptop.

Macross: early Japanese Anime cartoon, named Robotech in the US.

mask: short for photographic mask; part of the process used to make integrated circuits.

meep: an exclamation of being overwhelmed.

memory map: the representation of how different devices are mapped to their memory in a computer system.

MHz: megahertz or 1 million times per second.

milliamp: a measure of current; one one-thousandth of an amp.

MMU: Memory Management Unit, the main controller for how various memory and IO circuits are mapped into memory.

modem: MOdulator DEModulator, the hardware that interfaces to the phone system to send and receive information.

MOS 6526 I/O chip: a general purpose multi-port input output chip used in the Commodore 64 and in the Commodore 128.

MOS 6529 I/O chip: a general purpose single-port input output chip used in the TED series of computers to scan the keyboard.

MOS: Metal Oxide Semiconductor, later known as CSG (Commodore Semiconductor Group), was a semiconductor design and fabrication company based in Norristown, Pennsylvania; famous for the 6502.

NMOS: N Channel Metal Oxide Semiconductor.

noise, dynamic: moving patterns of noise which can be highly distracting.

noise, static: non-moving patterns of noise that are visible on the display monitor.

noise/sparkle: small flickers in the computer display as seen on a monitor.

nor gate: a gate exhibiting inverted "OR" logic.

NTSC: National Television Standards Committee, the committee that determines the specifications for broadcast television.

ohm: unit of measurement in electrical resistance.

one-off PC board: a single-use PCB that will not need to be remade at a later date.

opcodes: short for operational codes, the language of microprocessors.

open collector gate: a specialized gate in TTL logic that only pulls down; can be connected to other open collector gates and a pull-up resistor.

oscilloscope/scope: a piece of test equipment that allows the engineer to see electronic signals.

pachinko parlor: a Japanese business where Pachinko is played, much like a Pinball Hall in the States; very noisy with lots of lights.

PAL: Phase Alternating Line, the standard for color TVs in Europe.

parallel bus: an interface designed to communicate with peripherals, such as printers and disk drives; uses multiple pairs of wires to send information in parallel as opposed to sequentially/serial.

passivation: a layer of silicon nitride that protects an integrated circuit from the environment.

PCB: Printed Circuit Board, the main structure that most components are mounted to in a computer system.

PERT: Program Evaluation Review Technique, using a chart with circles or rectangles (nodes) to represent project events or milestones. These nodes are linked by vectors, or lines, that represent various tasks. PERT charts allow managers to evaluate the time and resources necessary to manage a project.

phantom key: a falsely detected key closure when too many keys are pressed in an array of keys.

phase lock loop: a circuit that generates a clock based on a mathematical relationship to another clock.

Phi clock: the main clock signal in a 6502-based computer system.

pincer movement: a military maneuver in which the two wings of the attacking army simultaneously converge on the enemy to surround it.

PLA: Programmable Logic Array, a fixed architecture logic device with programmable AND gates followed by programmable OR gates.

Plus/4: CBM home computer, TED series, originally the C264, 64 kB RAM, BASIC 3.5, built-in productivity software, 40-column color display, 1984-86.

poly: short for polysilicon, one of the layers in an NMOS IC.

power resistor: a resistor of higher wattage to dissipate power in the form of heat.

probing: a test and troubleshooting method of inserting test probes into a chip while under a microscope.

prototype: an early sample, model, or release of a product built to test a concept or process.

pull-up: a resistor tied to a positive voltage meant to keep signals from floating around in illegal states.

purple creeping crud: slang for the corruption that would occur on a poorly passivated IC. It looks purple under the microscope.

RAM: Random-Access Memory, the dynamic memory where temporary variable and information is stored.

rev: revision

RGBI: the color monitor interface consisting of Red, Green, Blue and Intensity signals.

ROM: Read-Only Memory, permanent memory that contains the operating system and other static data.

ROM monitor: a built-in program that allows the user to examine and modify memory.

RPN: Reverse Polish Notation, developed in the 1920s by Jan Lukasiewicz; a formal logic system which allowed mathematical expressions to be specified without parentheses by placing the operators before (prefix notation) or after (postfix notation) the operands. Hewlett Packard adopted this for their pocket calculators.

RS-170A: the NTSC specification for color video in the US.

schematic: a drawing of electronic circuitry showing how things are connected.

Schottky parts: high speed logic utilizing Schottky transistors internally.

sector: a section on a floppy disk that is loaded at one time and includes a checksum to verify accuracy.

serial bus: an interface designed to communicate with peripherals such as printers and disk drives; uses minimal number of wires and sends information sequentially or in series as opposed to parallel.

shift register: converts various inputs to a data stream.

Shinu mousugu: Japanese for "soon to die", or saying that one is exhausted.

silicon: slang for all integrated circuits which are grown on a silicon substrate. ICs in general.

silicon-controlled rectifier: a semiconductor switch.

silicon nitride coating: see passivation.

slew rate: how fast a signal rises or drops.

soft output: a type of electrical output that can be shorted to ground without damage.

soft-tooled: a way to produce plastic housings quickly using wood and other soft materials to cast the plastic.

Spidey Sense: most often portrays a pending sense of doom.

Squid: nickname for Navy sailor.

standard cell gate array: utilizes a library of preconfigured circuits or cells as opposed to true custom.

STASH: BASIC 7.0 statement used with the REU on the C128. It moves the contents of memory into the REU.

substrate: the physical material on which a microcircuit is fabricated.

super line: slang for the final production assembly line at West Chester, Pennsylvania.

SWAP: BASIC 7.0 statement used with the REU on the C128. It swaps the contents of the computer's internal RAM with the contents of the REU.

switching power supply: a power supply that uses energy storage and semiconductor switches to create power; more complex and expensive than a "linear" supply, but more efficient.

sync signals: synchronicity, being of the same time base where assumptions can be made about the relationship between multiple signals.

TED: TExt Display integrated circuit made by MOS Technology; video chip that also contained sound generation hardware, DRAM refresh circuitry, interval timers, and keyboard input handling. It was used in the TED family of computers, including the well-known Plus/4 and C16.

terms: equations for programmable logic.

test jig: a device for testing components and circuit boards.

Texan Write: Commodore slang for having to write a register twice in a row to make it work correctly.

Texans' register: a register that needs a Texan Write.

the hand: holding a hand up to interrupt someone.

tiger team: a small group of experts with diverse skills whose purpose is to solve or recommend solutions to a problem, after which they return to their prior work assignments.

Tornado Alley: an area of the central United States where tornadoes are most frequent, including Bil's early home state, Indiana.

trace: an interpretive diagnostic method which provides an analysis of each executed instruction and writes it on an output device as each instruction is executed.

transistor: an active component of an electronic circuit consisting of a small block of semiconducting material to which at least three electrical contacts are made. It may be used as an amplifier, detector, or switch.

UART: acronym for Universal Asynchronous Receiver Transmitter, a device used to interface a parallel controller or data terminal to a bit-serial communications network.

UNTIL: see DO/LOOP/WHILE/UNTIL/EXIT.

Valkyrie: an imaginary type of craft described in Macross.

Variable AC transformer: a piece of test equipment that can simulate a variety of voltages on the AC mains power.

vias: conductive traces through a PCB to get from one side to the other.

VIC: Video Interface Chip, originally used in the VIC-20.

VIC-20: CBM home computer using the VIC chip, 5 kB RAM, BASIC 2.0, 22-column color display, 1981-85.

VIC-II: Video Interface Controller, the main chip in the C64 and the source of its game playing magic.

VICE: Versatile Commodore Emulator, a collection of programs that allows a variety of non-Commodore computers to run programs on 8-bit CBM computers, such as the VIC-20, C64, C128, and Plus/4. See https://vice-emu.sourceforge.io/.

volt: the international unit of electromotive force equal to the product of current and resistance. See also "electromotive force."

voltage: the potential difference or electromotive force measured in volts. See also "electromotive force."

VT100: popular serial terminal in the 1980s.

wafers: the substrate that integrated circuits are produced on.

WHILE: see DO/LOOP/WHILE/UNTIL/EXIT.

white noise: random noise; sounds like static.

wirewrap: a way of connecting circuitry without having to produce a printed circuit board.

WORM: Write Once Read-Only memory, predecessor to the CDROM.

Z: short for any of the Datsun Z series of cars.

Z Lounge: slang for the private area built by the Z8000 engineers with furniture stolen from the lobby.

Z80: an 8-bit microprocessor popular in the 1980s, used for running CP/M.

Parting Shots

Right: Bil at CBM Christmas Party. Back in the day.

Left: At the release of *8 Bit Generation: The Commodore Wars* documentary (2016) that Bil narrated. From left to right: Chuck Peddle (father of the 6502), Leonard Tramiel, and Bil Herd.

Right: Marg with C128, writing for *RUN Magazine* about the computers that Bil and his team designed. Back in the day.

Fig. 8-1 Montage 1.
Photos courtesy of Dave Haynie (top), Chris Collins (center), Deborah Porter-Hayes (bottom).

Fig. 8-2 Bil Herd 2017.

About Bil Herd, Outside of Commodore

Bil has been busy since he left Commodore. He designed the backup sensor in 1986 which is found on many modern cars, co-authored a patent on machine vision in 1990, and founded an ISP in 1995. He designs high-speed computers, does consulting for hardware design, and owns Mercury Consulting Group (mcgllc.com) doing IT architecture and support.

In the vintage computer world, Bil is very active. He participates in the Vintage Computer Federation (vcfed.org), does videos for Hackaday (hackaday.com), is a keynote speaker for Altium (altium.com), and does guest spots on media, such as The 8-Bit Guy (the8bitguy.com). He contributed to Jeri Ellsworth's C64 Direct-to-TV product. Bil narrated *The Commodore Wars* in 2016 and *Easy to Learn, Hard to Master - The Fate of Atari* in 2017, two documentaries from 8-Bit Generation (www.8bitgeneration.com), and he was in the movie, *The Commodore Story* in 2018. He also hosts C128.com for Commodore enthusiasts, as well as Herdware.com, devoted to old-school electronics and new technologies.

Bil lives a quiet life in the country with his family and a whole menagerie of farm animals, and still drives a Z when the weather is right. He can be reached at c128.com.

Printed in Great Britain
by Amazon